JOSSEY-BASS TEACHER

Jossey-Bass Teacher provides educators with practical knowledge and tools to create a positive and lifelong impact on student learning. We offer classroom-tested and research-based teaching resources for a variety of grade levels and subject areas. Whether you are an aspiring, new, or veteran teacher, we want to help you make every teaching day your best.

From ready-to-use classroom activities to the latest teaching framework, our value-packed books provide insightful, practical, and comprehensive materials on the topics that matter most to K–12 teachers. We hope to become your trusted source for the best ideas from the most experienced and respected experts in the field.

Making Thinking Visible

HOW TO PROMOTE ENGAGEMENT, UNDERSTANDING, AND INDEPENDENCE FOR ALL LEARNERS

Ron Ritchhart
Mark Church
Karin Morrison

Foreword by
David Perkins

JOSSEY-BASS
A Wiley Imprint
www.josseybass.com

Published by Jossey-Bass
A Wiley Imprint
One Montgomery Street, Suite 1200, San Francisco, CA 94104-4594—www.josseybass.com

Jossey-Bass books and products are available through most bookstores. To contact Jossey-Bass directly call our Customer Care Department within the U.S. at 800-956-7739, outside the U.S. at 317-572-3986, or fax 317-572-4002.

Jossey-Bass also publishes its books in a variety of electronic formats. Some content that appears in print may not be available in electronic books.

Library of Congress Cataloging-in-Publication Data

Ritchhart, Ron, 1958- author.
 Making Thinking Visible : How to Promote Engagement, Understanding, and Independence for All Learners / Ron Ritchhart, Mark Church, Karin Morrison.
    p. cm
  Includes bibliographical references and index.
  ISBN 978-0-470-91551-6 (pbk.), ISBN 978-1-118-01501-8 (ebk.), ISBN 978-1-118-01502-5 (ebk.), ISBN 978-1-118-01503-2 (ebk.)
  1. Thought and thinking--Study and teaching. 2. Critical thinking--Study and teaching. 3. Cognition in children. I. Church, Mark, 1970- II. Morrison, Karin, 1951- author. III. Title.
  LB1590.3.R63 2011
  370.15′2--dc22
                                  2010049619

Printed in the United States of America
FIRST EDITION
PB Printing   20 19 18 17 16 15 14 13 12 11

CONTENTS

LIST OF FIGURES AND TABLES

Figures

Tables

DVD CONTENTS

Please note: The video content can be accessed online at www.wiley.com/go/makingthinkingvisible. When prompted, enter your email address and use access code 15516.

The Explanation Game: Debbie O'Hara, Kindergarten Art
International School of Amsterdam, The Netherlands

Chalk Talk: Leeland Jennings, Grade 2 Science
St. Charles Elementary, Michigan

See-Think-Wonder and Sentence-Phrase-Word: Lisa Verkerk, Grade 5 Humanities
International School of Amsterdam, The Netherlands

Connect-Extend-Challenge: Mark Church, Grade 6 Social Studies
International School of Amsterdam, The Netherlands

CSI: Color-Symbol-Image: Melyssa Lenon, Secondary Chemistry
Chesaning Union High School, Michigan

Generate-Sort-Connect-Elaborate: Ravi Grewal, Grade 12 English Literature
Bialik College, Melbourne, Australia

Looking at Students' Thinking Protocol: A Professional Learning Group Looks at Students' Thinking in Grade 7 Science
Bialik College, Melbourne, Australia

FOREWORD

Have you ever listened to one side of a conversation and wondered, "Where did that come from?" A number of years ago, I had a signal experience of this sort. I was walking slowly across the Cambridge Common toward my office at the Harvard Graduate School of Education. A man was sitting on a park bench talking loudly on his cell phone: "I have to! He lied to me and he lied to you! What did he tell you on the phone? Everything's A-okay, he said. Well everything's not A-okay!"

I felt a powerful temptation to ask, "Where did that come from?" but an even more powerful inhibition against intruding on a stranger's life. So I swallowed my curiosity and strolled along, memorizing what the stranger said and writing it down as soon as I got to my office. Several times in the ensuing years I've reread my note and wondered about the story behind the man on the park bench. This small experience has come to symbolize for me how much remains to be revealed when we hear just half a conversation . . . and hearing half a conversation happens a lot in our lives, especially when we interpret "conversation" broadly.

Thinking is a good example. We do not generally hear other people's thinking, just the results of their thinking—an idea, an opinion, a plan. The messiness of "what if," "on the other hand," "but I worry that," or even just "my gut says" all happens on the other end of the line. What the person says to us may sometimes sound like the whole story, but it is only half or much less than half of the internal conversation. That's why we sometimes have to ask ourselves, "Where did that come from?"

Often we could ask that same question about our own thinking. Research suggests that most people are not sharply aware of how they go about figuring out a problem or coming to a position on an issue. If this seems strange, let's compare with why coaches are so important in athletic learning. A coach, besides having expertise the athlete does not, can pay attention in ways the athlete cannot—from the outside and without having to perform physically at the same time.

All this signals why the ideas about *Making Thinking Visible* are so important to education. In broadest terms, these ideas call for externalizing processes of thought so that learners can get a better handle on them. To this end, the authors foreground a range of ideas about questioning, listening, documenting, naming, and more, including many specific strategies and a general approach to establishing a positive, engaged, and thoughtful culture of learning in classrooms. Ron Ritchhart, Mark Church, and Karin Morrison have been deeply involved for many years, along with me and a few other colleagues in various combinations, in developing these ideas and fostering their practice. Here they bring us the wisdom of their experience.

However, more is at stake here than learning to think better. The mission addressed by this book is not only learning to think but thinking to learn. To elaborate, there is an uncomfortable question I like to ask people from time to time: "What ideas did you learn during your pre-university education that are important in your life today?" Some people have a hard time identifying much beyond a list of facts, but others report knowledge they have found to be tremendously important to who they are, how they understand the world, and how they behave. For instance, I recall one person mentioning the French Revolution, not for its details but for how it had served as a lens to look at conflicts of all sorts. I remember another person discussing ecological understandings that influenced substantially not only what policies the person supported but the conduct of everyday life. In general, when people bring forward themes that have mattered to them, they mention themes to think *with*, not just themes to think *about*—think *with* the French Revolution to understand other conflicts or think *with* your ecological knowledge to revise some of your everyday behaviors.

Thinking with is two important steps beyond just knowing information, the focus of far too much education. One step beyond is thinking about a topic, often interesting and valuable but in itself leading toward rather specialized understandings. When learners get comfortable thinking with the ideas in play, those ideas become far more meaningful. Horizons of application open up . . . everything from managing everyday relationships or making a smart purchase to making sense of global warming on a personal level.

The place of thinking about and thinking with what is learned gives us a second reason why making thinking visible and related themes are so important to learners. Back to that park bench one more time: in the complex, conflicted, and sometimes precarious world of today and tomorrow, the better people think about and with what they know, the more likely they will be able to make sense of the half conversations we all encounter. And the more prepared they will be to enter meaningfully into the whole conversation.

David Perkins

PREFACE

In 2005, my colleagues at Harvard Project Zero and I had just finished a five-year project exploring how to cultivate thinking dispositions in school settings. The project, Innovating with Intelligence, unfolded at Lemshaga Akademi in Sweden with the financial backing of the Carpe Vitam Foundation. Drawing on a long line of research on dispositions and enculturation, we developed a set of thinking routines: simple strategies for scaffolding thinking that were designed to be woven into a teacher's ongoing classroom practice. These routines formed the foundation of our intervention and became the core practice of an approach we eventually called "Visible Thinking." We documented our efforts and presented a set of initial routines to the world via a website: www.pz.harvard.edu/vt.

Almost immediately the website became a hit with the teachers with whom we had been working as well as a valuable resource for our colleagues and ourselves in our ongoing work. Teachers who had been involved with Teaching for Understanding saw the thinking routines as short understanding performances that enhanced their efforts with students. Colleagues Shari Tishman and Patricia Palmer found them useful in supporting an initiative, Artful Thinking, focusing on arts integration. Faculty at the Harvard Graduate School of Education found them to be useful tools for actively engaging students with complex ideas. Some colleagues even used the routines as structures for reflecting on and writing about the ideas they were developing. Facilitators at our annual summer institutes gravitated toward the routines for supporting adult learning in much the same way they might use a protocol to structure a professional discussion.

At the same time, David Perkins, Mark Church, Karin Morrison, and I were beginning the Cultures of Thinking project at Bialik College, a pre-K through grade 12 independent school in Melbourne, Australia, with the financial support of Abe and Vera Dorevitch. We felt that thinking routines would be a good starting place for teachers to begin their own thinking about the forces shaping classroom culture. Although our broader goal was to focus teachers' attention on the issue of developing a culture of thinking, we had noticed in our earlier research that as teachers worked with thinking routines in earnest and over time, they soon found themselves thinking about the other cultural forces at play; most notably time, language, opportunities, and interactions (for more on these, see Chapter Seven).

Not long after the VT website's debut, educators we didn't even know began to write us about how they were using the thinking routines and to express an eagerness for more: more routines, more stories from classrooms, more video illustrations, and more examples of teachers' efforts at different grade levels and subject areas. In short, more support for learning designed to enhance the effectiveness of routines in their educational settings. Although educators shared how valuable the website was as a resource, they kept expressing a desire for a book that would take their learning deeper: a collection that they could set on their desks as a ready resource and thumb through at their leisure, something that they could bring to planning meetings, share with colleagues, and mark up with their own notes and tips. Some teachers admitted to having gone so far as to print off the entire website and bind it together in order to fulfill this need.

This outpouring of interest and enthusiasm led Mark, Karin, and me to begin thinking about creating a book that would both extend and complement the Visible Thinking website. In our early conversations we identified several goals that we thought such a book would need to fulfill. First, we thought it was important to capture the development that had occurred in our own thinking as researchers, developers, and facilitators since we originally debuted the idea of visible thinking back in 2005. Our ongoing research and conversations with colleagues had expanded our thinking about visibility beyond just the use of routines, and we wanted to share these additional strategies. We present these ideas in Chapter Two.

Second, we felt an obligation to share the many stories of teachers who were making use of thinking routines in novel ways. Over the years, we have worked with thousands of educators, and we never cease to be amazed at their inventiveness. However, we wanted to find a way to tell these stories that would help readers see the power of the routines to support thinking and learning and not just as clever activities. As the popularity and use of thinking routines has spread, we have seen a few too many examples of their ineffective use and wanted to help people better understand the conditions under which the power of thinking routines is realized. Consequently, in designing our template for writing up the routines, we decided to emphasize the importance of selecting appropriate content along with some ideas for the formative assessment of students' thinking, something we had not dealt with explicitly in our earlier work. You'll find more about this new template in Chapter Three. Drawing on the wealth of examples gleaned from teachers, both through the Cultures of Thinking project at Bialik College and elsewhere, we crafted rich "pictures of practice" that highlighted each teacher's thinking as he or she planned, implemented, and reflected on his or her use of that thinking routine. These stories are found throughout Chapters Four, Five and Six.

As an accompaniment to the original Visible Thinking website, we had also produced a DVD that became available in 2005. This video collection highlighted teachers from the International School of Amsterdam and has become a popular resource for educators who want to share what Visible Thinking is all about with their colleagues. We had seen the power of these videos to present an embedded teaching practice that highlights the interactive quality of routines and the importance of using them with powerful content. Consequently, Mark, Karin, and I wanted to include as part of this book a DVD containing video stories from a more diverse range of classrooms that would highlight teaching done by teachers in the United States, Australia, and Europe. We reference the seven videos captured on the included DVD throughout this book and hope that this resource will enhance your reading and understanding of the ideas presented.

Another goal we identified for our writing was to situate the use of thinking routines and other tools within the larger enterprise of teaching, addressing such goals as fostering engagement, uncovering understanding, and promoting independence within a classroom culture of thinking. In Chapter One, we unpack thinking and discuss the critical role it plays in learning, making the case that promoting thinking isn't a nice extra but is central to learning. We then situate the thinking routines and visibility strategies presented throughout the book within three case studies: one from a classroom, one from a museum, and one from a professional group, which we present in Chapter Seven. These cases demonstrate how strategies for making thinking visible exist within the larger mosaic of a culture of thinking. Finally, we conclude this volume by pulling together our "Notes from the Field" in Chapter Eight. Here we present some of our research on how teachers learn to use routines and work with them over time, as well as a collection of tips, triumphs, and hints for moving forward with your own use of visible thinking practices.

Throughout this book, we have sought to weave together narrative threads from a diverse set of classrooms. This array of perspectives adds to the richness of the larger story we have been able to tell here. But the story isn't over. There are always more voices to add, more tales to tell. We continue to learn with and from teachers throughout the world; educators like yourself who are continually looking for ways to engage learners, develop understanding, support thinking, and promote independence. Since you are reading this book, we assume you are one of these inspired educators. And so, we hope that you will add your own voice to the chorus of teachers working to make thinking visible. Take these ideas and make them your own, embedding them within the culture of your classroom. Use this book as a resource, but stretch beyond it. Take risks in your teaching. Most of all, have confidence in every learner's ability to think and your capacity to nurture that thinking. The results will amaze and energize you.

Ron Ritchhart

ACKNOWLEDGMENTS

At the core of this book rests the idea that it is important to nurture thinking in the daily lives of learners and to make it visible so that a culture of thinking can be built and a strong learning community established in organizations, in schools, and in classrooms. Although this is an idea easy to embrace, it takes something more to bring it to fruition. It takes hard work, dedication, continual reflection, and most of all a willingness to take risks and reach outside the comfort zone of established practices. This is both an individual endeavor and a collective process, recognizing that one learns as much from others' practice as from one's own. We thank all of those who joined us in this journey of nurturing thinking and who were willing to dig in to the work of making thinking visible.

We are greatly indebted to Abe and Vera Dorevitch and the Bialik College School Council for the financial support provided. They have been the political visionaries who recognized the potential of these ideas to transform schools and classrooms. They were willing to support seven years of ongoing professional learning for the teachers at Bialik College to take ideas first developed as part of the Visible Thinking Project, funded through Carpe Vitam Foundation, and the research on Intellectual Character, supported by the Spencer Foundation, and advance them through on-the-ground, in-the-classroom exploration as part of the Cultures of Thinking Project. Their dedication to advancing the education happening not only at Bialik College but also around the world has produced far-reaching benefits and ripple effects around the globe. In addition, Dow Chemical has financially supported the teachers of mid-Michigan in their application of these ideas; ATLAS Learning Communities provided support for teachers in New York City; Lemshaga Akademi in Sweden and the International School of Amsterdam have facilitated the coming together of teachers from around the world to share their experiences. And so, from the vision of just a few individuals willing to think big, we have seen a dramatic impact that continues to grow, nourishing our collective and ongoing development as educators.

The journey with these ideas plays out in real schools. All busy places with too much happening and too many agendas to serve. And yet, we have been blessed to find school leaders who valued this work and who have been willing to do the hard work to make sure the mission of making thinking visible could take hold at their schools. In particular, at Bialik College, Genia Janover carved out a central place for the Cultures of Thinking Project and ensured that teachers had time to meet regularly to share, discuss, and explore these ideas in depth. Her commitment and dedication to teacher learning have been instrumental in moving these ideas forward. Also at Bialik College, Daphne Gaddie and Tosca Mooseek brought these ideas into the ongoing discussion of teachers. In mid-Michigan, Rod Rock and Geralyn Myczkowiak provided the inspiration and leadership to bring together a diverse collection of teachers to pursue these ideas in a wide scale initiative across many public school districts. In Traverse City, Michigan, Jayne Mohr, Pam Alfieri, and Julie Faulkner made it possible for many teachers from Traverse City Area Public Schools to be a part of this work. In New York City at Vanguard High School, Principal Louis Delgado embraced these ideas and supported his teachers' work with them. In Clover Park School District in Washington state, Patty Maxfield facilitated the ongoing exploration of these ideas within the district. In Marblehead Public Schools in Massachusetts, Beth Delforge and Paul Dulac advanced a whole-district focus on thinking. Linda Gerstle embraced these ideas early on and integrated them into ATLAS Learning Communities' work around the United States. Julie Landvogt first saw the power of these ideas in 2000 and established a network of schools in Melbourne, Australia, to explore them. At Melbourne Grammar School, Chris Bradtke, Alan Bliss, and Roy Kelley took up the charge. And the list goes on and continues to grow.

As we have tried to move these ideas forward in our research and development work, we have been inspired by their broad applicability. The idea of making thinking visible and the assorted thinking routines that support that mission have found a place across a range of subject areas, in assorted organizations, in diverse settings, and with varied types of learners. The heart of this book is contained in these Pictures of Practice. We only have been able to tell a relatively few number of stories here; however, we acknowledge all the other dedicated professionals who have been a part of this journey. Their stories serve as daily examples and inspiration for students and colleagues. In particular we thank the teachers of Bialik College, Saginaw Intermediate School District in Michigan, Traverse City Area Public Schools, Vanguard High School, Marblehead Public Schools, International School of Amsterdam, Lemshaga Akademi in Sweden, Brighton Primary in Tasmania, and Melbourne Grammar School, Methodists Ladies College, and Wesley College, all in Melbourne. These represent just a small number of the many schools and teachers at them who have journeyed with us.

In the writing of this book we have to thank the conceptual visionaries who pushed our thinking and contributed greatly to the formation of the ideas presented here through their ongoing dialogue with us. At Project Zero at the Harvard Graduate School of Education, we thank our colleagues David Perkins, Terri Turner, Becca Solomon, and Linor Hadar, who have been key in developing these ideas as part of the Cultures of Thinking Project. Shari Tishman and Patricia Palmer, who were part of the original Visible Thinking project in which an initial set of thinking routines were developed. Steve Seidel, Mara Kerschevsky, and Ben Mardell have all made us think about issues of visibility and documentation further and deeper through their work in the Making Learning Visible project. In addition, Tina Blythe and Julie Landvogt pushed our thinking forward on more than one occasion.

For Michael, Jean, and Kevon.

Thank you for pushing us to love, laugh, live, and think more deeply.

You've made us better teachers and better people for being in our lives.

ABOUT THE AUTHORS

Ron Ritchhart has been a principal investigator at Project Zero, Harvard Graduate School of Education since 2000. Before coming to Project Zero, he was a classroom teacher working in a variety of subject areas ranging from art to mathematics, at grades ranging from elementary to secondary school, and in settings as diverse as New Zealand, Indiana, and Colorado. The thread running through all of Ron's work as an educator and researcher has been and continues to be the importance of fostering thinking, understanding, and creativity in all settings of learning. He is the author and producer/director of many articles, books, and videos that address these topics.

In 2002, Ron published the book *Intellectual Character*, which put forth the idea that a quality education is about much more than scores on tests; it is about who students become as thinkers and learners as a result of their time in schools. Ron's classroom-based research, for which he was recognized by the Spencer Foundation, unpacked the important role school and classroom culture plays in nurturing the development of students' thinking dispositions. His identification of the forces shaping the culture of groups and organizations resulted in a framework now being used widely to help educators both in and out of the classroom think differently about teaching and learning.

Ron's ideas and their application have now found a strong following in many schools and organizations. Since 2005, Ron has been applying these ideas at sites all over the world but most notably in Melbourne, Australia, through the Cultures of Thinking Project funded by Bialik College and Abe and Vera Dorevitch.

Mark Church has been an educator for nearly twenty years and has a particular interest in helping teachers and school leaders think deeply about their efforts to cultivate thinking and learning opportunities for students. A skilled facilitator, he works with schools and districts throughout the world, encouraging efforts to create rich communities of practice for educators committed to being mindful students of those they teach and lead. In his work, Mark draws on his extensive and diverse teaching background, having taught elementary and middle school students in the United States, Japan, Germany, and The Netherlands.

After several years overseas, Mark returned to the United States to consult with ATLAS Learning Communities and Harvard Project Zero's Visible Thinking projects. Mark has also been an online course coach, developer, and instructor for WIDE World online learning at the Harvard Graduate School of Education as well as a faculty member for the annual Harvard Project Zero Summer Institute. Mark has presented on issues of thinking, learning, and understanding at conferences throughout the world, especially emphasizing classroom work with middle-years learners. Currently Mark is a district administrator supporting professional growth and development in the Traverse City Area Public Schools in northwestern Michigan. Additionally, he serves as a consultant for various Harvard University Project Zero Cultures of Thinking initiatives in the United States and abroad.

Karin Morrison is an enthusiastic and passionate educator interested in the thinking and learning of both teachers and children. Her work has focused on providing the environment and structures needed to support deeper thinking and greater understanding and engage students in learning in a relevant and meaningful way. She is currently director of the Development Centre at Independent Schools Victoria (ISV), Australia. Karin also serves as the instructor for the WIDE World online learning course, Making Thinking Visible, developed at the Harvard Graduate School of Education.

Karin was instrumental in developing the collaboration between Project Zero and Bialik College that led to the creation of the Cultures of Thinking project at Bialik. Karin was the in-school leader of this project for its first five years. While at Bialik, she was director of the Rosenkranz Centre for Excellence and Achievement in Education and director of Teaching and Learning. Karin has long been an avid supporter of thinking on the world scene. She was co-convenor for the Twelfth International Conference on Thinking in Melbourne in 2005, the Australian delegate to the World Council for Gifted and Talented Children, past president of the Victorian Association for Gifted and Talented Children, and a committee member of the Reggio Emilia Australia Information Exchange. Karin has also been a faculty member at the annual Project Zero Summer Institutes and the ATLAS Learning Communities Summer Institute in Vermont.

PART ONE

SOME THINKING ABOUT THINKING

CHAPTER 1

Unpacking Thinking

According to the *Oxford English Dictionary*, there are somewhere in the neighborhood of a quarter of a million distinct words in the English language—if one uses a somewhat strict definition of distinct words, that is ("Facts About Language," 2009). Of course, of this vast number of linguistic options, we use only a small percentage on a regular basis. It is estimated that a mere 7,000 words account for 90 percent of our day-to-day usage. With these numbers in mind, where do you imagine the word *think* resides in terms of frequency of use? That is, with what relative incidence do you believe you use, hear, or read the word *think* each day? What rank does it hold in our average use? Does it make the top 1,000 or is it much further down the list?

Drawing on information from several lists, *think* as a word ranks somewhere around the top 125 to 136 in terms of frequency in print (Fry, Kress, & Fountoukidis, 2000). If one considers just verbs, *Oxford English Dictionary* rates the word *think* as the twelfth most used verb in the English language! Clearly the word *think* plays an astonishingly prominent role in our speech and writing, but for all this usage, how well do we understand what it actually means to think? When we use the word *think*, what meaning do those listening to us infer? When we tell someone we are thinking, what is it we are actually doing? Although no data is available, one might expect the word *think* to occur even more frequently in classrooms. When teachers use it, what do they intend? When students hear it, how do they interpret it? Does it lead to any actions on their part?

If we want to support students in learning, *and* we believe that learning is a product of thinking, then we need to be clear about what it is we are trying to support. What kinds of mental activity are we trying to encourage in our students, colleagues, and friends? When we ask teachers in workshops, "What kinds of thinking do you value and want to promote in your classroom?" or, "What kinds of thinking does that lesson force students to do?" a large percentage of teachers are stumped. They simply haven't been asked to look at their teaching through the lens of thinking before. They ask their students to think all the time, but they have never stepped back to consider just what it is they specifically want their students to do mentally. However, if we are going to make thinking visible in our classrooms, then the first step will be for us as teachers to make the various forms, dimensions, and processes of thinking visible to ourselves.

BEYOND BLOOM

When we ask teachers to identify the thinking required in their lessons, we frequently get the response, "Do you mean Bloom's taxonomy? Is that what you're after?" Most teachers have learned about Benjamin Bloom in their teaching training courses. Although his taxonomy focused on three domains—affective, psychomotor, and cognitive—it is the cognitive domain that most teachers remember. Bloom identified a sequence of six learning objectives that he felt moved from lower-order to higher-order thinking: knowledge, comprehension, application, analysis, synthesis, and evaluation. However, these ideas were just a theory and were not based on research on learning. Nonetheless, they have become codified into the way many teachers are taught to think about thinking. Teachers are often admonished to make sure some of their questions or lessons require the "higher levels" of thinking, though generally this is taken to mean anything above comprehension.

Although Bloom's categories capture types of mental activity and thus are useful as a starting point for thinking about thinking, the idea that thinking is sequential or hierarchical is problematic. Bloom suggests that knowledge precedes comprehension, which precedes application, and so on. However, we can all find examples from our own lives where this is not the case. A young child painting is working largely in application mode. Suddenly a surprise color appears on the paper and she analyzes what just happened. What if she does it again but in a different place? She tries and evaluates the results as unpleasing. Continuing this back and forth of experimentation and reflection, she finishes her work of art. When her dad picks her up from school, she tells him about the new knowledge of painting she gained that day. In this way, there is a constant back and forth between ways of thinking that interact in a very dynamic way to produce learning.

In the 1990s, two of Bloom's former students revised his taxonomy, and a new list was published using verbs rather than nouns. However, the idea of a sequence was kept. Moving from lower- to higher-order skills, Anderson and Krathwohl (2001) identified remembering, understanding, applying, analyzing, evaluating, and creating. Once again a potentially useful list, but it remains problematic if one takes it as a set sequence to guide instruction for learning. Looking at the thinking actions that Anderson and Krathwohl associated with these six, one might question whether the "testing" they say is involved in evaluating is really more difficult or higher order than the "describing" they list under remembering. For instance, looking carefully to notice and fully describe what one sees can be an extremely complex and engaging task. Such close observation is at the heart of both science and art. Analysis and speculation depend on careful noticing.

Our colleague Steve Seidel (1998) has written about both the importance and challenge of description when looking at student work. Because the mind is designed to detect patterns and make interpretations, slowing it down to fully notice and just describe can be extremely challenging. In contrast, one can test the ability of a paper airplane to fly, the accuracy of a proposed mathematical algorithm, or the strength of a toothpick bridge pretty quickly and easily.

What these examples illustrate is that it makes little sense to talk about thinking divorced from context and purpose. Furthermore, the idea of levels might best be considered with regard to the thinking itself. Rather than concerning ourselves with levels among different types of thinking, we would do better to focus our attention on the levels or quality within a single type of thinking. For instance, one can describe at a very high and detailed level or at a superficial level. Likewise, one can simply test something out to determine if it will fail, or one can fully test the limits and conditions of that failure. Analysis can be deep and penetrating or deal with only a few readily apparent features. Watch any major television news show and contrast it to the more in-depth stories one might hear on radio and see in print, and you will see different levels of analysis at play.

One can argue that there is a bit of category confusion in both of the Bloom's lists as well, since not all items seem to operate at the same level. This can most readily be seen in the way "understanding" is framed. Since the 1970s, many researchers and educational theorists have focused on the complexities of teaching and learning for understanding, as opposed to just knowledge retention (Bruner, 1973; Gardner, 1983, 1991; Skemp, 1976; Wiske, 1997). Some researchers have made the distinction between deep and surface learning (J. B. Biggs, 1987; Craik & Lockhart, 1972; Marton & Saljo, 1976). Surface learning focuses on memorization of knowledge and facts, often through rote practices, whereas deep learning has a focus on developing understanding through more active and constructive processes. Today, most educators would argue that understanding is indeed a very deep, or at least complex, endeavor and not in any way a lower-order skill as the revised taxonomy suggests (Blythe & Associates, 1998; E. O. Keene, 2008; Wiggins & McTighe, 1998). Indeed, understanding is often put forward as a primary goal of teaching.

Research into understanding, much of it conducted with our colleagues at Project Zero, indicates that understanding is not a precursor to application, analysis, evaluating, and creating but a result of it (Wiske, 1997). Recall the brief illustration of the young girl painting mentioned earlier. The understanding or insight she develops into painting are the direct result of much and varied activities and the associated thinking that went along with those activities. Thus, we might consider understanding not to be a type of thinking at all but an outcome of thinking. After all, one cannot simply tell oneself to understand something or direct one's attention to understanding versus some other activity. Ellin Keene (2008) writes about the complexity of the process of understanding in the process of reading and the need to develop explicit thinking strategies to support those efforts. Likewise, James Hiebert et al. (1997) write about how learning mathematics for understanding is fundamentally a different task than memorizing procedures.

The same argument put forth about understanding—that it is a goal of thinking rather than a type of thinking—applies equally well to the process of creating. How does one go about the process of creating anything? It is not necessarily a single direct act but a compilation of activities and associated thinking. Decisions are made and problems are solved as part of this process. Ideas are tested, results analyzed, prior learning brought to bear, and ideas synthesized into something that is novel, at least for the creator. This creation can be simplistic in nature, as with the child creating a new color; useful, as in the invention of a new iPhone app; or profound, such as new methods of producing energy from never before used materials.

As these brief critiques point out, the idea of levels is problematic when it comes to parsing thinking and ultimately less useful than one might hope. Thinking doesn't happen in a lockstep, sequential manner, systematically progressing from one level to the next. It is much messier, complex, dynamic, and interconnected than that. Thinking is intricately connected to content; and for every type or act of thinking, we can discern levels or performance. Perhaps a better place to start is with the purposes of thinking. Why is it that we want students to think? When is thinking useful? What purposes does it serve? We pick up on these issues in the following section of the chapter.

BEYOND MEMORIZATION, WORK, AND ACTIVITY

In the preceding discussion of Bloom's taxonomy, we made the argument that understanding isn't a type of thinking one does but is in fact a chief goal of thinking. As most teachers are aware, understanding is one of the major thrusts of current educational practices. The Teaching for Understanding (TfU) framework (Blythe & Associates, 1998) and Understanding by Design (UBD) (Wiggins & McTighe, 1998) are two current curricular planning tools that help teachers focus on understanding. It would be nice if we could merely take for granted that all teachers adopt this goal and strive to teach for understanding, but we all know that the reality of most schools and classrooms is quite different. Within the high-stakes testing environments in which educators today operate, there is often pressure to cover the curriculum and to prepare for the test (Ravitch, 2010). Although lip service may be paid to the idea of teaching for understanding, there are pressures that work against it. These pressures aren't necessarily anything new. Schools, having been built on an industrial model, have long focused on imparting skills and knowledge as their chief goal.

In most school settings, educators have focused more on the completion of work and assignments than on a true development of understanding. Although this work can, if designed well, help to foster understanding, more often than not its focus is on the replication of skills and knowledge, some new and some old. Classrooms are too often places of "tell and practice." The teacher tells the students what is important to know or do and then has them practice that skill or knowledge. In such classrooms, little thinking is happening. Teachers in such classrooms are rightly stumped when asked to identify the kinds of thinking they want students to do because there isn't any to be found in much of the work they give students. Retention of information through rote practice isn't learning; it is training.

The opposite side of this same coin is a classroom that is all about activity. In the often misunderstood notion of experiential or inquiry-based learning, students are sometimes provided with lots of activities. Again, if designed well some of these activities can lead to understanding, but too often the thinking that is required to turn activity into learning is left to chance. Other times, the activity itself is little more than a more palatable form of practice. Playing a version of *Jeopardy* to review for a test may be more fun than doing a worksheet, but it is still unlikely to develop understanding.

At the heart of this view of teaching is the notion that curriculum is something that teachers deliver to students and good teachers are those most effective at that delivery. Reflecting on his own evolution as a teacher, Mark Church recounts how prevalent this view was in his own teaching:

> In my early years of teaching I was "the fun teacher" bursting with confidence and more than a bit of hubris. I kept my students entertained. They liked me. They liked my class. Whatever was to be covered became an object of knowledge that I, as the expert, would deliver by way of gimmicks and glamour to my students. Consequently, I judged my teaching by the ease with which I was able to transmit information along a linear, one-way path of knowing. My idea of good teaching was to focus on the creation and delivery of palatable, hands-on, though not necessarily minds-on, activities. Becoming a good teacher meant mastering a set of delivery techniques and knowing all the answers to my students' questions. In those years it had not yet occurred to me that good teaching hinged upon what I knew and understood about

the learners themselves and about how learning happens. However, it was not until I really examined the issue of what is understanding and how does it develop that I actually began the process of becoming a teacher. Only then did I recognize that work and activity are not synonymous with learning.

Let's return to the key question with which we began this chapter: "What kinds of thinking do you value and want to promote in your classroom?" And the associated question, "What kinds of thinking does this lesson force students to do?" When classrooms are about activity or work, teachers tend to focus on what they want their students to do in order to complete the assignments. These physical steps and actions can be identified, but the thinking component is missing. When this happens, the learning is likely to be missing as well.

Here's a quick exercise to help you identify the possible discrepancy between students' classroom activity and teaching that is likely to lead to understanding. Begin by making a list of all the actions and activities with which your students are engaged in the subject you teach (if you are an elementary school teacher, pick a single subject to focus on, such as math, reading, or writing). You might want to brainstorm this list with a couple of colleagues or teammates. Now, working from this list, create three new lists:

1. The actions students in your class spend most of their time doing. What actions account for 75 percent of what students do in your class on a regular basis?

2. The actions most authentic to the discipline, that is, those things that real scientists, writers, artists, and so on actually do as they go about their work.

3. The actions you remember doing yourself from a time when you were actively engaged in developing some new understanding of something within the discipline or subject area.

To the extent your first list—what students spend the bulk of their time doing—matches the other two lists, your class activity is aligned with understanding. If the three lists seem to be disconnected from one another, students may be more focused on work and activity than understanding. They may be doing more learning *about* the subject than learning *to do* the subject. To develop understanding of a subject area, one has to engage in authentic intellectual activity. That means solving problems, making decisions, and developing new understanding using the methods and tools of the discipline. We need to be aware of the kinds of thinking that are important for scientists (making and testing hypotheses, observing closely, building explanations . . .), mathematicians (looking for patterns, making conjectures, forming generalizations, constructing arguments . . .), readers (making interpretations, connections, predictions . . .), historians (considering different perspectives, reasoning with evidence, building explanations . . .), and so on, and make these kinds of thinking the center of the opportunities we create for students. Furthermore, these kinds of thinking need to be among the primary expectations we hold for students: that they can and that they will engage in the kinds of thinking necessary to build disciplinary understanding.

A MAP OF THINKING INVOLVED IN UNDERSTANDING

In the preceding section we listed a few types of thinking that were central to different subject areas, such as making and testing hypotheses in science or considering different perspectives in history, but are there particular kinds of thinking that serve understanding across all the disciplines? Types of thinking that are particularly useful when we are trying to understand new concepts, ideas, or events? When you thought about the kinds of thinking you did to develop your own disciplinary understanding, you probably identified some of these. Ron Ritchhart and colleagues David Perkins, Shari Tishman, and Patricia Palmer set themselves the task of trying to identify a short list of high-leverage thinking moves that serve understanding well. Their goal was not to come up with all the different kinds of thinking that were involved in understanding but to identify those kinds of thinking that are essential in aiding our understanding. They wanted to identify those thinking moves that are integral to understanding and without which it would be difficult to say we had developed understanding. They came up with the following six:

1. Observing closely and describing what's there
2. Building explanations and interpretations
3. Reasoning with evidence
4. Making connections
5. Considering different viewpoints and perspectives
6. Capturing the heart and forming conclusions

We feel that these six all play important roles in fostering understanding of new ideas. If we are trying to understand something, we have to notice its parts and features, being able to describe it fully and in detail. Identifying and breaking something down into its parts and features is also a key aspect of analysis. The process of understanding is integrally linked to our building explanations and interpretations. In science, we label these as *theories* and *hypotheses*. In mathematics, we sometimes call them *conjectures* or *generalizations*. In building these explanations, we draw on and reason with evidence to support our positions and try to arrive at fair and accurate positions that can be supported. When we encounter anything new, we make connections between the new and known, drawing on our past experience. These connections help us to link ideas and find where the new ideas fit within the subject area and out. Our connections might also be about application and where the new ideas or skills are used. All of these connections aid our retrieval of information and help ensure that new information is not static or inert (Whitehead, 1929). If one were only to look at new ideas or situations from a single perspective, we would say that one's understanding was limited and sometimes even biased. Awareness of the different perspectives or takes on an idea gives us a more robust understanding. Capturing the heart or core of a concept, procedure, event, or work ensures that we understand its essence, what it is really all about. We want to make sure we haven't lost the forest for the trees and that we notice the big ideas in play.

These types of thinking are by no means exhaustive of all the kinds of thinking we want to make visible in classrooms. However, they do provide a good and useful list with which to begin. Many teachers working to make thinking valued and visible in their classrooms have found that posting these thinking moves in their classrooms can be extremely useful. The list helps draw students' attention to what they will be doing to learn. To help ensure that work and activity don't swamp students' learning, teachers often pause class either before or after an assignment to discuss the types of thinking that will be or were involved in the assignment. As students become more aware of their own thinking and the strategies and processes they use to think, they become more metacognitive (Ritchhart, Turner, & Hadar, 2009a).

Since all of these thinking moves directly support the development of understanding, this list can be useful to teachers in planning units. Over the course of a unit of study, students should be engaged in all of these types of thinking on more than one occasion to help them develop their understanding. If students haven't been actively engaged in building explanations, reasoning with evidence, making connections, or having the opportunity to look at things from more than one perspective, then there would likely be significant holes or gaps in their developing understanding. Just as the six thinking moves can help to develop understanding, they can also be useful in assessing understanding. Fredrik Pettersson, a secondary history teacher at Lemshaga Akademi in Sweden, found that the six thinking moves were exactly the qualities he was looking for in a historical essay and decided to use them as an assessment rubric that he gave to his students. The sixth grade team at the International School of Amsterdam decided that if they were really trying to make thinking visible in their classrooms, then students should focus on their thinking and not only their performance on tests and quizzes. All sixth graders were charged with creating a visible thinking portfolio in which they collected samples that demonstrated where and when they had engaged in each of the six thinking moves. These portfolios were then presented to parents as part of a student-led conference at the end of the year.

Since identification of the six thinking moves that support understanding, what we sometimes call the "understanding map," we have added two additional thinking moves:

7. Wondering and asking questions

8. Uncovering complexity and going below the surface of things

The importance of curiosity and questioning in propelling learning is easily seen in our experience as learners. We know that when our curiosity is sparked and we have a desire to know and learn something, our engagement is heightened. Many teachers are familiar with the use of essential questions as vehicles to propel students' learning. However, questions are also an ongoing part of developing understanding. The questions we ask at the outset of a learning journey change, morph, and develop as that journey moves forward. Even after extensive efforts to develop understanding, we find that we may be left with more questions than when we started. These new questions reflect our depth of understanding. This depth and our ability to go below the surface of things is a vital part of our ongoing development of understanding. Rather than look for or accept the easy answers, we push to identify the complexity in the events, stories, and ideas before us. In this complexity lay the richness, intrigue, and mystery that engage us as learners.

While these eight represent high-leverage moves, it is important to once again stress that they are by no means exhaustive. We offer up this list as a useful starting place, and no more. You can probably think of other kinds of thinking that are useful, such as visualization, taking stock of what you understand, looking for cause-and-effect relationships, and others. Furthermore, you can probably identify many thinking moves that further flesh out the key eight in ways that are useful. For instance, comparing and contrasting ideas is a specific type of connection making, as is thinking metaphorically. Classifying extends our description and noticing. We've chosen the broad terms of explanation and interpretation, but these are certainly related to inferring, explaining, and predicting. You might well ask, Where is reflection? Structured reflection has been shown to be a way to enhance understanding and problem solving (Eyleer & Giles, 1999).

The answer is that a structured reflection—that is, reflection that goes beyond voicing one's opinion or feelings—involves describing the object of reflection and noticing its key features, connecting what is new to what one already knows, and examination of the event or object of reflection through various lenses or frames, which is perspective taking (Colby, Beaumont, Ehrlich, & Corngold, 2009).

OTHER KINDS OF THINKING

Of course, understanding is not the sole goal of thinking. We also think to solve problems, make decisions, and form judgments. Many of the eight key thinking moves come in handy when we are doing those activities as well. Looking at things from new perspectives, identifying the parts, and reasoning with evidence certainly play a role. Making connections to our prior knowledge so that we can draw on it and use it effectively is useful as well. Forming conclusions and identifying the essence are also important. Some additional types of thinking we haven't mentioned that seem useful in the areas of problem solving, decision making, and forming judgments include:

1. Identifying patterns and making generalizations
2. Generating possibilities and alternatives
3. Evaluating evidence, arguments, and actions
4. Formulating plans and monitoring actions
5. Identifying claims, assumptions, and bias
6. Clarifying priorities, conditions, and what is known

Again, these six are not meant to be exhaustive, merely useful moves in terms of directing our mental activity and planning our instruction. Each of the six could be further elaborated with associated kinds of thinking. For instance, brainstorming is a useful strategy to help one generate possibilities and alternatives, and taking stock would be a part of clarifying priorities, conditions, and what is known. Formulating plans and actions connects with the idea of being strategic just as evaluating evidence is a part of being skeptical. Reviewing this list, one might get the impression of a very thoughtful mathematics or science classroom in which problem solving plays a central role. In learning mathematics and science actively, it is important that one gets used to looking closely, noticing patterns, and generalizing from those patterns to create procedures, algorithms, and theories. Of course, these theories and conjectures must be carefully evaluated and tested.

The preceding list might also give one the impression of a civics class in which students are exploring current political, social, or ethical issues. In these situations, getting clear about priorities, conditions, and what is known and unknown is an important starting place. Being sensitive to assumptions and bias that might be clouding our perception is also crucial. Of course, in such situations one must also look at things from a variety of perspectives, drawing on one of the kinds of thinking discussed in the understanding map. Depending on the situation, one might also find oneself generating possibilities and alternative takes on the situation and/or making plans to carry out and monitor.

The combination of the preceding list with the eight thinking moves in the map of understanding goes a long way to helping us unpack what we mean by thinking. By being clearer in our own minds as teachers about the kinds of thinking we want our students to do, we can be more effective in our instructional planning. We can create opportunities for the kinds of thinking we value and want to make an expectation in our classrooms. Being clear about the thinking students need to do to develop understanding or to solve problems effectively allows us to target and promote those kinds of thinking in our questioning and interaction with students. Now that we are clearer about what we mean by thinking, we turn our attention toward how we can make students' thinking about thinking visible.

UNCOVERING STUDENTS' THINKING ABOUT THINKING

When schools take on the mission of cultivating students' thinking and enculturating the habits of mind and dispositions that can support lifelong learning, the issue of how students construe thinking and their general metacognitive awareness comes to the fore. It's one thing for us as teachers to articulate the kinds of thinking we are seeking to promote; it is another for students to develop a greater awareness of the significant role that thinking plays in cultivating their own understanding. The important function of this awareness is highlighted by Biggs (J. B. Biggs, 1987), who stated, "To be properly metacognitive, then, students have to be realistically *aware* of their own cognitive resources in relation to the task demands, and then to plan, monitor, and control those resources" (p. 75). Biggs refers to this awareness of one's own learning processes and one's control over them as "meta-learning," a subcomponent of metacognition. Others have labeled it "meta-strategic knowledge," that is, knowledge about the strategies one has at one's disposal to facilitate and direct one's own learning (Zohar & David, 2008). As you have been reading through this chapter, your own meta-strategic knowledge has most certainly come to the foreground as you have thought about the processes one uses to think and learn.

As a part of the Cultures of Thinking project at Bialik College, the research team of David Perkins, Terri Turner, Linor Hadar, and this book's authors was interested in exploring students' explicit awareness of the process of thinking and how these conceptions of thinking might change as their teachers worked to make thinking more visible in their classrooms. Specifically, the team was interested in uncovering students' awareness of thinking moves they might undertake that could facilitate their learning, problem solving, decision making, and judgment. Although this includes study skills and the recognition of memorization and knowledge retrieval strategies, it goes beyond them to look at students' awareness of those thinking strategies that can build understanding, such as looking at material from a different perspective, making connections with one's prior knowledge, generating alternative hypotheses, and so on. But, how does one uncover students' thinking about thinking? How does one unearth their conceptions of what thinking is and the mental moves it encompasses? How can this be done in an open way that captures individual responses and growth over time rather than constraining students' responses to a predetermined set of categories?

Our research team developed a methodology using concept maps that teachers across a variety of grade levels could use in their classrooms as a platform for launching a discussion about what thinking is and the kinds of thinking that would be emphasized in their classrooms. Our prompt for the map was purposely general in an attempt to support and not inhibit students' responses. It asked students, "What is thinking? When you tell someone you are thinking, what kind of things might actually be going on in your head?" Two examples were given: "Making a mental picture of things" and "Comparing one thing with another." The term *thinking* was written in the middle of the page, and students were asked to record their ideas about thinking. We specifically chose the phrasing, "What is going on in your head?" as opposed to "What are you doing?" to focus students on cognitive actions rather than physical ones. We chose two specific examples that likely would be familiar to students in order to further promote a focus on cognitive acts.

As both educators and researchers, we found this technique and prompt readily accessible to students. As such, it is something you might like to try yourself in your classroom. Teachers in our study generally allowed between 5 and 10 minutes for students to complete their maps and then followed up with some sort of discussion of the maps. One way some teachers did this was to have students form small groups and create a joint concept map on thinking, drawing from their individual maps. This allowed students who struggled with the map construction to hear the ideas of others. In other classrooms, teachers made a concept map as a whole class after students had completed their individual ones. This allowed the teachers to engage students in a discussion of which ideas might group together and was particularly effective at focusing in on thinking rather than some of the peripheral ideas that emerged on students' maps. However it was debriefed and built upon, teachers found looking at students' conceptions of thinking as revealed through these maps fascinating. In every classroom there was a huge range and variety of responses. Examples of a fourth grade, sixth grade, and tenth grade map are provided in Figures 1.1, 1.2, and 1.3.

Looking through hundreds of maps from students in grades 3–11, the research team identified four main response types: associative, emotional, meta, and strategic. *Associative responses* are those associated with thinking but do not describe or identify the act of thinking. Comments such as "in math class," "when I'm traveling," and "what will happen next" spoke to the when or where of thinking, as well as "what I am thinking about." These comments did not describe actual thinking processes or the nature of thinking but rather people, places, and things. Other associative remarks included very general comments about "what I think with," or "how I think," such as "thoughts in my mind" or "brainwaves." Likewise, *emotional responses*, those comments revealing an affective connection to thinking, were not strictly about thinking either. Frequently students included affective words and phrases such as *unsure, joy,* and *hard when there is time pressure.*

When researchers first administered the concept map task at the beginning of our work, we found elementary students' responses were frequently 70 percent associative and 10 percent emotional. Even middle and high school students' maps were close to 50 percent associative and 10 percent emotional. The point here is that students don't have much knowledge of the strategies they might employ to facilitate and direct their thinking. Without this knowledge, they are likely to be less effective, less independent, less engaged, and less metacognitive as learners. You can read more about this study and the findings in "Uncovering Students' Thinking About Thinking Using Concept Maps," *Metacognition and Learning* (Ritchhart, Turner, & Hadar, 2009b). If you do this activity with your own students and notice a high level of associative or emotional responses in their maps, don't be alarmed or worry that they aren't responding to the prompt accurately. People can only deliver those things they know and have access to, and rather than being incorrect, these responses reveal that an awareness of thinking simply hasn't been developed for these particular students.

There were a few responses on students' concept maps that spoke to a greater awareness of the nature of thinking, though not strictly about the thinking process. These were labeled *meta responses*. Rather than specifying an action, these comments focused

Figure 1.1 A Fourth Grade Student's Concept Map on Thinking

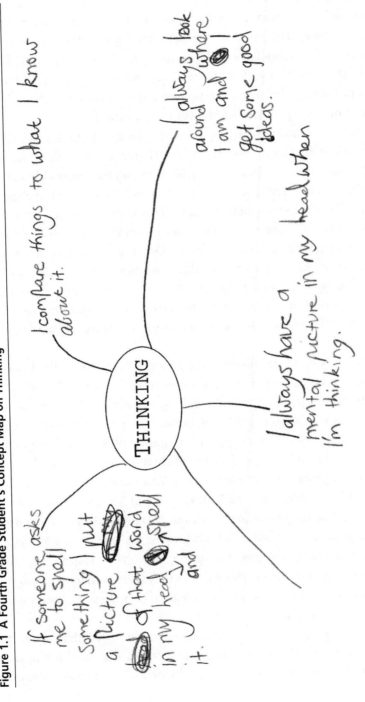

THINKING

I compare things to what I know about it.

I always look around where I am and get some good ideas.

I always have a mental picture in my head when I'm thinking.

If someone asks me to spell something I put a picture of that word in my head and spell it.

Figure 1.2 A Sixth Grade Student's Concept Map on Thinking

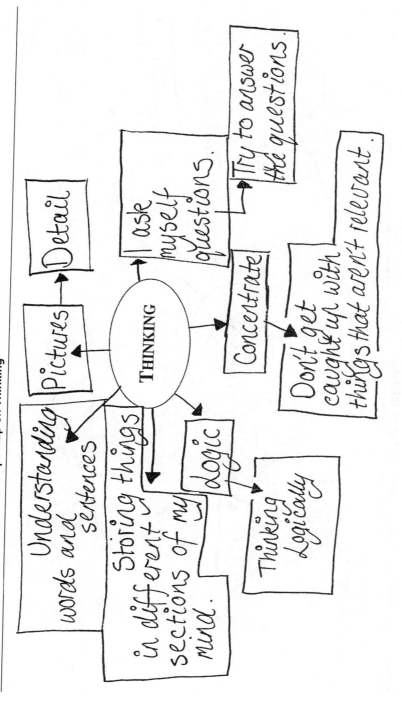

Figure 1.3 A Tenth Grade Student's Concept Map on Thinking

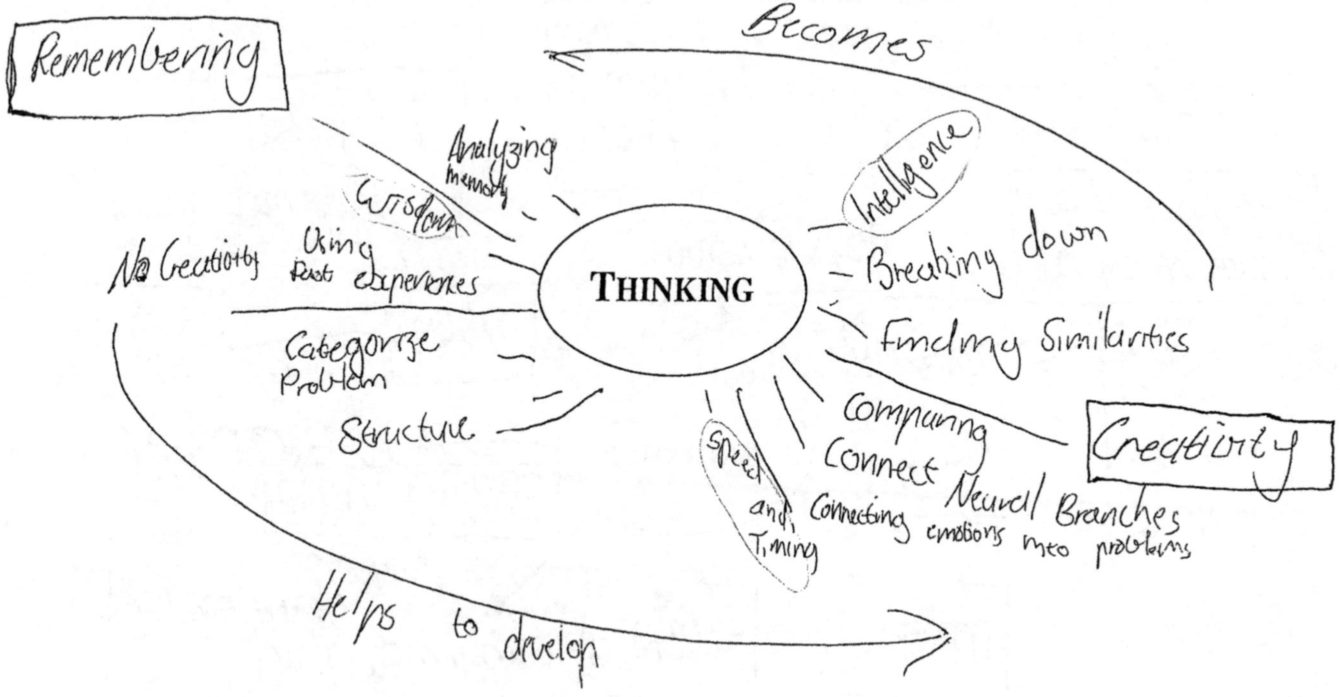

on epistemology, the nature of understanding, and conceptualizations of building knowledge. This meta type of response included comments such as "There is always more to learn," "You can't ever fully understand something," and "Remembering helps to develop creativity." Look for these in your own students' maps as partial indicators of a greater awareness of the purpose and complexity of thinking, learning, and understanding.

Of course, the type of responses we as teachers would like to see students deliver are *strategic responses*. However, even here not all strategies are equal. As was discussed earlier in this chapter, people have thinking moves that can be directed at knowledge retention and memorization as well as those that can be used to help one understand. The Cultures of Thinking research team identified four categories into which students' strategic responses might be grouped:

1. *Memory and knowledge-based strategies*. These related to surface learning and focus on storage and retrieval of information, such as "Look in books" or "Practice it over and over again."

2. *General and nonspecific strategies*. These stood out as a category due to their very general nature. Items in this category often sounded good but did not reflect specific actions one could take. For example, "Think logically" is clearly related to thinking but it is ambiguous in terms of its actions when coming from a fifth grader. So too are items like "Problem solve," "Metacognition," or "Understand."

3. *Self-regulation and motivation strategies*. This category of responses reflected students' understanding that thinking needs to be motivated and managed, and included responses such as "Clear your mind of all other worries" and "Tell myself I can do it."

4. *Specific thinking strategies and processes*. This category relates to deep or constructive approaches to learning that are about making meaning, building understanding, solving problems, and making decisions. These included such responses as "Consider different perspectives" or "Expand on other questions that may arise from the previous one."

In this book, when we talk about making thinking visible, we are generally referring to those specific thinking strategies and processes students use to build deeper understanding. These are the processes that need to live at the center of classroom activity, directing the work of both teachers and students. As we make thinking—our own as well as that of our students—visible, we draw attention to the mechanisms by which individuals construct their understanding. To the extent that students can develop a greater awareness of thinking processes, they become more independent learners capable of directing and managing their own cognitive actions. But, how likely is it that just making thinking visible through the various strategies discussed in the following chapters will enhance students' awareness of thinking processes and strategies? In our concept map research done at the outset of the Cultures of Thinking Project, we found that on average students at every grade level made statistically significant gains in their reporting of specific thinking strategies on the concept map task, from a 250 percent increase in responses for the younger students to 65 percent for high school students. On average, all students in the sample made gains that exceeded normally developmental projections by more than 68 percent.

One major goal of making thinking visible is to facilitate greater understanding among students. Another aim is to enhance students' engagement and independence. This second goal is accomplished, at least in part, through the development of students' meta-strategic or meta-learning knowledge. As this research shows, the tools presented in this book clearly have an impact on students' learning about learning and their thinking about thinking. The Pictures of Practice woven throughout the book to illustrate the use of strategies provide evidence of the types of understanding that can be elicited through the use of thinking routines and effective questioning. As you work with these ideas yourself, keep these goals in mind and continually look for ways your own students are demonstrating greater understanding, becoming more engaged, and displaying their independence as learners.

CHAPTER 2

Putting Thinking at the Center of the Educational Enterprise

How does one learn to teach? More to the point, how does one learn to teach well? We have to say the more time we spend in education, the more vexing we find this question. Not because there aren't ready answers out there, but because the answers often seem to be too ready, too simplistic, and self-perpetuating in nature. It is easy to think of the job of teaching as delivering the prescribed curriculum to students. Indeed, when we train to be teachers we often focus on the methods of delivering content. There are even courses at the university level referred to as "methods" courses. In our early years of teaching we often struggle with getting the curriculum across and agonize over failed lessons aimed at doing just that. This view of teaching is ubiquitous, generally shared by parents and students as well as teachers themselves. We see it playing out in our language when we talk about teacher "training," which usually means training in new methods. We see it in policymakers' efforts to improve education, which generally focus on changing the curriculum with the assumption that teachers will then deliver that curriculum and schools will improve as a result. We see it in the calls for enhanced content knowledge for teachers, an important thing to be sure, but oftentimes promoted as sufficient for effective teaching in and of itself.

We believe this view of teaching, as little more than the delivery of content, is not only an overly simplistic view of teaching but also a dangerous one in that it puts the focus on the teacher and not the learner, casting the learner in a passive role and assuming that learning is merely taking in what has been delivered. As a result of this view of teaching and learning, assessments focus on the degree of absorption by the student of what the teaching has delivered. Thus, we create a distorted view of teaching that is self-reinforcing and divorced from what we know about supporting effective learning. We judge teaching effectiveness based on student absorption of material, and teaching becomes defined as the delivery of that material. The educational system becomes distorted, being more concerned with producing effective test takers than successful learners (Gallagher, 2010). Consequently, the answer to the question "How does one learn to teach?" becomes, "By mastering the content and developing some delivery strategies." Oh, and you might want to learn some good classroom management techniques to deal with students' rebellion against their imposed passivity.

In contrast, when we place the learner at the hub of the educational enterprise, our focus as teachers shifts in a most fundamental way that has the potential to profoundly affect the way we define teaching. With the learner at the center of the educational enterprise, rather than at the end, our role as teachers shifts *from the delivery of information to fostering students' engagement with ideas.* Instead of covering the curriculum and judging our success by how much content we get through, we must learn to identify the key ideas and concepts with which we want our students to engage, struggle, question, explore, and ultimately build understanding. Our goal must be to make the big ideas of the curriculum accessible and engaging while honoring their complexity, beauty, and power in the process. When there is something important and worthwhile to think about and a reason to think deeply, our students experience the kind of learning that has a lasting impact and powerful influence not only in the short term but also in the long haul. They not only learn; they learn how to learn.

In Chapter One, we shared how this deeper understanding of the educational enterprise was pivotal in Mark Church's evolution as a teacher. He is not the only one for whom this is true of course. The literature on teacher change suggests that this shift from a focus on teaching to that of learning is a central aspect of many teachers' professional growth and integral to the process of learning to be an effective practitioner (Hatch, 2006; Intrator, 2002, 2006; McDonald, 1992; Palmer, 1998). Rather than seeing learning as the passive taking in of information, we must honor the fact that learning occurs as a result of our thinking and active sense making. Consequently, as teachers interested in both students' learning and understanding, we have two chief goals: (1) creating opportunities for thinking and (2) making students' thinking visible. Although these goals are not the same, they are synergistic and interdependent. When we create opportunities for thinking, we establish both the context and the need for making students' thinking visible.

In his book *Smart Schools,* our colleague David Perkins (1992) makes a case for the importance of developing opportunities for thinking: "Learning is a consequence of thinking. Retention, understanding, and the active use of knowledge can be brought about only by learning experiences in which learners think about and think with what they are learning. . . . Far from thinking coming after knowledge, knowledge comes on the coattails of thinking. As we think about and with the content that we are learning, we truly learn it" (p. 8). Thus, thinking is at the center of the learning enterprise and not a mere add-on, something to do if there is time. We as teachers must acknowledge that when we reduce the amount of thinking we ask of our students, we reduce the amount of learning as well. However, even when we create opportunities for thinking, we must realize that students' thinking may still be invisible to us. To make sure thinking isn't left to chance and to provide us with the information we need in order to respond to students' learning needs, we must also make their thinking visible.

HOW DOES VISIBILITY SERVE BOTH LEARNING AND TEACHING?

When we make thinking visible, we get not only a window into what students understand but also how they are understanding it. Uncovering students' thinking gives us evidence of students' insights as well as their misconceptions. We need to make thinking visible because it provides us with the information we as teachers need to plan opportunities that will take students' learning to the next level and enable continued engagement with the ideas being explored. It is only when we understand what our students' are thinking, feeling, and attending to that we can use that knowledge to further engage and support them in the process of understanding. Thus, making students' thinking visible becomes an ongoing component of effective teaching.

The Harvard Smithsonian Center for Astrophysics has famously documented how teachers' inattention to students' thinking leads to superficial learning and ingrained misconceptions about science even for students who succeed at the highest level. In their *Minds of Our Own* video, an honors chemistry teacher admits that "I don't like asking 'why' questions on tests. I spend so much time covering the concepts then I ask the question, 'Why?' and I get back so many different answers. It's sometimes very depressing to see some of the answers that you get back when you ask 'Why?' questions. They are valuable, but as a teacher it is sometimes very frustrating to see some of the reasons students think a certain scientific phenomenon takes place." This teacher, far from being cavalier or uncaring, is expressing the bind that he finds himself in when teaching for the test. He knows his students don't really understand what is being taught, but in the delivery paradigm of education he focuses on covering the material for the test and keeps their thinking invisible so as to allow for the semblance of learning, an illusion that equates scores on a test with evidence of learning. However widespread and ubiquitous this practice is—and make no mistake, teachers all over the world have been forced into accepting this compromise—this illusion, some might say delusion, about what real learning is serves no one well, least of all students who wind up being ill prepared for future learning (Schwartz, Sadler, Sonnert, & Tai, 2009). It also robs the teacher of the ability to confront students' misconceptions and design experiences to advance their understanding.

In contrast, our colleague Tina Grotzer, who directs the Complex Causality Project at Harvard Project Zero, has designed a series of modules on scientific concepts that directly confronts students' misconceptions and seeks to reveal their thinking so as to restructure it. For instance, in a unit on density, students watch as the teacher drops two candles of equal diameter, one short and one long, into two containers of liquid. The shorter candle floats while the larger candle sinks. Students are asked to write what they observed and explain why the event they witnessed happened. In doing so, students are encouraged to develop and put forth theories of explanation drawing on their scientific knowledge. Thus, at the outset students' thinking is surfaced through their words and drawings. The teacher then removes the candles from the two containers and switches them. This time the larger candle floats and the smaller one sinks; an unexpected outcome for most students. Again, students are asked to write about what they observed and to develop an explanation. Students then share their reactions and discuss how the simple experiment changed where they focused their attention. As the discussion unfolds, students become aware that though both liquids appear the same, they must differ in some respect and that sinking or floating is not a matter of simple linear causality in this instance but depends on the relationship between the liquid and the object placed into it.

By continually exposing students' thinking and pushing it forward through discrepant and unexpected events, the science teachers working with the Complex Causality modules stay in touch with students' developing understanding and are able to guide it throughout the lesson. At the same time, the teachers allow students' nascent theories to be the object of continual discussion, justification, and refinement, thus putting students in charge of developing their understanding and not merely providing them with information to memorize for the test. As this lesson demonstrates, making thinking visible benefits the teacher by providing an important assessment tool. At the same time, it helps to advance students' understanding.

Making students' thinking visible serves a broader educational goal as well. When we demystify the thinking and learning process, we provide models for students of what it means to engage with ideas, to think, and to learn. In doing so, we dispel the myth that learning is just a matter of committing the information in the textbook to one's memory. School no longer is about the "quick right answer" but about the ongoing mental work of understanding new ideas and information. Vygotsky (1978), writing about the importance of the sociocultural context of learning in providing models, stated, "Children grow into the intellectual life of those around them" (p. 88). As educators, this quote provides a powerful metaphor for what it means to educate another. Taking this quote seriously, we must then ask ourselves, What kind of intellectual life are we presenting to our students in our individual classrooms and in our school as a whole? What are my students learning about learning? What messages am I sending through the opportunities I create for my students about what learning is and how learning happens?

When we learn anything, we rely on models. We attend to what and how others are doing things, and we imitate them. This is as true and important for learning to learn and learning to think as it is for learning to dance or to play baseball. Imagine aspiring to be a great dancer without ever having seen great dancing. The novice imitates experts in an ever-advancing series of approximations of excellence, learning what works best for him- or herself along the way. Consequently, the students in our charge need to see an image of us as thinkers and learners that they can imitate and learn from. They need to see and hear others' perspectives, insights, and questions as they advance in their own understanding. Students need to see how others plan, monitor, and challenge their own thinking in ways that move them forward. Students need to see that all learners make mistakes and that learning often occurs from reflecting on those mistakes.

The important role that models of thinking and learning play helps us to see that an education is much more than the delivery of content. A quality education is also about the development of the habits of mind and thinking dispositions that will serve students as learners both in our own classrooms and in the future (Costa & Kallick, 2009; Ritchhart, 2002). For this to happen, teachers must help students to recognize the key features and contexts for the use of various types of thinking. This means we need to draw on our understanding of what thinking is and the types of thinking we seek to foster so that we can name, notice, and highlight thinking when it occurs in class: recognizing a student who puts forth a new point of view, offers up a nascent theory or conjecture, proposes an explanation, makes a connection, sees a pattern, and so on.

This naming and noticing is a central part of becoming capable in particular activities (Johnston, 2004). As Ellin Keene (E. Keene & Zimmermann, 1997) notes, until students can name a process they cannot control it. As our attention is drawn to thinking, we become more aware of it, its uses, and effects. This awareness of occasions for thinking is the foundation of all dispositions (Perkins, Tishman, Ritchhart, Donis, & Andrade, 2000; Ritchhart & Perkins, 2005; Tishman, Perkins, & Jay, 1993). We must first spot opportunities for thinking; only then can we activate our abilities. Without this noticing, our skills and knowledge lay inert and unused. As educators, we want students who not only can think but who *do* think. Thus, the visibility of thinking, both their own and others', provides the foundation for dispositional development. Once teachers start noticing and naming thinking, that is, making it visible, they as well as their students become more aware of thinking and it becomes difficult not to notice it in the future

(Harre & Gillet, 1994). When we make the thinking that happens in classrooms visible, it becomes more concrete and real. It becomes something we can talk about and explore, push around, challenge, and learn from.

In Lisa Verkerk's fifth grade classroom at the International School of Amsterdam, featured on the DVD, she frequently names and notices students' thinking as a way of providing specific feedback on learning rather than giving generic praise, that is, comments about good work or a job well done that only tell students they have pleased the teacher more than providing substantive information about their learning. Lisa draws students' attention to the thinking they have done. Commenting to two students who have worked to build their understanding of a series of photographs that highlight the plight of refugees, Lisa tells them, "I like how you have used your prior knowledge and what you already know to really build explanations of what is going on in these photographs. You've really looked closely and used evidence to back up your reasons." This kind of feedback provides students with a clear picture of the thinking they have done and a reference point they can draw on in their future learning.

HOW CAN WE MAKE THE INVISIBLE VISIBLE?

Making thinking visible is not without challenges. As we have discussed, we first must be clear in our own minds what thinking is. This allows us to make thinking visible by naming and noticing it as it occurs. In addition, for thinking to occur students must first have something to think about and be asked to think. We as teachers must create opportunities for thinking. However, even when opportunities for thinking are present, we must still recognize that thinking is largely an internal process, something that happens "under the hood" as it were. In the remainder of this chapter, we look at ways we as teachers can make students' thinking more visible through our questioning, listening, and documentation practices.

Questioning

The issue of asking good questions has long been a focus in education, particularly as it relates to students' thinking and the creation of opportunities for learning. Open-ended questions—as opposed to closed-ended, single-answer questions—are generally advocated as a means of pushing beyond knowledge and skill and toward understanding. In addition, Bloom's taxonomy, which was discussed in Chapter One, is often suggested as a template to help teachers ask better questions. The usual advice given is to make sure questions go beyond the knowledge level and push for application, analysis, synthesis, and evaluation. Moving beyond simple recall in questioning is certainly good advice and likely to create more opportunities for thinking. However, many teachers find that trying to ask more "higher-level" questions can feel stilted. Furthermore, teachers may find it hard to come up with such questions in the moment. Even when such questions are formulated and asked, they might not do as much to illuminate students' thinking as we might hope, particularly if it is perceived that the teacher is looking for a specific answer. In such cases, students will merely play the game of "Guess what's in the teacher's head."

A more flexible way of approaching the issue of questioning would be to think about how we as teachers can ask questions that (1) model our interest in the ideas being explored, (2) help students to construct understanding, and (3) facilitate the illumination of students' own thinking to themselves. Each of these represents not so much question types—though they may be classified this way—as they represent goals we have as teachers: to model intellectual engagement, to support students in constructing understanding, and to help students clarify their own thinking. In contrast, a lot of the questions asked in classrooms are about testing students' memory of what was taught. Such questions do not engage learners with ideas; they merely review content.

Modeling an Interest in Ideas.   Asking authentic questions—that is, questions to which the teacher does not already know the answer or to which there are not predetermined answers—is extremely powerful in creating a classroom culture that feels intellectually engaging. Such questions allow students to see teachers as learners and foster a community of inquiry. John Threlkeld, an algebra teacher at Colorado Academy in Denver, is a master of this. In observing his classroom over the course of a year, Ron Ritchhart often noticed he generally began his classes with questions such as, "You know, I was wondering if that pattern we looked at yesterday might be present in any of the other situations we have looked at in this unit. What do you think?" Or, "Yesterday, Amy found an interesting way of approaching the problem, and I was wondering if that would always work?" Martin Nystrand (Nystrand, Gamoran, Kachur, & Prenergast, 1997) and his colleagues have shown that these kinds of authentic questions, though exceedingly rare in most classrooms, have a positive influence on student engagement, critical thinking, and achievement. One can also think of authentic questions as being generative in nature. That is, they generate or help to promote class inquiry and discovery, framing learning as a complex, multifaceted, communal activity as opposed to a process of simply accumulating information. True generative questions have legs. They propel learning forward.

Good "essential questions" fall into this category of being generative as well. In her ninth grade humanities class, Kathy Hanawalt at Clover Park High School in Washington State uses a set of essential questions to focus her students on the fundamental issues of truth, perspective, and universality that lie at the heart of history and literature. Above her whiteboard on construction paper are five questions: What's the story? What's the other story? How do you know the story? Why know/tell the story? Where's the power in the story? These questions serve as the touch points for ongoing exploration of everything that happens in the class. When Kathy first began using the questions in her class, she found that her students were particularly captivated by looking at the notion of the other or hidden story to understand not only the events they were reading about but also those events around them. Even in simply sharing a recent event, she found that students were likely to ask the class, "Yeah, but what's the other story?" This question truly became essential and generative to students' learning. When reading accounts of history, current events, or political essays, the notion that there is another story and that uncovering it is necessary to truly understand people and events propelled learning and engaged students in Kathy's classroom. Using questions such as these supports students' learning of how to learn by sending messages that learning history involves uncovering the stories.

The provenance of authentic questions doesn't rest solely with the teacher, however. When students ask authentic questions, we know they are focused on the learning and not just the completion of assignments. Students' authentic questions are a good measure of their intellectual engagement. Middle school science teacher Paul Cripps in Wyoming says that students' questions are his best assessments of their learning. "I judge my students not by the answers they give, but by the questions they ask," he says. When observing in John Threlkeld's class Ron often heard him exclaim, "Great question!" At one point, Ron asked him, "What makes something a great question?" Without missing a beat he said, "Oh, a great question is one that gets us all thinking, including me." Through students' questions we get a glimpse into their thinking: What issues are engaging them? Where is there confusion? Where and how are they making connections? Where are they seeking clarification? Once one student has offered up his or her insights or confusion, we often see a ripple effect in the classroom that helps to produce the excitement and energy needed for learning.

Constructing Understanding. Our research team recently looked at teacher questioning in the Cultures of Thinking Project. We observed that when teachers focus on making thinking valued and visible in their classrooms, their questioning shifts away from asking review or knowledge-based questions to asking more constructive questions. (Note: More facilitative questions were also asked; these are discussed in the next section of the chapter.) Constructive questions can be thought of as those that help to advance understanding. These are questions that ask students to connect ideas, to make interpretations, to focus on big ideas and central concepts, to extend ideas, and so on. In studying teachers' questions in secondary mathematics classrooms, Jo Boaler and Karin Brodie (Boaler & Brodie, 2004) note that such questions not only serve to activate students' thinking but also to "guide students through the mathematical terrain of lessons" (p. 781). Constructive questions act, not as nice add-ons to make sure some so-called higher-order thinking is happening, but as the guideposts and goals for the lesson itself. Teachers' constructive questions navigate the important ideas and conceptual anchors in such a way as to ensure that they are not missed by students. Whereas teachers asking review-type questions tend to do so because they want to assess what students know and remember, teachers who ask constructive questions do so because they want to guide, direct, and push forward students' understanding of important ideas.

In her first grade class at the International School of Amsterdam, Stephanie Martin's students were learning about their senses. One of the goals of the unit was for students to be able to connect each of their senses with the kinds of information that can be gathered from it. In one lesson, Stephanie's students felt an object in a box and then described aloud what kinds of things they felt: squishy, soft, round edges, corners, and so on. Based on these responses, Stephanie then asked students to begin to make interpretations and assumptions: "What do you already know just by feeling it?" Followed up by "What do you not know by feeling it?" and "What does your feeling of it make you wonder?" These questions might not seem complex or difficult on the surface, but they go to the heart of what Stephanie wants her students to understand: What information do we get from each of our senses; and what can we do with that information? Without such questions, the activity of feeling a mystery object would be little more than a game and unlikely to yield much learning.

Cathy Humphrey in her middle school algebra class in California's Silicon Valley uses questions to make sure that students aren't merely learning rote procedures but are focusing on the underlying mathematics (Boaler & Humphreys, 2005). Two entire class periods are focused on the constructive question: Why is two times the quantity n minus 1, that is, $2(n - 1)$, equal to $2n - 2$? Cathy asks her students to explain in their own words why it is true and to develop arguments that will convince a skeptic: "If you were gonna try to prove to someone that this always would work, how would you do it?" Cathy's intent here is not to review the distributive property, which students haven't formally been taught, but to focus students on how to think about the idea of "quantities" as expressed when using the parentheses in mathematics. She wants students to be able to understand that such quantities are entities unto themselves that can be operated upon. In doing so, she is also pushing her students to go beyond arithmetic explanations; that is, trying to prove something true by simply substituting in a number for n to see if it works. As useful as such test cases might be, they don't really constitute a proof, so Cathy asks her students to think like a skeptic and try to prove the equality. Anthony shows his understanding when he responds, "Okay, it's just like you are doing those two (meaning the quantity $n - 1$)—you're doing n minus one twice and you're adding it together . . . and then it's the same thing as doing two n minus two because you're still gonna subtract two."

As these two examples illustrate, constructive questions frame the intellectual endeavor in which students are to be engaged and point them toward uncovering fundamental ideas and principles that aid understanding. This may seem like a tall order to place on teachers' shoulders. However, this is precisely where the thinking routines that will be presented in Part Two of this book can be useful. The steps of each of the routines outline a set of constructive moves that students can make to facilitate their understanding and make their thinking visible. For example, in Stephanie Martin's lesson mentioned earlier, she began her lesson by adapting the See-Think-Wonder routine into Feel-Think-Wonder. Her initial question, "What did you feel when you reached into the mystery box?" directs students to making observations based on touch. Then, "What do you think about what you felt?" moves students toward interpretations and the exploration of possibilities. Finally, Stephanie asked her students, "What are you left wondering about the object in the box given that we were only able to feel it?" When you read about other routines in Part Two, keep in mind their constructive nature that you as a teacher can direct toward the specific ideas and concepts you want students to explore and understand.

Facilitating and Clarifying Thinking. "What makes you say that?" This question is often one of the most fully integrated thinking routines in the classrooms of teachers with whom we have worked. You'll see many of the teachers featured on the DVD integrating this question into their interactions with students. (You can also read more about its use in Chapter Six.) At Bialik College, where teachers have formed professional learning communities as part of the Cultures of Thinking Project, one teacher remarked, " 'What makes you say that?' isn't just a teaching tool; it is a way of life." She said she learns so much more and has much deeper conversations with friends and family just by asking "What makes you say that?" instead of responding right away to people's comments. Teachers remark that the wording of this question seems to strike just the right tone with people and invites them to elaborate on and clarify their ideas in a nonthreatening way. Although "Tell me why?" or "Give me your reasons and evidence for that statement" serve the same role, they seem not to convey the same level of openness and interest.

This simple yet powerful question is a perfect example of the kind of question that can facilitate and clarify the learner's own thinking. In using facilitative questions, the teacher's goal is to try and understand students' thinking, to get inside their heads and make their thinking visible. Again, it is switching the paradigm of teaching from trying to transmit what is in our heads to our students and toward trying to get what is in students' heads into our own so that we can provide responsive instruction that will advance learning.

Jim Minstrell, a former secondary science teacher who now directs research efforts in science education aimed at uncovering students' thinking, studied his own teaching and carefully examined the way he interacted with his students through his questioning during his time at Mercer Island High School in Washington State. He coined the term "reflective toss" to describe the questioning sequence he uses to facilitate and clarify students' thinking (Zee & Minstrell, 1997). Traditionally, we have often characterized the discourse of the classroom as originating from the questions teachers ask. However, Jim takes students' comments and ideas as the starting point for dialogue. In the reflective toss, the teacher's first goal is to try to "catch" students' meaning and try to understand their comments. If meaning can't be grasped immediately, then a follow-up question, such as "Can you say more about that?" or "I'm not quite following you, can you say what you were thinking in a different way?" is asked. Once the meaning is grasped by the teacher, then the teacher "tosses" back a question that will push the student to further elaborate and justify their thinking, both to the teacher and to themselves. For instance, Jim might ask students, "What does that tell you then?" "What do you think you were basing that on?" or even our old standby, "What makes you say that?"

This sequence of questioning has a huge advantage over the traditional question, respond, evaluate pattern (Cazden, 1988) that we find with review-type questions in that it facilitates students clarifying their own thinking and ideas in such a way that new understanding is developed that the student owns. Rather than being a passive agent who merely takes in what the teacher has said, the student becomes an active agent in constructing his or her understanding. British researcher Douglas Barnes, who has studied the role of language in shaping learning throughout his long career, states that the more a learner "is enabled to think aloud, the more he can take responsibility for formulating explanatory hypotheses and evaluating them" (Barnes, 1976, p. 29).

Listening

Ron Ritchhart recalls a pivotal episode from when he was a mathematics coach. Rather than being a one-off, it was an episode that seemed to repeat itself over and over again at the various schools where he was working: "I would teach a mathematics lesson in one teacher's classroom with other teachers from the same grade level observing. After we had debriefed the lesson, the observing teachers were encouraged to teach the lesson and share their experience with the group in our next session together. Invariably, at these follow-up sessions a teacher would remark, 'I wrote down all the questions you asked, and I was very careful to ask the same questions, but my students didn't respond the same way as when you did it.' This happened enough times among the teachers with whom I was working that I decided to investigate what was happening."

What he observed was that indeed the teachers were doing their best to ask the same key questions—questions that were generally constructive in nature—he had asked at pivotal points in the lesson. However, students often gave short answers or seemed to be guessing rather than thinking mathematically. This wasn't a problem with the students, however, as Ron had rotated his demonstration teaching among all the classes. He also noticed that when students didn't respond the way the teachers had expected, the teachers were often stumped about how to respond and tended to just move the lesson forward. Ron concluded, "It is one thing to ask good questions, but one also has to *listen for the answers*." The teachers, in part because they were taking risks and trying new ways of teaching mathematics with which they were unfamiliar, were so focused on what they were going to do or say next that they often failed to listen to students. This had two effects on the class: first, it inadvertently sent a signal that the teacher was not as interested in hearing the students' thoughts as in hearing a specific answer. As a result, the students played "Guess what is in the teacher's head" rather than stating their true ideas and understanding. Second, by not listening, the teachers had trouble being responsive to students through appropriate follow-up (facilitative) questions. Good questions, that is, questions that drive learning, don't come from some prescribed list or set of guidelines; they arise in response to students' contributions. If we don't listen to those thoughts, we rob ourselves of the information we need to be able to ask good questions. If we don't first "catch" students' meaning, we will be hard pressed to "toss" back a question that pushes them to elaborate or clarify their thinking.

In the Reggio Emilia preschools of Italy, they espouse the idea of a pedagogy of listening. Carla Rinaldi, the director of the preschools and executive consultant for Reggio Children, holds that listening must be the basis of the learning relationship that teachers seek to form with students. Within such a learning context, "individuals feel legitimated to represent their theories and offer their own interpretations of a particular question" (Giudici, Rinaldi, & Krechevsky, 2001). Listening conveys a sense of respect for and an interest in the learner's contributions. When this is present, students are more willing to share their thinking and put forth their ideas, just as we as adults respond more when we know the person we are talking with is interested in us and our ideas. These same sentiments are eloquently expressed by poet Alice Duer Miller (1915) in her observation that "listening is not merely not talking, though even that is beyond most of our powers; it means taking a vigorous, human interest in what is being told us." This vigorous human interest allows us to build community in the classroom and develop interactions that pivot around the exploration of ideas. Our listening provides the opening for students to make their thinking visible to us because there is a reason to do so.

As teachers, our listening to students provides a model for our students of what it means to listen. In classrooms where teachers routinely ask, "What makes you say that?" they invariably notice that students soon pick this up as an appropriate and useful way to respond to one another's contributions. Developing active listeners isn't just a nice side benefit, however. Brigid Barron (2003) studied group interactions among sixth graders solving mathematics problems collaboratively to try to identify what made some groups successful while other groups floundered. In her paper, "When Smart Groups Fail," she found that group success was far less dependent on the academic skills of the group than it was in the group's ability to listen and respond to one another's ideas. Successful groups engaged with the ideas of the group members, echoing back the ideas that were presented and asking clarifying and probing questions of one another. In these groups, individual members did not just talk; they also listened and sought greater equality among all group members. This allowed them to build on one another's ideas and advance far beyond groups with academically more proficient students.

Documenting

Another tool for making students' thinking visible is the use of documentation: recording of the class's investigation on the whiteboard, photographs of students working, audiotapes of the class discussion, written notes of students' ideas and contributions, students' papers and drawings, and so on. To those new to documenting students' thinking, it might be easy to confuse documentation with merely recording what the class has done, a sort of archive of activity through the collection of various forms of documents. However, to be useful to both teachers and students, documentation must extend beyond this. At its heart, the documentation process, which has its origin in the Reggio Emilia preschools but has since moved to include all grade levels through the work of the Making Learning Visible project at Harvard, is focused on the learning process itself by trying to capture the events, questions, conversations, and acts that provoke and advance learning over time.

Our Project Zero colleagues, Mara Kerchevsky, Terri Turner, Ben Mardell, and Steve Seidel, have been investigating how documentation supports students' learning from early childhood through secondary school. They define *documentation* "as the practice of observing, recording, interpreting, and sharing, through a variety of media, the processes and products of teaching and learning in order to deepen learning" (Given, Kuh, LeeKeenan, Mardell, Redditt, & Twombly, 2010, p. 38). Embedded in this definition is the idea that documentation must serve to advance learning, not merely capture it. As such, documentation includes not only what is collected but also the discussions and reflections on those artifacts. In this way, documentation both connects to the act of listening and extends it. To capture and record students' thinking, teachers must be vigilant observers and listeners. When teachers capture students' ideas, they are signaling that those ideas and thoughts have value and are worthy of continued exploration and examination.

In Stephanie Martin's first grade class, as students share what they felt inside the mystery box, she records their individual contributions on sticky notes and places them on chart paper. This allows students to see that their ideas have value and exist as contributions to the class's discussion. The documentation of the class's observations about what was felt then becomes a foundation that Stephanie and the class can connect to as they move on to discuss what they think and wonder about those observations. The documentation demonstrates Stephanie's listening and provides the basis for the ongoing class conversation about the object in the mystery box. In Brigid Barron's (2003) study of successful groups, she found similar examples of documentation happening among students themselves. Documentation of the ongoing problem-solving process allowed all group members to access the thinking of the group and feel a sense of ownership of it. The documentation also allowed the group to monitor progress and make contributions and ask questions at appropriate points in the process that would advance the understanding of the group. In contrast, unsuccessful groups were often those where the written work of the group was done by a single member and not easily accessed by others. This practice led to disenfranchisement of some group members.

Documentation of students' thinking serves another important purpose in that it provides a stage from which both teachers and students may observe the learning process, make note of the strategies being used, and comment on the developing understanding. The visibility afforded by documentation provides the basis for reflecting on one's learning and for considering that learning as an object for discussion. In this way, documentation demystifies the learning process both for the individual as well as the group, building greater metacognitive awareness in the process. For teachers, this reflection on students' learning functions as assessment in the truest sense of the word. Documentation, while not used for grading, often provides a rich and potentially illuminating glimpse into students' learning and understanding. To uncover this richness, we often need more sets of eyes than ours alone. Sharing documentation with colleagues can lead to rich discussions of learning and allow us to see and notice aspects of students' thinking and implications for instructions that we, as teachers working on our own, might easily miss. We explore how this collegiality can facilitate rich professional learning in Chapter Eight as well as on the DVD clip of a professional learning group using the LAST protocol to discuss a piece of documentation.

When we as teachers frame our core activity not as delivering the curriculum to a passive group of students but as engaging students actively with ideas and then uncovering and guiding their thinking about those ideas, the strategies presented in this chapter take on a new sense of urgency and importance. We make students' thinking visible through our questioning, listening, and documenting so that we can build on and extend that thinking on the way to deeper and richer understanding. These core practices provide the backdrop for our discussion of thinking routines in Part Two of this book. Rather than seeing the routines as separate practices, it is important to view them as structures that grow out of and extend our ongoing practice of questioning, listening, and documenting. As you will see, thinking routines are effective and really come alive in classrooms when they emerge from and are linked to enduring efforts to make thinking visible. Look for these connections as you read through the Pictures of Practice accompanying each of the thinking routines in Part Two of this book.

USING THINKING ROUTINES TO MAKE THINKING VISIBLE

CHAPTER 3

Introduction to Thinking Routines

In this chapter, we formally present the idea of thinking routines and look at how this special kind of classroom routine can further help us as teachers to make thinking visible and support students' development of understanding. Routines can be thought of as any procedure, process, or pattern of action that is used repeatedly to manage and facilitate the accomplishment of specific goals or tasks. Classrooms are dominated by such routines. Teachers have routines that serve to manage student behavior and interactions, to organize the work environment, to facilitate transitions, or to maintain rules for communication and discourse. In earlier research, we found that teachers who are successful at promoting students' thinking tend to develop, adapt, and make use of specific routines to scaffold and support students' thinking (Ritchhart, 2002). These simple procedures, usually consisting of only a few steps, provide a framework for focusing attention on specific thinking moves that can help to build understanding. Just as routines for lining up or handing in homework become engrained, thinking routines also become part of the fabric of the classroom over time. To understand how thinking routines operate in the classroom and how you might use the routines presented here, as well as how you might create your own, it is helpful to look at routines from three perspectives: as tools, as structures, and as patterns of behavior.

THREE WAYS OF LOOKING AT THINKING ROUTINES
As Tools

Thinking routines operate as tools for promoting thinking. Just like any tool, it is important to choose the right tool for the job. If a hammer is needed, a saw doesn't work very well and feels awkward. Extending this metaphor further, one doesn't make big pronouncements about the use of a tool as much as one identifies and focuses the crew on a goal or objective to be achieved and puts the appropriate tools to use to achieve it. In Chapter One, specific types of thinking that promote understanding were discussed. These included observing closely and describing what is there, building explanations and interpretations, reasoning with evidence, making connections, considering different viewpoints and perspectives, capturing the heart and forming conclusions, wondering and asking questions, and uncovering complexity and going below the surface of things. Each of the routines presented here in Part Two is a tool for promoting one or more of these kinds of thinking. For instance, the Think-Puzzle-Explore routine asks students to think about what they *think* they know about the topic at hand, which is making connections to prior knowledge; to identify what is *puzzling* to them, which is wondering and questioning; and then to begin the process of planning out an *exploration* of one of those puzzles, which is formulating plans. Therefore, as teachers we must first identify what kind of thinking we are trying to elicit from our students and then select the particular thinking routine as the tool for that job.

Identifying the thinking at the outset also helps us to focus our assessment of students' responses within the routine. Although the routines are open-ended and aren't used to elicit specific responses, there is still a place for ongoing, formative assessment. For instance, if we know we are looking for reasoning with evidence, then we can push students to back up their assertions with evidence if they fail to do so. Or, if the routine focuses on connection making through metaphorical thinking, then we want to push students to go beyond the obvious connections to those that are more nuanced. Each of the routines is written to help you keep thinking at the forefront. The "Purposes" section of each routine highlights the kinds of thinking the routine is designed to elicit. The "Selecting Appropriate Content" section provides further information on the kinds of classroom situations and subject matter content for which the routine might be useful. In the "Assessment" section, tips for formative assessment are given regarding what to look for and attend to in students' responses both in the moment and over time. In addition, suggestions are provided about how you might push students' thinking further.

Finally, since the thinking routines operate as tools for thinking, this means that they should be useful to students as well as teachers. Rather than just activities that help teachers engage their students more actively, thinking routines are tools that students can use to support their own thinking. The routines exist both as public practices that can be useful in groups at school and as private practices to be used by individuals. Indeed, this is the true power of the routines in developing students as thinkers and learners. For instance, a teacher can ask you, "What makes you say that?" But it is also useful to recognize when one has made an assumption in one's own speech, writing, or reflection and ask oneself, "What makes *me* say that?" When this occurs, students are acting as independent learners and truly demonstrating the development of thinking dispositions.

As Structures

The thinking routines that the Visible Thinking and Cultures of Thinking teams of researchers have developed and used in classrooms throughout the world have been carefully crafted to support and structure students' thinking. The steps of the routine act as natural scaffolds that can lead students' thinking to higher and more sophisticated levels. For instance, in developing the Generate-Sort-Connect-Elaborate routine for concept mapping, we first looked at what kinds of thinking needed to happen to create a concept map that would help a student to both construct and display his or her understanding. First, we identified that it was necessary to generate ideas broadly, almost in brainstorming mode. Then, to make use of the graphic nature of concept maps, those ideas needed to be sorted in some way. This sorting was a key step that many students were not doing because they had been taught to just write their ideas on the paper as they occurred. Consequently, a key thinking move was being excluded. Once the ideas were sorted, perhaps around importance or centrality to the topic, then connections between ideas could be made and some significant areas of the map elaborated.

Just like Generate-Sort-Connect-Elaborate, the steps in all of the routines follow a natural progression in which each step builds on and extends the thinking of the previous one. Therefore, in using the routines the goal is never simply to fill out or complete one step and move on to the next but to use the thinking occurring at each step in the subsequent steps. This sequential aspect of routines can be helpful as you begin trying the routines out in your classroom. Think about how you will use students' responses and connect them to the next step of the routine, continually looking for how good thinking at one stage sets up good thinking in the next stage. For instance, in See-Think-Wonder, the close observations of the "See" stage provide the foundation for well-grounded inter-pretations at the "Think" stage. If the class has failed to notice much in the way of detail and nuance, then often the thinking is little more than unsupported opinion or guessing.

In the description of each routine presented in Part Two, the thinking moves of the routine are presented concisely in bullet-point form at the beginning so that you can quickly get a feel for how the routine operates from the learner's perspective. These are the learner's actions. These steps might be written out for the learners or in some cases posted in the room for future reference. Other times, a teacher may seamlessly weave in the steps of the routine within the flow of a lesson. Each of these thinking moves are then elaborated further in the "Steps" section, in which suggestions are given for the initial use of the routine by the teacher, the teacher's actions as it were. The "Tips" section provides further pointers about things to consider, or in some cases watch out for, in using the routine.

Another way thinking routines operate as structures is that they often become structures for whole-class or small-group discussions. Sometimes, we as teachers struggle with how to support students in worthwhile and meaningful discussions on their own. Such discussions may be inhibited due to a lack of listening, as was discussed in Chapter Two, or by an over-focus on work completion. If students feel like the group's job is to fill out the worksheet, then they focus their attention on the worksheet rather than the discussion. Once a thinking routine is well known to students, the routine itself can become useful in structuring the group's discussion. For example, the 4C's routine and Connect-Extend-Challenge, which you can view being used for both whole-class and small-group discussion on the DVD, are useful routines for supporting small-group discussions around readings or presentations.

As Patterns of Behavior

At Project Zero we have often been asked why we have chosen to call these practices "thinking routines" and not thinking strategies. This is not just a cosmetic shift in language. The idea of thinking routines must be understood within the broader notion of classroom routines as culture builders (Leinhardt, Weidman, & Hammond, 1987; Ritchhart, 2002; Ritchhart, Palmer, Church, & Tishman, 2006). Routines are a useful way of thinking about the practice of teaching in that they recognize that effective teaching depends on more than the design of units and delivery of lessons, as discussed in Chapter Two. All instruction takes place within a context, and routines contribute to the establishment of that context through the creation of socially shared, scripted slices of behavior (Leinhardt & Steele, 2005; Yinger, 1979). Whereas an instructional strategy may be used only on occasion, routines become part of the fabric of the classroom through their repeated use. Effective teachers of thinking address the development of students' thinking in this way, by developing a set of routines that they and their students can use again and again (Ritchhart, 2002). Since the routines are "shared scripts," students are able to use them with increasing independence.

Although the word *routine* carries with it notions of ordinariness, habit, and ritual, it would be a mistake to characterize thinking routines as simply mundane patterns of behavior. Classroom routines are practices crafted to achieve specific ends in an efficient and workable manner. While these practices do become "our way of doing things," their adoption as routines—that is, as patterns of operating—grows out of teachers' recognition of them as effective tools for achieving specific ends. With use, these tools become flexible rather than rigid, continuously evolving with use. Consequently, we observe that the teachers with whom we have worked are continually adapting the routines to better serve the learning at hand. In the "Pictures of Practice" section of each routine, you'll see how teachers have used each of the thinking routines flexibly and to good advantage to support their goals for students' thinking and learning. These stories usually highlight teachers' evolving use of routines over time and give you a glimpse into how the routine has become a pattern of behavior in the teacher's classroom. In the "Uses and Variations" section of each routine, short examples of additional ways teachers have used the routine that might not immediately occur to you are also provided.

When thinking routines are used regularly in classrooms and become part of the pattern of the classroom, students internalize messages about what learning is and how it happens. For instance, one of the things you will notice in many of the routines is that they are designed not to elicit specific answers but to uncover students' nascent thinking around the topic. This sends the message that learning is not a process of absorbing others' ideas, thoughts, or practices but involves uncovering one's own ideas as the starting point for learning. Learning then becomes about connecting new ideas to one's own thinking. Another key thinking move in many of the routines is wondering and questioning as an ongoing part of learning. Often we as teachers begin units by asking questions but pay less attention to questions as an evolving and ongoing part of the learning. Indeed, teachers may give the impression that learning is a matter of finding answers to one's questions and that once those answers are found the learning stops. Through ongoing use of the routines, this idea that questions not only drive learning but also are outcomes of learning becomes embedded in the learning process. In Chapter Seven, this idea of creating a classroom culture in which students learn how to learn and thinking is made visible is taken up further.

HOW ARE THE THINKING ROUTINES ORGANIZED?

There are many ways one might organize the twenty-one thinking routines presented here. Originally the Visible Thinking Project, funded by Carpe Vitam and conducted with colleagues David Perkins, Shari Tishman, Ron Ritchhart, and Patricia Palmer, grouped the routines around four key thinking ideals: understanding, truth, fairness, and creativity. Other times the routines have been organized around specific types of thinking, such as looking closely, reasoning, or building explanations. On other occasions, it has been useful to organize the routines around those most commonly and widely used at a particular level or subject area. Some routines work particularly well with adults in facilitating group learning and problem solving, and this presents yet another possible grouping. Here we have chosen to group the routines into three major categories: Introducing and Exploring, Synthesizing and Organizing, and Digging Deeper. These categories reflect the way teachers often plan for and attend to the different parts of a unit of study.

In working with teachers over the years, our team has found that the routines, while useful individually, take on more power when used to support students' ongoing learning across a unit, that is, to build an arc of learning rather than to craft a single episode. To facilitate this process of planning and developing a unit, we grouped the routines from those that tend to be used early in a unit, to those that come in the middle, to those that often serve a more culminating function. In Chapter Four we pull together thinking routines that are useful for introducing and exploring new ideas. These are the routines teachers often use at the beginning of units to develop interest and begin the process of inquiry. In Chapter Five, we present those routines that are useful for organizing and synthesizing information. These routines take students beyond their initial exploration of a topic and are often useful in making sense of new information that students have read, discussed, or viewed during a unit of study. In Chapter Six, we look at routines that go a step further and push students to go below the surface of things and consider the complexity of issues and ideas. A brief overview of the routines presented in each chapter, their key thinking moves, and a brief explanation is presented in Table 3.1.

As you read through Part Two of the book and identify routines that you think will be useful tools in your classroom, you may well find that a routine that we have identified as good for introducing a topic is also useful for digging deeper or culminating a unit of study. We encourage such flexibility and broad thinking when situating the routine properly in the classroom. Likewise, our intention with the "Pictures of Practice" stories and the "Uses and Variations" sections is to stimulate new possibilities for you rather than limit your thinking. Working with educators across all grade and subject levels, including those at universities and in museums, we are continually amazed at the inventive way teachers, facilitators, and leaders have taken the routines we have developed and combined or adapted them to support their learners' thinking and understanding in unique ways. In describing the routines, we often refer to "students"; however, we have found the routines work well with adults in situations when the facilitator or leader desires to make the group's thinking visible. In whatever context you choose to use them, many educators find that when first using the routines it is useful to try them in a straightforward format so that both they and their students can get used to the steps of the routine and understand how they operate to facilitate thinking. Once the teacher is comfortable with the use of the routine, not as an activity but as a vehicle for promoting thinking, then meaningful adaptations and variations often begin to emerge.

Table 3.1 Thinking Routines Matrix

Routine	Key Thinking Moves	Notes and Brief Description
	Chapter Four: Routines for Introducing and Exploring Ideas	
See-Think-Wonder	Describing, interpreting, and wondering	Good with ambiguous or complex visual stimuli
Zoom In	Describing, inferring, and interpreting	Variation of STW using only portions of an image
Think-Puzzle-Explore	Activating prior knowledge, wondering, planning	Good at the beginning of a unit to direct personal or group inquiry and uncover current understandings as well as misconceptions
Chalk Talk	Uncovering prior knowledge and ideas, questioning	Open-ended discussion on paper; ensures all voices are heard, gives thinking time
3–2–1 Bridge	Activating prior knowledge, questioning, distilling, and connection making through metaphors	Works well when students have prior knowledge but instruction will move it in a new direction; can be done over extended time during the course of a unit
Compass Points	Decision making and planning, uncovering personal reactions	Solicits the group's ideas and reactions to a proposal, plan, or possible decision
The Explanation Game	Observing details and building explanations	Variation of STW that focuses on identifying parts and explaining them in order to build up an understanding of the whole from its parts and their purposes
	Chapter Five: Routines for Synthesizing and Organizing Ideas	
Headlines	Summarizing, capturing the heart	Quick summaries of the big ideas or what stands out
CSI: Color, Symbol, Image	Capturing the heart through metaphors	Nonverbal routine that forces visual connections
Generate-Sort-Connect-Elaborate: Concept Maps	Uncovering and organizing prior knowledge to identify connections	Highlights the thinking steps of making an effective concept map that both organizes and reveals one's thinking

(continued)

Table 3.1 *(continued)*

Routine	Key Thinking Moves	Quick Notes and Brief Description
Connect-Extend-Challenge	Connection making, identifying new ideas, raising questions	Key synthesis moves for dealing with new information in whatever form it might be presented: books, lecture, movie, and so on
The 4C's	Connection making, identifying key concept, raising questions, and considering implications	A text-based routine that helps identifies key points of complex text for discussion; demands a rich text or book
The Micro Lab Protocol	Focusing attention, analyzing, and reflecting	Can be combined with other routines and used to prompt reflection and discussion
I Used to Think..., Now I Think...	Reflecting and metacognition	Used to help learners reflect on how their thinking has shifted and changed over time
Chapter Six: Routines for Digging Deeper into Ideas		
What Makes You Say That?	Reasoning with evidence	A question that teachers can weave into discussion to push students to give evidence for their assertions
Circle of Viewpoints	Perspective taking	Identification of perspectives around an issue or problem
Step Inside	Perspective taking	Stepping into a position and talking or writing from that perspective to gain a deeper understanding of it
Red Light, Yellow Light	Monitoring, identifying of bias, raising questions	Used to identify possible errors in reasoning, over-reaching by authors, or areas that need to be questioned
Claim-Support-Question	Identifying generalizations and theories, reasoning with evidence, making counterarguments	Can be used with text or as a basic structure for mathematical and scientific thinking
Tug-of-War	Perspective taking, reasoning, identifying complexities	Identifying and building both sides of an argument or tension/dilemma
Sentence-Phrase-Word	Summarizing and distilling	Text-based protocol aimed at eliciting what a reader found important or worthwhile; used with discussion to look at themes and implications

CHAPTER 4

Routines for Introducing and Exploring Ideas

⚙ SEE-THINK-WONDER

Looking at an image or object:

- What do you see?
- What do you think is going on?
- What does it make you wonder?

In and out of the classroom, we've seen the power of evocative images and complex art to spark students' interest and thinking. The See-Think-Wonder (STW) routine emerged out of our interest in harnessing the power of looking closely, not only at art but also with a wide variety of objects and stimuli, as a foundational element of much of our learning. This routine was designed to draw on students' close looking and intent observation as the foundation for greater insights, grounded interpretations, evidenced-based theory building, and broad-reaching curiosity.

Purpose

This routine emphasizes the importance of observation as the basis for the thinking and interpretation step that follows the close looking. At the beginning of this routine, students spend a few minutes silently looking at a work of art, image, or some kind of artifact. This "Seeing" provides the opportunity to look carefully, to more fully observe, and to notice before interpreting. The placement of "Wonder" as the final step of the routine ensures that learners have had time to take in new information through careful observation, think about and synthesize this information, and then identify additional wonderings. These wonderings can open up whole new areas of exploration and thinking initiated by the students themselves. Consequently, this routine is a favorite choice of teachers in starting a unit of study as it allows questions to be raised that might guide future inquiry.

Selecting Appropriate Content

Although the term *image/object* is used for the sake of this explanation, the learners may be asked to look carefully at a painting, photo, artifact, video clip, excerpt of text, political cartoon, chart, found object—in fact, almost anything that can be observed, interpreted, and wondered about. However, selecting an evocative, engaging stimulus is critical. Since the first step of the routine focuses on careful observation, there need to be significant elements in the image/object to see and notice to ensure the routine is relevant. This generally means that the image/object has some ambiguity to it, is not already known to students, offers many different layers of explanation, and possesses a degree of detail that is likely to emerge only after extended looking. A good test is to ask yourself whether the image/object engages you. Can you look at it for several minutes and notice new things? Does it spark your curiosity?

Steps

1. *Set up.* Present the chosen image in a way that allows students to see the image/object in as much detail as possible: projecting it on a screen in a darkened room, having a large printed copy that the whole class can see when seated together, or multiple copies that pairs can look at. Allow sufficient silent time for close observation, 2 or 3 minutes, before any talk or discussion.

2. *See.* Ask learners to state what they noticed. Emphasize that you are not looking for interpretations at this stage, only what they observe. A useful prompt is to tell students that an observation is something you could actually put your fingers on within the image/object. One method of debriefing the "I see's" is to have students do a Think-Pair-Share. Then the class discussion might start with sharing those things your partner noticed that you hadn't.

3. *Think.* Ask learners what they think is going on in the image/object. This general, interpretive question may be modified to suit the image/object. For instance, you might ask, "Based on what we are seeing and noticing, what does it make us think? What kinds of interpretations can we form based on our observations?" The goal here is to build up layers of tentative interpretation rather than merely naming the subject matter. Push students for alternatives and additions: "What else is going on here?" It is often effective to respond to students' responses with "What do you see that makes you say that?" This encourages learners to provide supporting evidence. In time, this develops more considered responses, helping move students away from guessing or unsubstantiated opinions.

4. *Wonder.* Ask learners what they are now wondering about based on what they have seen and have been thinking. Initially, students may find it hard to separate "thinking" from "wondering." For instance, they may wonder whether their interpretations are correct: "I wonder if she really is his sister." Or their initial "thinks" may be framed as tentative and conditional wonderings: "I wonder if that object in the corner is a boat?" To help address this confusion, you might suggest that wondering is about asking broader questions that push us beyond our interpretations to look at issues and ideas raised by the image/object.

5. *Share the thinking.* In this routine, students are generally sharing their thinking at each step along the way before moving on to the next one. This allows the class to build on the group's thinking at the previous stage and often results in richer discussions than might be had alone. It can be very useful to document the thinking at each stage as it happens, though it is not always necessary. If the use of STW is to generate interest in a topic and raise questions, then wonderings can be written down and posted around the room to encourage ongoing consideration, and students can be encouraged to add to the wonderings over time as new ideas occur.

Uses and Variations

Depending on the image/object, the STW steps can be completed one at a time (as just described) or by using the three prompts—See, Think, Wonder—together at the same time. This means students begin by naming something they "see," stating what they "think" about it (their interpretations of that observation), and then raising a question. For instance, "I see a lot of black in the image. I think that means it is nighttime. I wonder if the darkness is also reflective of the artist's mood?" At Bialik College, June Kamenetzky's grade 1 students used STW this way during their unit on communication. June brought in various images of hieroglyphics, cave drawings, and symbols on ancient coins for her class to examine. Their observations of each detail followed by thoughts about these then led students to many new puzzles and wonderings. The opportunity for students to express their wonders led to new pathways of investigation and a much richer unit of inquiry.

During a unit on identity in grade 2, Nellie Gibson, also at Bialik College, gave each child a sheet with a picture of themselves on it and asked them to do a See-Think-Wonder individually. Students were engrossed in the topic—themselves—and were quite good at completing the routine independently. Nellie's objective was to raise wonderings that might be explored later, and students' responses didn't disappoint: "I wonder wot [sic] it looks like inside your eyes?" "I wonder if my nose is like my parents or grama's or granpa's?" "I wonder why my mum and dad have dark brown hair and I have light brown hair?" "How does your tongue allow you to talk?"

Another colleague, Zia Freeman, used STW to help her preschool students engage in an ongoing exploration of the idea of a "princess." Zia was interested in helping students break commercial and gender stereotypes and found that engaging students in looking at and discussing different images, many of which were nontraditional, of princesses helped them to do so. In one particular episode, these four-year-olds were able to look at and discuss one image for more than 40 minutes.

A variation on STW has been used to structure teachers' classroom observations. Teachers from a professional learning group at Bialik College, a private preK–12 school in the suburbs of Melbourne, Australia, visited each others' classes and made a list of what they saw and heard, carefully avoiding interpretations such as "Everyone was engaged" or "Students were off task." Having had experience using STW in their classrooms, they were aware of the importance of just observing without judgment or interpretation. Later when they met as a group and discussed their observations, teachers would begin with something they had seen or heard, make a couple of possible interpretations, and raise a question about it. Having the structure of this routine for the visits ensured respectful and focused conversations centered on trying to understand the complexity of the classroom rather than evaluating the effectiveness of a particular lesson. Consequently the teachers being observed felt more respected and invited into the goal of understanding rather than defending the lesson.

Assessment

In students' "See" responses, look for improvement in their ability to notice details that take them deeper into the image rather than getting stuck on immediate surface features. In the "Think" step, pay attention to the kinds of support students are able to provide for their interpretations in response to the "What makes you say that?" prompt. Are students drawing on evidence from their observations to create a coherent link, or are they merely making assertions based on beliefs and opinion? In the "Wonder" step, look for questions that are broad and adventurous rather than limited to those that require very specific factual responses. It may take students time to develop these types of responses, and they may need models of what it means to wonder if they are not used to asking themselves open-ended questions. The type and depth of questions posed also can illustrate students' understanding of the topic, as their questions tend to reach more to the heart of core issues the more they understand.

You can get a feel for how students can engage in STW at a very independent and high level of performance by watching Lisa Verkerk's grade 5 students at the International School of Amsterdam on the DVD. Lisa has students work in small groups of three to look carefully at art work from Rod Brown before reading the text Julius Lester has written to go with the images. Lisa's students have used the routine extensively in both her classroom and at previous grade levels. Thus, they are used to giving themselves time to look closely and generate possible explanations based on evidence.

Tips

Make sure you give enough time to looking closely and noticing details. You may be tempted to move on to the interpretive "Think" stage, but the "See" stage not only has the advantage of making everyone more aware of what is in the image; it provides the foundation students will draw on in making their interpretations. Don't be afraid to add your own contributions, but do this as a fellow learner. For instance, you might say, "One of the things I didn't notice when I first looked at this was . . ." Even so, you may find your students initially struggling with making interpretations rather than observations; don't treat this as an error, as that may shut students down. Instead, redirect students by asking them to show you where they are looking or by asking them what they see that makes them say that.

As tempting as it may be, avoid turning this routine into a worksheet for individuals to complete. It has been our observation that when worksheets are used, students give short responses and fail to notice because they just don't want to write it all down. This routine really benefits from hearing and building on the ideas of others. Instead of a worksheet, use Think-Pair-Share to get students talking.

A Picture of Practice

As a high school history teacher, Lesley Ryder has always felt that visual analysis was an essential skill. And yet, even in this highly visual age, she noticed that her tenth grade students at Methodist Ladies' College in a suburb of Melbourne struggled with it. Some of this she recognized was due to students not being able to interpret symbolic or abstract imagery as it might appear in a political cartoon or historical art work. However, Leslie also felt there was another issue impeding their interpretive skills. "There is a problem of being able to *see* the relevant detail in a visual image, whether a painting, cartoon, drawing, or photograph. In fact, it is really two problems: *seeing* the detail and discerning what is *relevant detail* in a particular context." Lesley decided to engage in an action research project in her classroom to see if the routine See-Think-Wonder would help improve her students' skill at visual analysis. Having experienced the routine herself in various professional development settings and in the classroom of colleagues, Lesley noted, "The accessibility and simplicity of See-Think-Wonder belies its power as a stimulus to deep thought and reflection."

As a first step in this process, Lesley had to do some rethinking of the unit she was teaching. Traditionally, she had structured the unit, which focused on the representation of women in the Middle Ages, by carefully leading students toward analysis by building up an understanding of context and skills using a range of primary written and visual sources presented in PowerPoint workbooks. This led to a culminating assessment of a late medieval tapestry. However, Lesley stated, "I soon realized that using STW would mean reversing this approach and decided to begin the unit with a STW on a painting from an earlier medieval artist. The class would then go on to explore the changing historical context before proceeding to the final assessment on the tapestry."

Lesley chose a black and white image of *The Temptation of St. Anthony* with which to start (Figure 4.1). Projecting the image on the screen for everyone to see, she asked the students to write lists of what they could see, what they thought these visual details might mean, and finally what wonders or questions were raised by the drawing. Although initially excited by the students' activity and eager writing, Lesley's enthusiasm quickly diminished as students began to share. The list of "sees" lacked detail and were often interspersed with interpretations. Lesley realized that she needed to help students discern the difference between seeing and interpreting as well as offer greater encouragement to seek out details and ambiguities in the image rather than merely assume that seeing was the same as being able to name the major features.

Drawing on this experience, Lesley regrouped for her efforts with the next class. "I was more explicit about what was required in each of the stages and asked the students to avoid interpretations where possible and just record the actual things they could 'see' under the first heading." She also took time to debrief each step separately before going on to the next. In this way, all students benefited from the ideas of others and were able to approach the next stage of the routines with a more robust background than they might have if just working individually.

When sharing their "sees," something quite interesting happened. Students began recounting various details such as the wine, the Bible, the woman's clothes, the different types of trees, the slope of the hillside, the staff, the bell tower, thatched hut, and so on. Then one student remarked, "What are those funny

Figure 4.1 Temptation of St. Anthony

Source: Courtesy of Sir John Soane Museum, London.

stick things under her dress? They look like chicken feet." Another student quickly responded, "Oh, I saw those but it seemed too silly to write down." This piqued the interest of the rest of the class, who were now all examining the image with renewed interest as one student remarked, "I didn't see them. What are they?" At this point Lesley took a quick survey to find that approximately a third of the students had recorded the "sticks," another third saw them but didn't record them because they thought they couldn't be important, and the remaining third hadn't noticed them. Lesley herself confessed to the class she hadn't seen them even though she had looked at the image quite a bit.

The observation of the "sticks" led beautifully into the "Think" part of the routine, in which students were asked to make interpretations about what they thought might be going on in the image. Suddenly the class was intent in making sense of the "sticks." A student made a leap that catapulted the class's thinking: "Maybe that isn't a woman at all, maybe those are the feet of the devil." Jumping on this idea, another student began to provide supporting evidence: "Look at the dress. See how it curls up at the end? Maybe that is the devil's tail." To which a third student responded, "I think you're right. I was wondering why the dress was like that. It didn't look quite right to me but I didn't know why." Of course, students didn't make this grand leap without some background knowledge. Students knew this was a religious image, and many were familiar with stories of temptation generally, if not that of St. Anthony in particular.

This experience gave Lesley pause and made her recognize how hard it is to see. In her own reflections after the lesson she wondered, "Could it be that we do not 'see' (or choose to ignore) what we do not understand or cannot interpret; that we do not 'see' the objects that have no connection to the ideas, beliefs, and values operating in our context?" Lesley was interested in investigating this notion further and in the next lesson asked her students what was the difference between "seeing" and "thinking." Specifically, what was going on in their heads in each case? One student summed up the difference by stating, "When we are 'thinking' we are making links to what we already know." This prompted a discussion about how one's beliefs might shape what one sees and the challenge of really looking closely and without judgment at anything. A rich discussion about metacognition and thinking about one's own thinking ensued as the class sought to understand why so many had missed the "sticks" as a significant detail and why it was so difficult to stop the mind and just see without always interpreting.

Reflecting on her experience in an essay titled, "Wondering About Thinking and Seeing: Moving Beyond Metacognition" (Ryder, 2010, p. 5), Lesley commented:

> Over the next couple of years I continued to work with STW in both Year 10 and 11 History, and across a variety of topics in each course. Even if the images studied did not always elicit the same complexity of response as "The Temptation of St Antony," I was usually able to steer the conversation towards consideration of the differences between the mental moves of "seeing" and "thinking." . . . The flexible ease with which I was gradually able to do this came from a clear understanding of the mental

or epistemic moves involved in the STW routine. "Seeing" requires looking closely, discerning detail, and suspending the constant tendency to interpret and evaluate; "thinking" involves interpretation of that detail by making links to what you already know; and "wonder" requires us to remain open to the possibility that the image may contain details for which we cannot make a connection, and moreover, that these may have held important meanings for others in different times and cultures. The stage is then set for a wider exploration of historical context. However, students also need to be conscious of the dangers of over-interpretation. Not all unexplained detail necessarily held deeper meanings for the artist; sometimes a visual element is there for aesthetic reasons only. A close study of other primary sources, and the historical context, helps us to differentiate the extraneous from the essential. Sometimes a "stick" is just a "stick"!

⚙ ZOOM IN

Look Closely at the Small Bit of Image That Is Revealed

- What do you see or notice?
- What is your hypothesis or interpretation of what this might be based on what you are seeing?

Reveal More of the Image

- What new things do you see?
- How does this change your hypothesis or interpretation? Has the new information answered any of your wonders or changed your previous ideas?
- What new things are you wondering about?

Repeat the Reveal and Questioning Until the Whole Image Has Been Revealed

- What lingering questions remain for you about this image?

This routine was originally created by Marc Perella, a middle school teacher in Fairfax, Virginia. It was further adapted by Rhonda Bondie of Primary Source Learning, an organization in northern Virginia devoted to helping teachers use the resources of the Library of Congress. Rhonda was interested in helping students to learn history from primary source documents in an engaging and meaningful way and created many digital versions, under the title "Crop It!" We present our own adaptation of this routine here, which we call Zoom In. Like See-Think-Wonder, this routine focuses on looking closely and making interpretations. The difference is that this routine reveals only portions of an image over time. The idea that our interpretations in history, as well as in other disciplines, are tentative and limited by the information we have at hand is a metaphor about learning embedded in the routine itself.

Purpose

The routine asks learners to observe a portion of an image closely and develop a hypothesis. New visual information is presented, and the learner is asked to again look closely and then reassess his or her initial interpretation in light of the new information.

Because learners must deal with limited information, they know their interpretations must be tentative at best and might change as new information is presented. The process of making such tentative hypotheses enables learners to see that not only is it okay to change your mind about something, but in fact it is important to be open-minded and flexible enough to change your mind when new and sometimes conflicting information is available and the original hypothesis no longer holds true.

By revealing only portions of the image at a time, the routine fosters engagement with the source material in a way that seeing the whole image at once sometimes does not. Learners must act as detectives to build up meaning both individually and collectively.

Selecting Appropriate Content

When selecting content for this routine, keep in mind that only sections of the image will be visible until the end. This means that you might be able to use a familiar image depending on which sections you reveal initially. Whatever you are considering, ask yourself, "Are there separate areas of the image that tell a different story? Are the various parts as potentially interesting as the whole?" The content might be a scene with many people doing different things with the initial focus on just one person or activity. You might select a section of a complex painting, a photograph of a geological site, a data display, graph or chart, or even a poem. To ensure that Zoom In isn't just a game, you'll want to choose content that is meaningful to your subject area and that will pull students in to your topic of study.

Once you have chosen an image, consider what information will be conveyed by each part of the image you choose to reveal at each stage. Bear in mind that each new part revealed should add significantly to the meaning of the section of the image originally displayed and challenge students to think in new ways. Consider when you might reveal something that is surprising or that will force new interpretations. You can then create a Zoom In using presentation software to make slides of each section or by enlarging the image and creating masks that you can peel off for your reveals.

Steps

1. *Set up.* Display a section of the selected image and invite learners to look attentively at it, allowing time for careful observation. You might want to begin with observations before moving to invite learners to develop hypotheses or interpretations based on what they have seen. They can do this individually, in small groups, or as a whole class.

2. *Reveal.* Uncover more of the image and again ask learners to identify anything new they are seeing and consider how this new information affects their previous interpretations and hypotheses. Depending on the stimulus, you may ask more pointed questions: "What do you think the relationship is between these two people? What feelings are you getting from the words revealed so far? Do you have a prediction of what the next section of data will look like?" At this stage, you may want to ask students about their wonderings as well.

3. *Repeat.* Continue the process of revealing and interpreting until the entire image has been revealed and invite learners to state any lingering questions they have. Encourage the learners to discuss their different interpretations and reflect how their thinking has changed with each piece of additional information.

4. *Share the thinking.* Discuss the process with learners. Ask them to reflect on how their interpretations shifted and changed over time. How did seeing more of the image influence their thinking? What parts were particularly rich in information and had a dramatic effect? Which were more ambiguous? What would the effect have been if the reveals had happened in a different order?

Uses and Variations

As a reading teacher, Anthony (Tony) Cavell was interested in students immersing themselves in text. When his grade 6 students at Bialik College began their study of *Mao's Last Dancer* by Li Cunxin, Tony decided that zooming in on an illustration by Anne Spudvilas of Li's arrival at the train station in Beijing could help his students gain a greater understanding of the context and setting of the novel. Tony restricted the first image to the child standing alone with no background visible. As the students examined the image, Anthony asked his students to take the perspective of the child in the image and posed additional questions. He asked, "What can you feel? What can you see, smell and hear? What can you notice?" The students individually recorded their responses. With each new reveal Tony repeated the questions, asking students to integrate the new information into their developing sense of the setting.

Paul Velleman wanted his grade 4 class at Bialik to learn more about the multitude of languages spoken by indigenous Australians and decided to do this by building up a sense of wonder through looking at maps of Australia in succession, each time adding an overlay onto the map that added more information. Paul did not exactly Zoom In on the map itself but built up layers of new information by superimposing more and more cartographic information, thus building a sense of anticipation, curiosity, and wonderings as the initial map developed from one with only the outer perimeters evident to a map with more and more divisions that eventually showed where every indigenous language had its origins. Each time the students tried to deduce what the map depicted as each new piece of information challenged their prior thinking. By not revealing all the information in the first place but encouraging students to develop hypotheses along the way, Paul built excitement and mystery. Reflecting on the experience, the class remarked on how readily assumptions can be made based on limited information and how those assumptions can change.

Assessment

Look for how students pay attention to detail when formulating their hypotheses and how they support their assumptions by referring to what they have seen and noticed. Are students synthesizing the new information as it is provided to develop new or modified hypotheses, or are they unwilling to move from their initial theories? Do students build on the ideas of others, or do they limit their thinking to only their own ideas? Are they able to reflect on how and why their thinking has changed throughout the process?

Tips

While there is no set number of "reveals" to use throughout a Zoom In, walk yourself through your proposed sequence of reveals to question what you are seeing and how much and what type of information is revealed each time. Will it challenge students' thinking? As developing flexible thinking is an important goal for this routine, encourage students to make connections to other situations when their thinking has changed as they have found out more about a situation or something they have learned previously. In the Picture of Practice following, the teacher used an interactive whiteboard to present the image and produce the reveals.

A Picture of Practice

Caitlin Faiman had been using a few thinking routines with the students she sees as a mathematics resource teacher at Bialik College. Previously, some of these students had been introduced to Zoom In as part of Tony Cavell's English and social science classes, and Caitlin was intrigued by it. At the same time, she questioned its use in mathematics.

One of Caitlin's goals for her grade 5 mathematics class was to see the big picture of mathematics and realize that mathematics is all around them. She decided

Figure 4.2 M. C. Escher's *Day and Night*

she might try a Zoom In using M. C. Escher's *Day and Night* image (see Figure 4.2) to see if it would prompt a rich discussion. Caitlin was curious how it would go: ''The total image is certainly captivating but will they be able to see the math in it or will it be too limiting showing only a piece at time?''

For the first reveal, Caitlin chose what appeared to be a single bird flying. She selected this because she wanted students to begin the process with something clear and relatively unambiguous so that she could focus their attention on making mathematical connections. Caitlin reminded students of their experience doing Zoom In with Mr. Cavell and asked them to begin by looking closely, take a few minutes of thinking time to write down some of the things they saw and noticed, keeping in mind that this was a mathematics lesson.

Students immediately noticed the bird and a rectangle. Caitlin asked them what the image might be about, reminding them that these were only beginning ideas and it was okay to be tentative and conditional in their thinking. Students responded in rapid-fire succession: ''It could be a bird trapped.'' ''Rectangles are the main shape for cages in the world.'' ''I think it might be a bird in a cage.'' Joshua added a more elaborated idea to the discussion: ''I think it is going to end up as an array, an array of birds, leading to a multiplication question." Marne connected with the shapes. "I see a bird. I think we are doing this to make us really look at shapes and see how shapes are made because in that bird I can see the head is a circle and the beak is a triangle.... It is in a blue rectangle ... and I can see an oval—the body, a different type of triangle is there as well ..."

As each new reveal was presented, Caitlin asked her students about what they could see, how their ideas or interpretations had changed, and how the new information had changed their hypotheses or created new wonderings. With each new piece of visual information, the discussions became richer, with observations moving from comments about birds such as, "It looks like the birds are flying over the sea because the birds are flying and you can see in the corner something that looks like land. Maybe it is winter ... or whenever they fly," to responses predominantly in the language of mathematics: "It now looks more like a pyramid [than an array]. It looks like those two extra heads are coming in between."

By the third reveal, the students had discussed rows, columns, vertical, horizontal, and diagonal lines and started making statements about factors. "To find all of the arrays [of a number] you just need to find all the factors.... 1, 2, 4, and 8. 1 row of 8 and 8 rows of 1, 2 rows of 4, and 4 rows of 2." Each new comment provided Caitlin with teaching opportunities to introduce or revise mathematical concepts.

"Students saw so much math! I was really amazed at their insights," Caitlin commented. "Our conversation touched on symmetry, transformation, direction, triangular numbers, congruency, reflection, and 2D and 3D shapes. It was amazing how students connected to their previous experiences and understandings. I didn't want it to stop." However, Caitlin did need to stop because the class period had ended before the entire image had been revealed.

The next day, Caitlin picked up where the class had left off. She recapped their previous observations and tried to push their thinking even further: "So we have shapes on this side that are transforming into white birds and shapes on this side that are transforming into black birds. How can we describe the direction the birds are sliding in? How can we describe it mathematically?"

As the discussion continued with talk of verticals, horizontals, flips, and sliding figures transforming, Caitlin noticed students were discovering a new mathematics concept that they didn't yet have language to name. She stepped in: "The mathematical word we are all describing is tessellate. It's when shapes fit together without leaving any gaps. What shapes are tessellating here?"

Once the entire image had been revealed and discussed, Caitlin concluded the lesson by asking, "If you were the artist of this picture what title might you give this piece? Remember we have explored this picture through a mathematical lens so your title should include this perspective." Some responses included "Day and Night Through a Line of Symmetry," "Bird's Eye of Symmetry," "Symmetrical Transformation," "Time Passing," "A 3D Depth of Birds," and "Tricks of Symmetry and Arrays."

All told, the Zoom In discussion continued for two 1-hour class periods. In reflecting on the lesson, Caitlin noted how excited her students were with the mystery of hidden information and remarked, "They were so comfortable taking risks, hypothesizing, and guessing and they didn't forget that they needed to offer support for their ideas." Some questions and challenges were raised for Caitlin as well. Chief among these was, "How long do I spend on each image?" However, Caitlin seemed to have answered this question for herself even as she raised it: "Just long enough to develop enough ideas to attain the level of thinking I was aiming for but not too long so as to drag the activity out and risk the students tiring of or resenting the next image being shown."

⚙ THINK-PUZZLE-EXPLORE

Consider the subject or topic just presented.

- What do you *think* you know about this topic?
- What questions or *puzzles* do you have about this topic?
- How might you *explore* the puzzles we have around this topic?

This routine developed out of our wish to make one of the most widely used classroom routines, Know–Want to know–Learned (KWL), less fact driven and more inquiry and process oriented. In KWL, students are asked, "What do you *k*now about this topic? What do you *w*ant to know? What have you *l*earned now that our study is over?" One pitfall in asking students what they "know" about a topic and making a list of such things is that often they give some misinformation or may say they don't know anything. In Think-Puzzle-Explore (TPE), by asking, "What do you *think* you know?" the teacher labels students' ideas as tentative or partial knowledge or as ideas that might be explored. In addition, asking, "What puzzles you about this topic?" rather than, "What do you want to know?" pushes students to think more broadly in terms of inquiry rather than fact collection. The "Explore" part of the routine then directs students' attention to how those puzzles might be investigated.

Purpose

This routine invites students to connect to their prior knowledge, to be curious, and to plan for independent or group inquiry. Think-Puzzle-Explore can provide teachers with a sense of students' current understanding of a topic and thereby influence the shape and structure of subsequent teaching and learning. As such, it sets the stage for deeper inquiry and is usually positioned at the beginning of a unit. However, the routine also may be revisited throughout a unit as well to identify new puzzles and plan further inquiry.

It is also powerful to incorporate at the conclusion of a unit, with the first step of the routine used almost as a reflective tool showing the students how their understanding has grown and what they think they know now. Revisiting the "Puzzle" section of the routine reminds students that learning is an ongoing process, and even after spending considerable time and thought exploring a topic, there is always more to understand.

Selecting Appropriate Content

Due to the nature of the routine, the puzzles raised about a topic are usually specific in nature; however the selection of complex and rich topics will lead to questions that seek more than the obvious in responses and invite multiple interpretations to be explored. The subject can range from a big idea, a specific topic in mathematics, an item in today's newspaper to almost anything that is relevant to your students and is worth developing an understanding of at a deeper level.

Steps

1. *Set up.* Since this routine helps to shape future inquiry and is often used as a reference point at the start of a unit, you'll want to plan some form of documentation. This could be done by students themselves working in small groups, by you on a whiteboard, or through the use of sticky notes to gather and collect students' ideas.

2. *Ask, "What do you think you know about . . . ?"* After asking the question, give students time to think and gather their ideas and to draw on past recollections and experiences. You can have students either say or jot down their thoughts and ideas. Oftentimes, students will build on one another's ideas, so recognize that new ideas will emerge as the public sharing begins.

3. *Ask, "What questions or puzzles do you have?"* Push the thinking further by inviting the students to wonder more about the topic with additional questions, such as "What would be interesting to investigate and learn more about? What are you wondering about? Are there things about this topic about which you are curious?" Ask students to articulate, either aloud or on sticky notes, the questions or *puzzles* they have about the topic.

4. *Ask, "How can we explore these puzzles?"* Ask students to identify a puzzle from the list, or at times you might want to highlight a couple of puzzles for the class, and ask students how the class or an individual might explore those puzzles further. "Whom might you ask? Where could you get further information? How would you frame your search key words? What sources would be worth tapping? What could you do yourself to investigate the puzzle other than look up information? How could you find ways to answer your own puzzles?"

5. *Share the thinking.* Much of students' thinking is shared when this routine is being done as a whole group. If it is done in small groups, then you might want to have groups report out, perhaps focusing on the puzzles. Alternatively, you might ask students to review the class's responses and group together puzzles that have similar themes or have strong connections. Students could then elect to work in pairs or small groups to plan the exploration of the questions or puzzles they found most interesting. Their exploration plans could then be shared with the group for feedback.

Uses and Variations

Grade 1 teacher Kathleen Georgiou, working with arts and technology specialist Helene Oberman at Bialik, decided to use the "Think" and "Puzzle" sections of TPE as one way to help students look at works of art depicting water and its uses as part of a unit on water as a resource. Prior to their class visit to the National Gallery of Victoria to view these paintings, drawings, and sculptures, the teachers invested time showing photos of artworks to their students and using the routine to structure their discussions of it. With each image, they asked, "What do you think you know about this? What puzzles you and what are you wondering?" Kathleen and Helene also met with the parents who would be accompanying small groups on the field trip and taught the parents the routine, showed them examples of how the students had responded, and encouraged them to discuss the responses with the students while at the museum. At the gallery, the students were given clipboards with photos of the new artworks they would be observing along with the questions from the routine to guide their exploration. Students' familiarity with the routine led to much discussion about their thoughts and wonderings.

After an extensive study of leadership with her grade 5 students at Bialik, Karen Glanc was interested to see what her students were now thinking about leadership. She was also very keen for them to understand that leadership is so much more than a topic to be studied, that even when the unit was "finished" there was still much more to discover. She chose the routine Think-Puzzle-Explore as a reflection tool to uncover what students think they know about leadership now, what new puzzles had emerged, and to get students to think about how they could continue their learning.

Assessment

The listening, reading, and/or documenting of learners' responses to the first section of this routine, "Think," provides an opportunity for the teacher to become aware of the misconceptions students may have about a topic. Instruction will need to address these misconceptions if understanding is to be developed. The "Puzzles" uncovered in the second section of the routine provide insights into the sorts of ideas students are interested in exploring further. Look to see if students are able to frame inquiry questions and express broad curiosity about a topic as opposed to just gathering facts. Often this takes time to develop. It is not that factual questions need to be discouraged, only that they need to be complemented by broader and more adventurous types of questions that get to issues of understanding. The "Explore" section provides an opportunity to look at students' ability to plan out an inquiry.

Tips

TPE may seem like only a cosmetic change from KWL since both have very similar goals. However, the language teachers use influences students' thinking. What appears to be very subtle changes in word choice nonetheless can have a huge impact on the ways students respond. Asking "What do you know about . . . ?" can immediately shut down the student who is not confident about the subject, whereas "What do you think you know about . . . ?" gives permission to have a go, raise possible responses to the question, safe in the knowledge that you are not guaranteeing that you have the absolute facts but rather some thoughts about it. Likewise, discussions of puzzles and wonderings help students to be more open-ended in their framing of questions and can support their curiosity.

As educators become more familiar with the routine and its language, they become more flexible in their applications of it. It is not unusual for a teacher to use only one part of the routine. For example, when coming across something unfamiliar in a news item, asking "What do you think you know about . . . ?" can lead to a very fruitful discussion. Alternatively, hanging chart paper up in the room for students to write their puzzles and wonderings about a topic on an ongoing basis can deepen the inquiry and arouse further interest and curiosity.

Some teachers are not sure how to handle the "Explore" section of this routine. One reason for that might be that they aren't used to asking students to plan and direct their own inquiry, and that is what this section asks students to do. To develop students' skills in this area, you might begin by collectively planning an inquiry as a class as a model, so that you are making the planning process itself visible. If students' only response to the "Explore" section of the routine is "Look it up on the Internet," you might push this to consider, "What kinds of sources would be credible? What keywords should be used? How will we decide if what is reported is true or not? Who else should we ask?" To push students thinking further you might ask, "If we can't find credible information in books or on the Internet, how might we find this out ourselves?"

A Picture of Practice

When Kiran Bansal was about to introduce the topic of time to her grade 2 class at Bialik College, she decided to commence with the question, "What do you think you know about time?" Kiran said she chose the Think-Puzzle-Explore routine "to activate prior knowledge and curiosity about the concept of time. I was hoping this routine would enable all students to contribute their ideas and generate curiosities with confidence."

Kiran explained how she carried out the routine: "I had students in groups of four or five with a large piece of paper and pencils at each table. They were given time and asked to put down their ideas and any thinking they had about time in the 'Think' section of the paper. We then shared all our ideas as a whole class. Next I asked the class if they had any wonderings or any questions that puzzled them about time. Students wrote these down on sticky notes in the "Puzzle" section. Students' thinking was collectively made visible on the board, which helped trigger more responses from the students. Then, as a class we took our wonderings and discussed as to how we could explore our questions in groups or as individuals." Students' responses are displayed in Table 4.1.

The students' thoughts and puzzles about "time" varied enormously, both in content and levels of understanding and sophistication. Topics raised included the mechanics of how clocks and watches work, different ways of measuring time, grappling with big philosophical issues about the role and importance of time, and big questions about the nature of time. Students' responses went far beyond facts and skills related to "telling time" and questions of how to tell time. As a result, Kiran found herself thinking totally differently about the unit she was about to teach.

After hearing and seeing all her students' responses, Kiran ensured that her planning for the unit addressed some of students' broader questions about the history, need, and importance of time as well as her standard objectives about telling time. Consequently, there were many rich discussions throughout the course of the unit. Kiran decided to have students work in small interest groups to explore some of the puzzles raised. These included a group looking at the insides of clocks and another on designing time machines. While students still learned the basics about seconds, minutes, and hours and telling the time, students' collective experiences with and understandings about time were so much more.

Table 4.1   Second Graders' Thoughts and Puzzles About Time

What do you think you know about time?	What puzzles do you have about time?
Time is day and night. Time is also morning and afternoon. You can see time on a clock. There are twenty-four hours in a day. Time can also be timetables. The time when the sun comes up is morning. The time when the moon comes up is night.	Who invented time?
	How was time created?
	Can you go backwards in time?
	What would we do if there was no time?
	When was the first clock created?
There is digital and analogue. There is bedtime, lunchtime, breakfast time. Day and Night, sunset, seconds and minutes.	Why is time called *time*?
	What is analogue?
Time can go fast, time can go slow. No one knows how it was created. If time stopped not even the slightest thing would move.	How long does it take for a tree to grow?
	How was time created?
There is digital time. There are also seconds. There is daylight and there is dusk. There are hours and minutes.	How does the clock know when to strike?
	Why is time so important?
There are 24 hours in a day. Bedtime, daytime and playtime. There is o'clock.	How does the big hand and little hand move?
The time it takes for a tree to grow. There is dinnertime.	Who thought of the word *time*?
	I would want to know about numbers and time and clocks.
When I think of time I think of how I grow up, multiplication, getting bored, waiting, bedtime, computer, my toys like how I grow out of my baby toys and get new, school time, hours and digital, sunrise and sunset and History.	I'm puzzled I don't really know anything about time
	Who made watches?
	What would happen if there was no time?

Kiran reflected on the difference TPE had made in her approach to the unit: "In my past experiences of teaching a mathematics unit of time, the teaching had always been based on a pretest and a post-test whereby the only skills I assessed were how well students could achieve the outcomes set in the curriculum. When I learned this routine myself, I was quite intrigued with the process that would give me a good understanding about the children's conceptual level and how the kids could venture into a journey of deeper understanding about this concept."

Kiran found that students' engagement in the unit was also quite different than in the past. "I was amazed to see that some of my students with learning difficulties also enjoyed sharing their thoughts compared to them being the passive learners in the past. Children were very enthusiastic and engaged during our journey of thinking, exploring, and learning. By making their thinking visible, children were able to track their learning, and this journey was packed with rich experiences such as opportunities given to children for listening, interaction, expectation of thinking, sharing, questioning, risk taking, and valuing each other's thoughts."

◎ CHALK TALK

Looking at the topic or question written on the chart paper:

- What ideas come to mind when you consider this idea, question, or problem?
- What connections can you make to others' responses?
- What questions arise as you think about the ideas and consider the responses and comments of others?

As teachers, we often want to ensure that we make room for all voices and invite all learners into the learning. However, it can sometimes be a challenge to give sufficient airtime to everyone in the group. Chalk Talk was developed by Hiton Smith of the Foxfire Fund to address this challenge while facilitating the nonlinear exploration of ideas. The routine is a "conversation" conducted silently on paper. Though sometimes referred to as a *protocol*, Chalk Talk is a useful tool for making thinking visible, and its simple structure focusing on reactions, connections, and questions fits within the definition of a thinking routine.

Purpose

This routine asks learners to consider ideas, questions, or problems by silently responding in writing both to the prompt and the thoughts of others. This "silent conversation" provides learners with time to follow through thoughts without interruption by choosing when they are ready to consider other points of view and make comments. It provides flexibility to move from one idea to another in a nonlinear way, to formulate questions as they arise, and to take the time needed to think through the collective information produced. The Chalk Talk process itself highlights the notion of building understanding in a collaborative way through putting forward ideas, questioning one another, and developing the ideas further. Its open-ended and exploratory nature makes it highly accessible to students. In addition, since individuals aren't asked to sign their comments, there is a degree of anonymity that will free up some learners to take more risks and offer ideas.

Selecting Appropriate Content

The prompt or prompts for a Chalk Talk can be single words or phrases related to a topic of study. However, often questions generate a richer level of discussion and interactivity.

Single words or the topic itself may encourage students to merely report what they know about that topic, whereas a question may invite more consideration and thinking. In formulating questions, consider those that invite multiple perspectives and reactions. For example, What is the relationship between revenge and reconciliation? How can we find out what really happened here? Should cloning be allowed? Don't shy away from controversial topics, issues, or questions. In fact, the Chalk Talk can provide a safe and calm environment for discussing issues that may be more difficult in a live, verbal discussion. Other sources of prompts may be the key ideas related to the topic being explored, questions that have arisen previously during discussions, or significant quotes from a text. In a large group, you might use multiple questions related to the topic at hand.

The Chalk Talk can also be used for reflection. As such, think about what issues, topics, or learning moments you want students to reflect upon. For instance, What have you been most surprised by in this unit of study? What is hard for you to master in this topic? Where would you most like to see improvement in yourself? What skills do you have around this topic that you could share with others? How do you know when you really understand something?

Steps

1. *Set up.* Write each prompt on a large sheet of chart paper or butcher's paper and place on tables around the room. Place markers at each table or pass them out to individuals. Decide whether you want to assign students to groups for the purposes of the Chalk Talk or you want them to freely move about the room. If students will stay together as a group, decide how much time you will give for the first round of the Chalk Talk.

2. *Present the Chalk Talk prompt.* Invite learners to think about their reactions to the prompt and record their ideas and questions. Encourage learners to read and add to each other's responses with additional comments and questions.

3. *Circulate.* Provide time for learners to circulate around the Chalk Talk paper, reading and adding to the prompts and responses as they build. If learners have been assigned to work in groups, you may want to have groups stay with one recording sheet for 5 minutes to allow time for the conversation to develop. You can then have groups rotate en masse to another group's paper, silently read what has been written there, and add their reactions and questions to the paper. This rotation often helps infuse new ideas into the "conversation" of a group who might be stuck.

4. *Facilitate.* You may need to prompt the group about types of responses they can make as they read: connecting ideas, elaborating on others ideas, commenting on what others have written, asking others to respond with more detail, and so on. There is no reason why you cannot be an active participant and model responding to comments and questions and posing new insights and wonderings. Toward the end of the session, indicate how much more time there is for responding.

5. *Share the thinking.* If people have rotated as a group, allow them to return to their original starting places to read what others have written on "their" Chalk Talk paper. Allow time for the group to review the various Chalk Talks if there is more than one. Ask the group what themes they noticed emerging. Where did they see common issues and reactions? What questions surprised them? Debrief the process itself, asking the group how their thinking developed during the Chalk Talk.

Uses and Variations

At List Elementary school in Frankenmuth, Michigan, physical education teacher Jill Waliczek used Chalk Talk to help second grade students reflect on what they were learning about bowling. Jill set up the gym in stations in which groups of four students would work. One student would be the bowler, one student the pin setter, one student would return the ball, and the fourth student would respond to the Chalk Talk prompt. Students rotated among each role until everyone had a chance; then the groups of four would move to the next station where everything was identical except for the Chalk Talk prompt. To get students to think about their learning, Jill selected the following prompts: What happens before the bowler releases the ball? What parts of bowling are you good at? What about your bowling is changing? How do you aim your ball?

Josie Singer, grade 7 English teacher at Bialik College, commenced the topic of humor with a whole-class discussion. During the discussion she noted some of the key questions raised by her students, questions such as, "If you do not find something funny, do you have a sense of humor?" "Is it acceptable to tell jokes based on gender, nationality, appearance, or disability?" "Can you learn to have a sense of humor?" and "Why is humor important?" She then asked the students to form small groups, and each group completed a Chalk Talk with one of the questions.

On the DVD, you can watch Leeland Jennings's grade 2 students at St. Charles Elementary in Michigan participating in a Chalk Talk, which his students renamed Pencil Talk, as part of their study of plants. Leeland shares how using the Chalk Talk and other routines over the course of the school year has changed how students talk about and discuss ideas often using more precise thinking language they have picked up from the routines.

Assessment

In learners' responses to the Chalk Talk prompts, look for the relevance of the contributions students are making. Are the contributions related to the big ideas or are they peripheral connections? Are students able to put forth their own ideas and original thinking, or do they hang back and echo the responses of others? Do the questions posed go to the heart and substance of the topic or are they tangential? How are students responding to the postings of others? Are they building their understanding by incorporating ideas and wonderings stated by others, or do they find it difficult to integrate the ideas of other students?

If students' responses seem stilted and limited, consider the effect the prompt might have had on their thinking. Was the prompt too narrow in scope? Did it focus more on stating what you know versus interacting with the ideas of others?

Tips

When setting up for Chalk Talk, learners can use their own pens, or you can place markers of various colors on the tables and invite learners to pick up the markers as they go around, changing colors if they wish to ensure anonymity. Alternately, if you want to track particular lines of thinking or particular students' responses, you can distribute the markers so that each student uses the same color throughout the process.

Although the Chalk Talk can work with people seated around a table or standing in front of a chalkboard, hence the name, there is something freeing about being able to walk around a table in a circular fashion, reading as one goes. This movement often helps to limit talk or fidgeting that may occur if students are asked to stand or sit in one place. In addition, many people find that reading a comment and then walking away from it gives them time to think about what they read and by the time they have returned to the comment they are ready to respond.

Time is very important in a Chalk Talk. You will need to monitor it and think about how long your students will need to reflect, read, and respond without getting bored. For example, adults often get a good start on a Chalk Talk after about 5 minutes and then may benefit from changing positions and reading and responding to another group for the next 5 minutes. However, younger students may need a bit more time for the reading and writing process.

Chalk Talk sheets can be placed where learners have access to them over the next weeks to enable them to revisit the ideas and add to them if desired. In fact, a Chalk Talk could be started in one session and continued in another session. This gives students even more thinking time for complex topics and issues.

A Picture of Practice

As an introduction to her grade 4 students' exploration of outer space, Corinne Kaplan at Bialik College showed a DVD on the launching of the first space rockets in the 1960s. After viewing the DVD, students were asked to think about "what stood out for them" in the documentary. A lively discussion ensued, and three aspects of space exploration surfaced as areas that most fascinated these grade 4 students: (1) that a monkey was first sent into space, (2) the competition between countries in the space race, and (3) the amount of money spent on space exploration.

Corinne believed that these topics were worth exploring more deeply. Consequently, she wanted to provide her students the opportunity to spend more time thinking about these ideas in a way that would enhance their understanding. Corinne remarked, "I decided that the Chalk Talk routine would provide an opportunity for the children to grapple with and think about some of the 'big ideas' that came out of our discussion." She believed the silent nature of the routine would give her students time to think through their ideas without interruption and also to stand back and look at others' thoughts and consider those as well. Corinne was conscious of the need for young children to move around, and the process of walking to and between the different questions written on the papers was viewed as a positive aspect of the routine.

Corinne spent time thinking about the prompts she would place in the center of the chart paper she would use for the Chalk Talk. Corinne recognized that she had very strong personal views about the sums of money spent on space exploration and was determined to be "mindful of any bias that may inadvertently slip in." Corinne brought this issue to her grade-level team meeting for discussion. Drawing on advice from colleagues, she began with a general prompt: "What are your ideas, thoughts, questions, and wonderings on ...?" She then had three prompts attached to this question stem: (1) "Sending animals before astronauts?" (2) "The government's spending so much money?" and (3) "The race into space?"

The questions were written on butcher paper and placed on tables positioned so that students could easily congregate around the tables to record and read responses comfortably. Corinne also wanted to make sure students could easily move among the three tables to contribute and think about each of the questions. Colored markers were also placed on these tables.

Although Corinne anticipated the Chalk Talk might last 10–15 minutes, she monitored students' engagement with the task to determine whether she needed to extend the time. She was amazed to find that students had so much to say about each question and that they were interested in reading and responding to other's comments that the session wound up lasting nearly an hour. During this time, students walked silently around the tables as they thought about these questions, wrote, connected, agreed and disagreed with their peers. There were no issues of talking or misbehavior because students were so engaged. "I was amazed that they were so interested in these big questions," commented Corinne.

Once the Chalk Talk had finished, the class took a close look at their thinking as displayed on the papers (see Figures 4.3 and 4.4). This examination led to another discussion as the class identified core themes and common concerns and thoughts. Corinne reflected, "Chalk Talk can be likened to 'equal opportunity time,' as the students who normally hold back verbally, due to a myriad of reasons, have a chance to be part of a very rich, yet silent dialogue. I love that aspect of this routine."

Figure 4.3 Fourth Grade Chalk Talk: The Race into Space

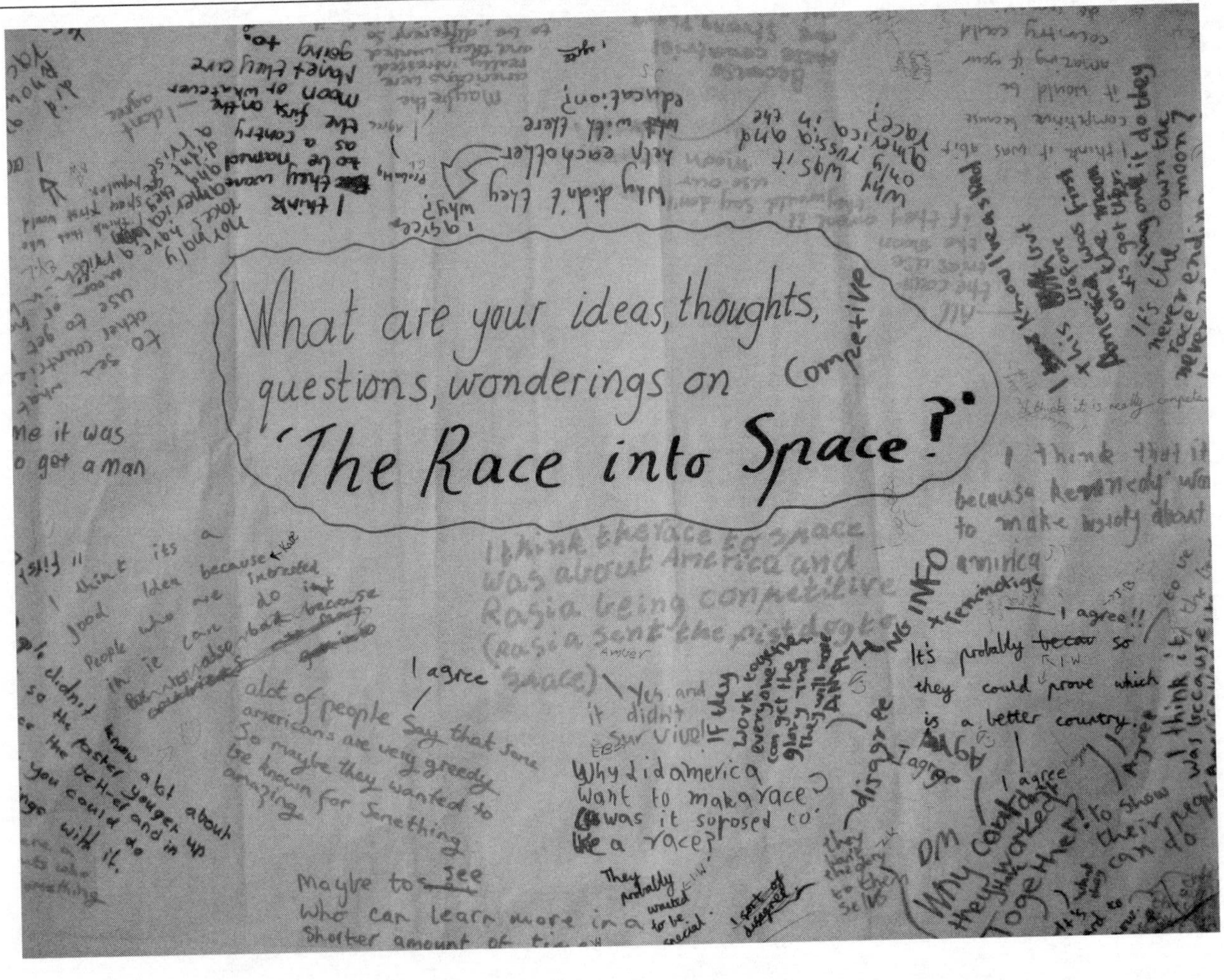

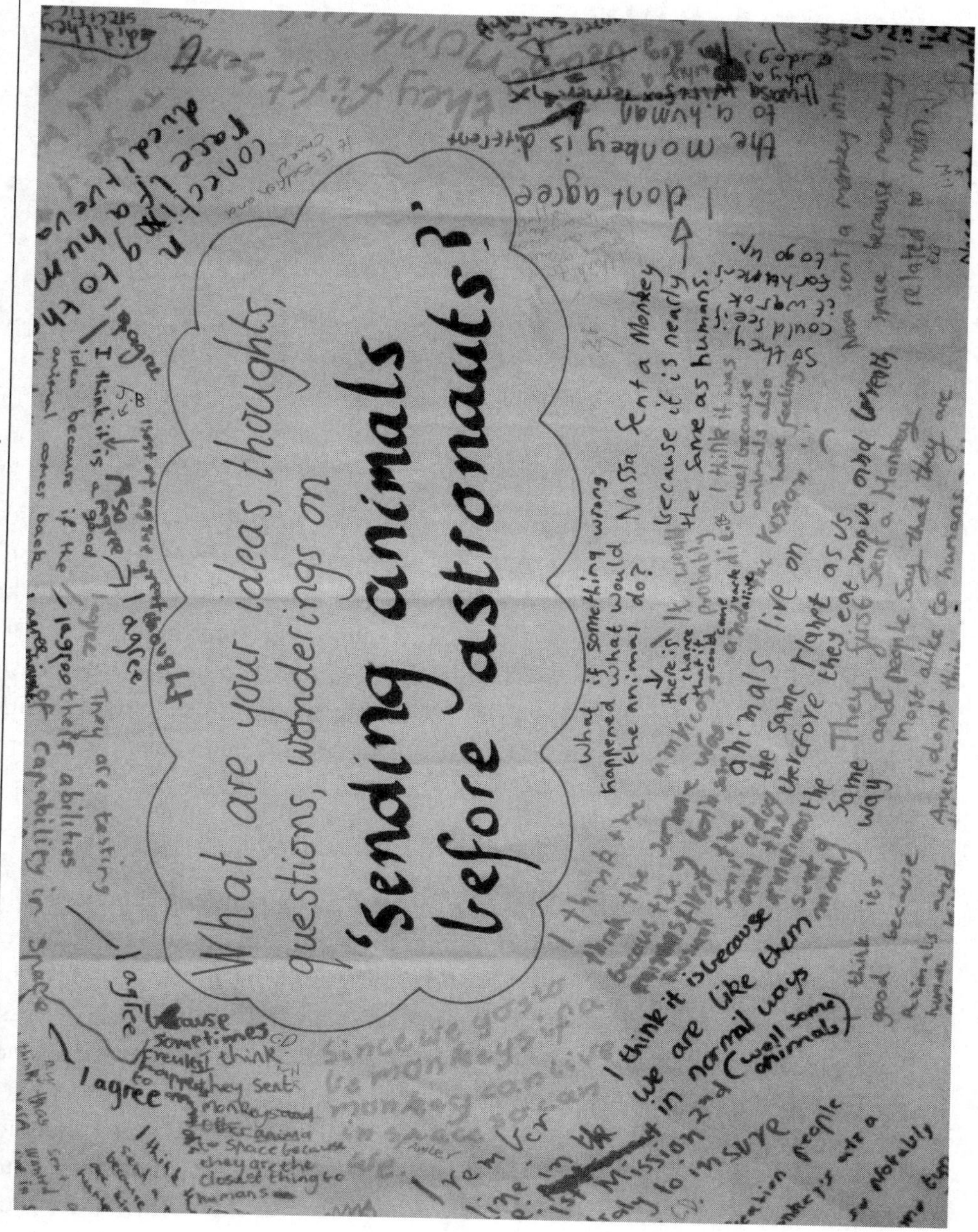

Figure 4.4 Fourth Grade Chalk Talk: Sending Animals Before Astronauts into Space

3–2–1 BRIDGE

Thinking about the key concept or topic, identify:

INITIAL RESPONSE	NEW RESPONSE
3 Words	3 Words
2 Questions	2 Questions
1 Metaphor/Simile	1 Metaphor/Simile

BRIDGE
Identify how your new responses connect to or shifted
from your initial response.

Teachers often begin the exploration of a new topic by trying to uncover students' prior knowledge of that topic. This routine came out of our interest in doing just that, but in a way that might push beyond revealing just the facts students might know. Instead, this routine focuses on the associations one has around the topic in terms of words, questions, and connections. The "bridging" part of the routine was designed to help students link their prior knowledge, questions, and understandings with the new ideas they develop as the unit progresses. This process helps them to understand themselves as learners.

Purpose

The first part of the 3–2–1 Bridge routine is all about activating prior knowledge before a learning experience begins. By starting with three words, the routine is very accessible in activating some basic ideas. The two questions push a bit further. Finally, the one metaphor or simile is a test of how one is understanding and framing a topic or issue.

After students' initial thoughts are generated, these ideas are set aside and not discussed. Instead, teachers begin the learning of the unit. The initial experience can be brief, a short reading or video, or it can more extended, a whole week of lab activity or other inquiry. After this initial period of learning, which should advance students' thinking on the topic and move it in new directions, students return and produce a second 3–2–1. At this stage, the key thinking done by learners is distilling their new ideas while assessing their current thoughts and understandings about the topic.

The purpose of the final part of this routine, the Bridge, is to help learners recognize and name their own learning and development. This helps to develop students' metacognitive ability, that is, the ability to step back and examine their own thoughts and learning. In the Bridge, students look at their initial responses (sometimes with a partner) and reflect on how those first impressions differ from their current take on things.

Selecting Appropriate Content

This routine works well when the topic or concept is one where all learners have some prior knowledge. There are many units in school that fit this requirement: planets, habitats, jazz, algebra, conservation, maps, erosion, fairy tales, and so on. If a topic is one that some students wouldn't recognize or know anything about it, it wouldn't be a good choice.

The selection of the instruction after the initial 3–2–1 is crucial in ensuring the effectiveness of the routine. Think about how your instruction will take students' thinking in a new and different direction that will extend it. If the routine were attempted on "fractions," this might not be effective if the instructional period is just a review of past knowledge and skills. Such instruction wouldn't change students' thinking about the topic of fractions. So, if the bridging instruction does not introduce any new ideas, it will have very little effect. It is instruction that is provocative, introduces new information, presents different perspectives, and challenges the learners' thinking that will serve to broaden and deepen understanding.

Steps

1. *Set up.* Decide how you will have students record their response. Since students will need to come back to their initial 3–2–1 after what might be an extended period of time, you want to make sure they won't lose their responses. Students might record their responses in a journal or on sheets you collect. Present the topic or concept to the learners in as simple and straightforward language as possible.

2. *Ask for three words.* Ask students to generate three words that quickly come to mind when they think of this topic. Encourage students not to overthink this; it isn't a test. You are just interested in some quick associations they are making with the topic.

3. *Ask for two questions.* Ask students to generate two questions that quickly come to mind regarding the topic. Again, remind them that these are questions that are pretty close to the surface for them and that don't need a lot of deep thought. Remind them that you are interested in merely uncovering their initial, surface ideas at this point.

4. *Ask for one metaphor or simile.* Ask the students to create a metaphor or simile for this topic. You may need to explain what a simile or metaphor is and use that language. For instance, "Planets are . . ." or "Planets are like . . ." You may need to provide a simple metaphor example as well. Remind students that metaphors and similes are nothing more than connections one is making, comparing one thing to another because they have important features in common.

5. *Provide an instructional period.* This may be a video, text, image, story, or experiment that conveys new information. There is no time limit on this instructional period. The main criterion is that it needs to be of sufficient substance to move students' thinking beyond their initial understandings.

6. *Perform the second 3–2–1.* Repeat steps 2–4 above. This time ask students to select words, questions, and metaphors prompted or encouraged by the instruction.

7. *Share the thinking: Bridging.* Invite learners to share with partners both their initial and new responses to the 3–2–1. In sharing, the partners should discuss what they are noticing about how their thinking on the topic shifted from the initial responses. Reiterate that their initial thinking is neither right nor wrong; it is simply a starting point. As a class or whole group, identify some of the new thinking and changes in thinking that have taken place. Try to capture these major shifts or changes. In some situations a more elaborate discussion of the metaphors might be worthwhile.

Uses and Variations

Bialik College teacher Tony Cavell incorporates 3–2–1 Bridge as a regular part of his sixth graders' book study. Beginning with just the book's title, Tony has students complete their first 3–2–1. Often students' initial questions are very general and are expressed as wonderings: "I'm wondering if it will be a mystery?" Their metaphors tend to be more basic connections and comparisons than true metaphors. For instance, "I think this book is going to be similar to . . ." Then, using each new chapter as the instructional period, students complete a 3–2–1 for each chapter. Students discuss the new connections they are making with the information in each new chapter and how they are currently understanding the novel.

Janis Kinda, a Jewish studies teacher at Bialik, was challenged in her teaching of the same religious festivals each year. She felt her students switched off and thought "Here we go again." Janis found the 3–2–1 Bridge routine provided a form of pretest by surfacing students' current understandings of the festivals and informed Janis of any previous teaching. She then searched for content that not only provided new information but also was challenging and engaging, something that would take students' thinking in new directions. Using 3–2–1 Bridge in this way forced Janis to think about finding the new in her topics. Janis found that in doing so, she awakened renewed interest and curiosity in her students. As a result, there were marked changes in the thinking demonstrated in the thoughts, questions, and metaphors produced in the second round of the routine and discussed in the bridging. Janis also found students' metaphors gave her insights into whether they understood the heart and significance of a particular festival as apart from its traditions of celebration.

Assessment

Introducing the first 3–2–1 at the beginning of a topic provides an effective, mini-preassessment. It provides an indication of where the learners' thinking is regarding the topic. Effective instruction should then build on this knowledge rather than repeat it. A secondary teacher in charge of a "Career Studies" module at his school decided to use the routine for the first time with his students. To his surprise he found that students' questions and metaphors were quite rich and advanced to begin with and that what he had planned for the module was likely to cover no new ground. Subsequently, he made the decision to rethink how he had organized the content of the course.

One caveat here about using 3–2–1 as a preassessment. Since the initial responses are meant to be quick, capturing what is close to the surface in students' minds, it would be unwise to read too much into weak or superficial responses, particularly in relation to the words and questions. A metaphor takes a bit more time and thought to develop, and therefore these often do reveal a layer of understanding or misunderstanding. For instance, Allison Fritscher at the International School of Brussels noticed her fifth graders initial metaphors on the digestive system were all linear in nature—a path, a road, a river, and so on. She noticed this when it happened initially and then attended closely to the shifts students made after three weeks of instruction. By that time the metaphors had become: like a watch, like a factory, like a vacation. These new metaphors were much more interactive and system-like in nature. The process of repeating the 3–2–1 steps after periods of new instruction enables teachers to see how readily learners are synthesizing and integrating new information into their thinking on the topic.

The routine can also elicit greater curiosity when used toward the end of a unit, when learners feel they have a good grasp of the topic and through the instruction can see that every topic can have new and surprising dimensions. In looking at students' new questions generated in the second or third iteration, look to see if the questions are those that reveal curiosity and engagement, propel learning, and get to issues of deeper understanding of the topic.

Tips

While metaphors and similes are suggested in the routine's guidelines, analogies work equally as well. Depending on the age and experience of the learners, some preteaching of analogies may be required, however. Some teachers of very young students have found it useful to provide lots of examples and regularly model the use of metaphors and analogies. Other teachers have chosen to emphasize the connection-making aspect of metaphors and have even used language such as, Write one connection or comparison between this topic and other things you know. What does it remind you of?

The choice of the instruction content that follows the first 3–2–1 is a critical factor in the effectiveness of the routine. Consequently, it is worth asking yourself, How will I take my students' learning in new and different directions? Are there interesting angles, aspects, or new discoveries around that topic that I could share that would totally surprise them? Consider consulting colleagues about the choice of content and working together to find some new and interesting material on familiar topics.

The "Bridge" or discussion of how responses have shifted or changed is a key aspect of this routine. It offers students a chance to be metacognitive. To facilitate this, it is often useful for learners to discuss their responses with a partner or small group. Oftentimes others can notice things in our responses that we miss because we are so close to them. For instance, it is not uncommon for people's first words to be nouns, as they are often naming things associated with the topic. With rich instruction, words often become more dynamic and may shift to more verbs or adjectives.

A Picture of Practice

As Andrea Miller's grade 3 students at Bialik were learning about their city, she realized that she wanted her students to be more aware of the cultural diversity of Melbourne and the role immigrants had played in shaping the city's past as well as its present. "The people of Melbourne" became the primary thrust of the unit. The class had already discussed many aspects of the city's geography and history when Andrea asked them to write three words, two questions, and a metaphor about the people of Melbourne. Many of these responses referred to the students' parents and grandparents, many of whom were immigrants to Australia.

At this time, the Australian media were featuring reports of refugees arriving in small boats, many under horrendous circumstances, to the country's northern shores. As Andrea thought about the sort of instructional opportunities that might further her students' understanding about the people of Melbourne, she decided to tap into this complex issue.

To launch this period of new instruction, Andrea decided to begin with a reading about a refugee camp in Afghanistan. Immediately, many students began to connect to news reports they had heard and asked many questions about the refugees. Andrea decided to invite a colleague, Nicky Dorevitch, to speak to her class. Nicky volunteered weekly in a detention center for asylum seekers and was passionate about the situation in which these people found themselves. Nicky described to the students her experiences in the detention center, with many stories about the people there. The students were engrossed and asked questions such as, "If you are a refugee in Australia, can you ever not be a refugee?" "Is it like a hotel?" "Would a baby born there (the detention center) be given Australian citizenship?" and "If you say the detention center is like a jail, how is it like prison if you don't do anything wrong?"

The discussions continued for several weeks with students bringing in newspaper cuttings about refugees, and parents and grandparents talking to their children about their families' histories and what it was like to be an immigrant to Melbourne. Throughout, there was continued interest in the plight of the detention center families.

Andrea asked the students to again write three words, two questions, and one analogy or metaphor about people living in Melbourne. This time students' responses, particularly their metaphors, showed how they were grappling with the complexities of the refugee issue:

- A refugee is like a rabbit hopping to get away from the fox.
- A refugee is like a bird fleeing from a cat on a wall.
- A refugee is like the wind.
- A refugee is like a bird.
- I think refugees are lonely. A refugee is like a begging dog.
- Rich is to president as poor is to refugee.
- A refugee is a homeless wanderer.
- Refugees leave for safety.
- Refugees leave their home to escape their lives.

Andrea was surprised and excited about the level of understanding her students demonstrated and was struck by how the routine helped hone in on the key issues in a clear and structured manner. Students' insight and empathy was evident. The routine provided a structure that enabled students to encapsulate their thinking in a powerful way. It also caused Andrea to think about the ways she had introduced the study of Melbourne in the past, how different this experience had been, and how much she valued the depth with which the students explored the topic.

Considering the idea, question, or proposition before you:

E = Excitements. What excites you about this idea or proposition? What's the upside?

W = Worries. What do you find worrisome about this idea or proposition? What's the downside?

N = Needs. What else do you need to know or find out about this idea or proposition?

S = Stance, Steps, or Suggestions. What is your current stance or opinion on the idea or proposition? What should your next step be in your evaluation of this idea or proposition? What suggestions do you have at this point?

This routine emerged from our focus on the process of decision making. The idea was that prior to making a decision about a new venture, policy, or proposition, one needed to explore the pluses and minuses of the situation and identify areas that needed to be further investigated. However, rather than just another pro/con list, this routine asks the group or individual who will act as the "decider" to identify things that excite them about the proposal and things that they find worrisome as their starting point. They then identify what they need to know more about in order to go forward. Having identified *Excitements, Worries,* and *Needs;* we noticed that we had three directions on the compass and so turned our attention to the compass point "South." Keeping with our original goal of helping individuals focus on decision making as a process and not just an outcome, the "South" on the compass became the final step of identifying *Stances, Steps,* or *Suggestions* for moving forward. Although the routine works well for decision making and proposal evaluation, teachers have found many more uses for it, as you'll see.

Purpose

Compass Points enables groups of learners to consider an idea or proposition from different angles. By exploring issues from multiple perspectives and identifying areas where more information is needed, individuals can avoid rushing into judgment. When we are very enthusiastic about an idea, it is very natural for our thinking to be influenced by our personal reactions to it. Consequently, it is easy to focus on all that is exciting without looking further. This routine validates that excitement while also inviting learners to consider what might be worrisome, thereby providing more balance to the thinking; this is followed by steps that are a "call to action" and require the learner to consider what he or she needs to know and then develop suggestions to move forward.

Working out "what you need to know" tends to be the most complex step of this routine; it requires reflective thinking to consider what is already known, analyze this, determine where the gaps are, and then develop the questions whose answers will help to fill these gaps. Sometimes it is useful to allow the group extended time to think about what was generated in the first three prompts before asking them to identify "Stances, Steps, or Suggestions."

Selecting Appropriate Content

Compass Points works well when the topic, idea, or proposition is one for which there are dilemmas or dissenting points of view or when some people are so attached to their perspectives it is difficult for them to consider the idea more broadly without some sort of structure to assist them in doing this. Since Compass Points looks at a proposition rather than debating an issue (there are other routines for that), the position to be considered needs to be well framed so that the issue in question or the event to be explored is clear. For instance, "Elimination of the dress code," "Our upcoming field trip," or "Doing your own independent inquiry project."

Steps

1. *Set up.* Frame the issue, event, or proposition and present it to the learners. If the proposition is new, allow for questions of clarification to ensure that learners have some sense of the topic. To document, place four large sheets of paper, one for each compass point, on the classroom walls. Label each sheet with one of the letters denoting the compass points. Alternatively, the proposition can be written on the whiteboard and the four points of the compass written around it. Distribute sticky notes for students to write their ideas on.

2. *Identify excitements.* Ask, "What excites you about this idea or proposition? What's the upside?" Allow time for learners to think, write, and post their ideas on the E chart or section. If learners are stuck in their own positions, you might phrase the question as, "What might people be excited about?"

3. *Identify worries.* Ask, "What worries would you have about this? What are your concerns? What's the downside?" Once students are ready, have them post their ideas.

4. *Identify needs.* Ask, "What do you need to know and gather more information about to help you better understand this issue or prepare for this event?"

5. *Ask for stances, steps, or suggestions.* Depending on the issue or event you are focusing on, it may be more appropriate to ask students to take a stance toward the proposal, identify next steps for actions, or make suggestions for enhancing the situation.

6. *Share the thinking.* Invite learners to review the comments made by others. This can be done at each juncture or at the end. However, often more powerful "needs" emerge if people are aware of the group's excitements and worries. The same can happen with the "steps, stances, or suggestions." Invite comments on the themes that emerged in each category. Were there commonalities in the responses? Spend some time on the "suggestions for moving forward" responses and develop a plan for putting into action at least some of the suggestions.

Uses and Variations

The steps outlined describe using the routine with a whole class, making the group's thinking visible and building on one another's ideas. However, learners can also move through the routine individually, thinking through their own responses and then discussing them with others. In this fashion, Sharon Berenholtz at Bialik College used Compass Points as a structure for reflection when her grade 10 class completed their study of Steinbeck's *Of Mice and Men*. Sharon directed students to complete the routine independently with the text in mind. For the "Suggestions," students were asked to propose other possible scenarios for the main characters. A colleague of Sharon's, Russell Kaplan, used the routine in a similar way to help students explore chromatography in a grade 7 science class. On the DVD you can watch teachers discussing the work Russell's students produced using the Looking At Students' Thinking (LAST) protocol.

Soo Isaacs found that Compass Points provided an avenue to open up a discussion about adolescence. At a grade 6, mother-daughter weekend for Bialik students, Soo met separately with the group of mothers and then the group of daughters and used the structure of compass points for them to respond to the following sentence starts: "As your daughter reaches adolescence...," and "As you reach adolescence..." The responses were very open and expressed many concerns and hopes. These led to ongoing discussions that could be directed at responding to the Worries, finding ways to maximize the Excitements and follow up on the Need to knows and Suggestions.

Compass Points can be very effective at faculty meetings when the introduction of a new program is being considered and it is important for everyone present to have some input in the decision-making process in a constructive manner.

Assessment

The Compass Points routine provides many opportunities to observe learners' flexibility in considering different aspects of a problem as they move from one step of the routine to the next. Are students able to think beyond their immediate reactions and positions? Are they able to generate multiple responses at each juncture or just one? Noticing how learners manage the "Need to Know" step enables teachers to see how their students are able to analyze the information they have and identify what else is needed to further their own and the group's understanding of the topic.

A Picture of Practice

The beginning of school is a significant time for students and parents. At Bialik College, preparatory year (five-year-olds) teachers Natalie Kluska, Kathleen Georgiou, and Emily Minter worked together as a team to devise plans for settling students into their new environments and for reassuring parents about the new school year. The group decided to use the Compass Points routine as a way to gather information about matters of interest and concern to both parents and students. Natalie explained her reasons for choosing this routine: "I felt this routine would help to highlight specific thoughts and concerns that the children had and that this could act as a basis for our understandings and support for them as they were beginning school. I also felt that it was very explicit and that this could help the children (and parents) to break down and identify some of their overwhelming thoughts and feelings. Similarly with the parents I felt that this would give me a clear indication of their thoughts and concerns and ways that I could best support them."

The team discussed ways to document the thinking of their young, prewriting stage students and decided to ask students to draw what they were excited about in starting school, what they worried about, and so on. Natalie began by introducing the idea of a compass. She then brought out a Hula Hoop that would become the compass. Natalie explains the rest of the procedure: "We began by looking at East as we wanted the students to share their excitement for their prep year. The students each completed their own drawings on a piece of paper and a teacher documented their explanations on the back of their work. These pictures were placed in the East section of our large Hula Hoop compass. Then, on another day, we looked at North. We first reviewed the East thoughts and then looked at North. Worries, West, were completed next and then the class finished with suggestions, South.''

The students in each of the three classes responded enthusiastically to the routine and their collective as well as individual responses proved most informative (see Figures 4.5–4.8). Although some responses were predictable—needing to know how to read and write, excited about making new friends, and so on—other responses were surprising—worries about parents forgetting to collect them after school, not knowing where and when to find older siblings, and such. Knowing students had fears about parents collecting them encouraged teachers to talk with their students about the processes in place to inform parents of the end-of-day procedures and to stay in touch: simple facts such as that parents had telephone numbers of the school and teachers and could easily get in touch with each other

Figure 4.5 A Student's ''Excitement'' from Compass Points

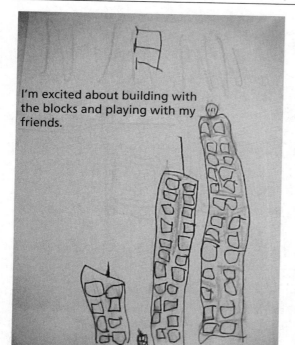

I'm excited about building with the blocks and playing with my friends.

Figure 4.6 A Student's "Worries" from Compass Points

I'm not worried about anything.

Figure 4.7 A Student's "Need to Know" from Compass Points

I need to know how to read and write more.

Figure 4.8 A Student's "Suggestions" from Compass Points

I need more quiet time.

if anyone was running late. The students' responses also enabled the teachers to make sure that the things students had identified as "exciting" were an integral part of school days.

"I'm absolutely amazed at how thoughtful the responses were," Natalie shared with her colleagues afterward. "I was struck by one child identifying that he was worried that other children would be better than him at stuff and this was a very big concern for this child. Identifying it and discussing it was helpful in this situation. The children really opened up and felt comfortable to share their thoughts. Since we reflected on the responses without names, we had the opportunity to hear them all and discuss them all in a nonthreatening way." Natalie was similarly impressed with students' suggestions: "I was amazed at how the children used the South, suggestions section, to respond to worries or needs to know that other children had raised in the other sections. This peer-peer support was very noticeable and was so incredible to see at the beginning of prep with a group of children who were together for the first time."

With all of the preps having completed the different sections of the routine, the teachers met to review the work and choose selected pieces for a documentation display through a digital photo story presentation. In making their choices, they tried to show a broad range of the students' thoughts while also representing all students' contributions. They wanted this documentation to serve not only the students but also the parents.

At the parent orientation night, the teachers decided to ask the parents to work through the Compass Points routine as well. Natalie described the process: "We briefly explained the Compass Points routine and asked parents to share some of their thoughts in response to each of the sections. They wrote their thoughts on sticky notes and added them to the children's thoughts." The anonymity of using sticky notes freed all parents to express their concerns and suggestions in a nonthreatening way, giving everyone a voice. Using the routine also had the benefit of making sure the evening wouldn't be hi-jacked by a few extremely vocal parents with issues. As a final step, the group watched the photo story the teachers had created with the sample of the children's compass points, and the parents had an opportunity to add any additional thoughts to their own responses after this.

The parents participated very willingly in this routine, and the notes posted identified patterns of concerns as well as clear indications of information that parents wanted to know. Many of the concerns and "need to knows" related to the children's social and emotional well-being, such as whether they were happy and making friends. There were also questions about what happens in a school day and how parents could support their children's early reading, and much excitement about their children commencing school and their new independence.

Natalie hoped that the routine would uncover thoughts of children and parents that she could use as a basis for creating their classroom community. She wanted students "to realize that they are not alone in their worries and concerns and through suggestions realize that we can all help each other—this came out strongly."

In reflecting on the experience, Natalie considered her learning from doing the routine with students over several years. "I think this is an invaluable tool that can be used as a reflection at a later date. With my last group we completed the Compass Point routine for their feelings about beginning grade 2. Once they had done this we reflected on the one from when they started prep (through the photo story). It was amazing to see the children's reflection and how they responded to their thoughts from two years earlier. This was an incredibly rich process and helped the children feel more at ease about their transition to grade 2. If they could now laugh about some of their concerns about starting prep, maybe this will also happen in grade 2 and they will see that there was no major reason for them to worry. Also for the parents to use this routine showed them an aspect of their children's learning—an example of how we do things—and it was great for parents to see each others' thoughts and concerns and to alleviate them. It also helped break the ice somewhat between parents at the orientation evening."

⚙ THE EXPLANATION GAME

Taking a close look at the object you are trying to understand:

- *Name it*. Name a feature or aspect of the object that you notice.
- *Explain it*. What could it be? What role or function might it serve? Why might it be there?
- *Give reasons*. What makes you say that? Or why do you think it happened that way?
- *Generate alternatives*. What else could it be? And what makes you say that?

Understanding often involves recognizing the parts of a thing, what they do, how they function, their roles and purposes. This thinking routine was designed to get students to look closely at features and details of an object or occurrence and then to generate multiple explanations for why something is the way it is. In this sense this routine is in part an exercise in the deconstruction of a thing or an exercise in understanding the whole by examining its parts.

Purpose

Like See-Think-Wonder, this routine involves looking closely and building explanations and interpretations. However, in STW learners generally are building up their understanding of an ambiguous image or object as they look closely and develop their interpretations. In contrast, in the Explanation Game, learners may already know what they are looking at but still not fully understand how it operates, functions, or is placed. Thus, students are generally focusing more on the parts than the whole in using this routine. For instance, students may know they are looking at a microscope but can use the Explanation Game to better understand the parts of this science apparatus. Likewise, students may examine the features of a mathematics diagram to determine what those features do or what purposes they serve.

In this way, the Explanation Game asks learners to build causal explanations for why something is the way it is and to understand the purposes or reasons why something functions the way it does. It is the noticing of parts and generating possible and even alternative theories and explanations about the relationships between those parts and the whole that makes this routine powerful for developing understanding.

Selecting Appropriate Content

The Explanation Game works well with content that has various parts and features that seem to call out for closer examination, requiring students to make interpretations and reason with evidence. Science phenomena, historical events, geographical images, and mathematical models are all possible areas where students might be asked to take a closer look at something and generate some explanations for why something is the way it is.

As with STW, it is helpful to play the Explanation Game yourself with the content you have chosen. What unique and slightly ambiguous parts or features do you notice in the image or object? Can you reasonably build some explanations about what purpose and role the parts might serve? Does understanding these parts and explaining them help you to build up an understanding of the whole?

Steps

1. *Set up.* Draw students' attention to an object you would like them to understand better. Resist asking the students to tell you what the object is if it is one they don't immediately recognize; rather, invite them to carefully look at the object to see all that they can possibly see, so that they can begin speculating as to how different features are related to one another.

2. *Name it.* Now ask students to share with their partners various features or aspects of the object they notice. It is important in this stage that students record all the different parts they are observing. This could be done on sticky notes. Working with a partner or in small groups affords students the opportunity to take notice of features they might miss individually.

3. *Explain it.* Once students have accumulated a list of various features they have noticed, ask them to begin explaining these features. It is important that you emphasize the name of this routine here: the *Explanation* Game. You want to focus the group's attention on the action of generating explanations, sharing with students that in this step their goal is to come up with as many different explanations as possible. Have students document their explanations.

4. *Give reasons.* Ask students to generate reasons why their explanations are plausible. This step is about pressing for evidence, asking students to articulate what they have seen in particular that makes them say why a certain feature could be explained a certain way.

5. *Generate alternatives.* In this step, ask students to press for alternative explanations than the ones they initially generated. The goal here is to keep student attention on the relationships between the features of the object they have noticed and why these features might be the way they are rather than coming too quickly to a fixed explanation. For each alternative explanation offered, students should ask one another, "What makes you say that?"

Uses and Variations

Debbie O'Hare, a kindergarten teacher at the International School of Amsterdam, has used the Explanation Game with her early learners for more than a few years. On the DVD you can watch her students playing the Explanation Game to explore a work of art as part of their study of how artists communicate. Recently, she used this routine to introduce her students to the postal system, part of their curriculum to help students get a sense of the communities in which they live. Debbie assembled "mystery boxes" full of postal instruments and asked each small group of students to take turns pulling an object from the box and speculating as to what it could be. Once all the objects were pulled from the box and placed on a tray, each small group then generated ideas about how all these objects might be connected in some way to one another. Debbie's intention was not only for students to become close examiners of each object but also to begin examining features and generating theories as to how these objects are related to one another.

The fourth grade team at the Inter-Community School of Zurich used the Explanation Game as part of their unit on Ancient Civilizations. The region has many archaeological sites, many of which date back to Roman times, that the teachers wanted to make use of in their study. However, they wanted students to understand that archaeology is not a straightforward process and entails building explanations to understand a particular artifact and thus a civilization. Prior to visiting these sites, the local museum loaned a set of replicas of some artifacts from the region to the class. The teachers used the Explanation Game to help their students think like archaeologists.

Assessment

Listen for the explanations given by students when looking at an object and take notice of the quality of their theories rather than their correctness. Do students simply state the obvious and scratch the surface of how things might be related, or do you hear them probing beneath the surface, stretching for connections and possible relationships? Do the explanations seem underdescribed, overly broad, and generalized, or do they seem rich in detail, evocative, nuanced, and descriptive? Do their explanations seem to capture important characteristics, themes, or elements, or do they seem to hover more on unimportant or disconnected details or ideas? As a whole, the class might engage in assessing the various explanations based on the best supporting evidence. This can help students see that it is not about guessing the right answer but about the evidence one can marshal in support of an idea.

Tips

A general tendency for students in the Explanation Game is to want to name the object and see whether they got it right. It is important to resist this urge as much as possible, keeping the focus on looking closely at features and constructing explanations for how things are related or what purposes these parts might serve. When students insist on telling what the object is, a teacher might redirect this by pressing for evidence, asking "What makes you say that?" and then offering the students a challenge by asking "If this weren't what you think it is, what else might it be?" The goal is to keep students in an explanation-generating mindset based on noticeable features. You can watch as Debbie O'Hara does this with her students on the DVD.

While the steps to the routine—Name it, Explain it, Give reasons, Generate alternatives—are clear, they can easily blend into one another. Although not entirely problematic, it is important that all these steps are distinct parts of the classroom discourse and documentation. When explanations are given without reasons, or when alternative explanations are missing, the Explanation Game can turn into "Guess what this object is." This undermines the goal of creating an environment for conjecturing and hypothesizing.

A Picture of Practice

By using the Explanation Game as an opening-day experience for his middle school students, Mitchell Gregory (a pseudonym as the teacher wished to remain anonymous) hoped it would set the stage for learning throughout the school year. He thought of the Explanation Game as much more than an activity; it was a pattern of thinking that he wished to foster among incoming sixth graders. Second, he knew the Explanation Game could help the sixth grade team jump right into a big subject matter issue with students around geography, a subject that each member of the team shared responsibility for teaching, and provide a common experience to build on the rest of the year. The Explanation Game could help students recognize geographic relationships by looking closely and generating explanations with reasons, something students would be asked to do all year. Finally, he wanted to use this routine to lay a foundation for ongoing dialogue, inquiry, debate, and rethinking. "Thinking about what kinds of cognitive behaviors are fundamental for understanding big ideas in social studies was a defining moment for us as a team in our joint planning," remembers Mitchell. "Once we focused our minds on the kind of thinking we wanted to encourage, deciding which thinking routines to use was much easier."

For Mitchell and the rest of the sixth grade team, geography was not only about naming facts about places around the world but also recognizing and explaining how natural processes and humankind interact and help give shape to our world. The kinds of thinking important to geographers reminded the team of what students were asked to do in their other subject areas: look closely both on and below the surface, generate explanations and theories for why things are the way they are, make claims and reason with evidence, and raise questions about evidence to help drive further inquiry. Consequently, the Explanation Game immediately struck Mitchell as the perfect way to launch the school year.

To begin planning, Mitchell and his colleagues searched magazines and the Internet for photos that captured dynamic images of people, places, and environmental processes. With all identifying captions removed, images were enlarged, posted around each classroom, and labeled with numbers. On the first day of school, when the new sixth graders came in and took their seats, the team of teachers welcomed them to the new school year and Mitchell asked who might like to start the year off with a bit of a game? Among cheers of "Yes!" and "Me!" all hands immediately shot up. Mitchell, the sixth grade team leader, informed students that they would need a bit of direction before setting off. "We're going to play a game today called the Explanation Game. Now, just what do you think we'll have to do in a game like that?" A student hesitantly offered, "Explain a lot?" Mitchell responded, "We're so glad you said that! That's music to your social studies teachers' ears! You'll be explaining a lot, just like geographers do!"

Mitchell continued his directions: "Around the room you see all sorts of images we've collected over the summer. Some look pretty cool and interesting. Others look quite ominous and a little bit frightening. What we'd like you to do is join with a partner and visit the images all around the place. Really take your time and see all that you can possibly see together with your partner. Two sets of eyes are better than one." He told the eager students, "Once you've seen and pointed out a lot of things to one another, we'll need you to take out your social studies journal and jot down a few notes."

Mitchell laid out the steps of the Explanation Game. "Record for us, just like geographers might, what things you are noticing—in other words, name the features you see. Then, explain it—just where or what you think it could be, and give us some reasons—what makes you give that explanation. If you think it could be something else because of something else you notice, then write that down too!" On the board, he wrote the four steps as a reminder for students. Mitchell decided not to prepare a worksheet for students to fill in on that first day; he wanted to use this opportunity to see how students naturally went about organizing their notes and thinking. The team could use this information to make future decisions about what kinds of organization it might be helpful to teach students.

Students partnered up and began visiting the images all around the room. Mitchell took a quick walk around to check whether any pairs needed more clarification about directions. Then, he took the opportunity to listen to students' conversations, something the whole team had come to value. "I used to think that my job was to give students directions, then go around and monitor their work. But more and more I'm finding it useful to listen in on students talking. I learn so much more about their thinking when I do that," Mitchell reflected later. "As soon as kids understood the steps to the Explanation Game, I found that I could go around and listen in to their conversations. This was just the start of our very first day, but their thinking blew me away!" he remarked. Figure 4.9 shows an example of students' journal entries for the Explanation Game.

After 45 minutes, Mitchell asked students to find seats so they could have some whole-group discussion. He intentionally used the steps of the Explanation Game to frame students' discourse. "So, we know there was a lot of good talking going on, so there must have been a lot of good thinking!" said Mitchell, speaking on behalf of the team. "We're wondering, could someone start us off and share with us what image captured their attention the most? Then share with us what it was, exactly, that you and your partner saw, where or what you think it could be, and what makes you say that?"

The first student shared her and her partner's thinking. Immediately other students' hands shot up as they were eager to share their explanations as to where or what they thought that very same image could be. Mitchell listened closely, recording each pair's thinking on the board while asking others to hold off a little as the teachers tried to follow the line of thinking being shared currently.

Figure 4.9 Sixth Grade Explanation Game Journal Entries

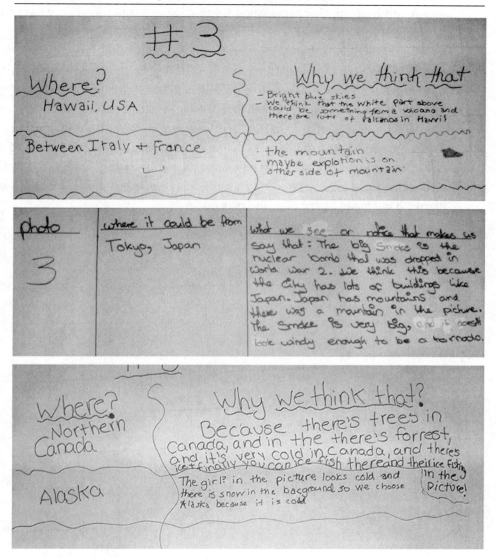

For the next student, one of the other teachers documented that student's thinking in a line stemming from the first person's explanations. When a student simply shared a judgment, such as, "It's Alaska," Mitchell would gently use the language of the routine to continue probing that student's thinking: "So you think it might be Alaska. Just what did you see or notice that makes you say that?" Once explained, he would ask, "Now that we've heard that explanation, we're wondering if someone else might have another explanation for that same image based on what you saw or noticed?"

The sixth grade students' thinking was rich, and Mitchell knew documenting it would be a means of reinforcing a type of thinking the class would use throughout the entire school year. "We were so pleased with how the Explanation Game helped us launch our school year," Mitchell recalled. "It became a sort of anchor activity that we continually referred back to across several units—not the images, so much, but the questions the routine asks: What do you see or notice? What could it be? What makes you say that? What else could it be and what makes you say that? The Explanation Game became so much more than one event. It became a process of thinking we made use of over and over again."

CHAPTER 5

Routines for Synthesizing and Organizing Ideas

⚙ HEADLINES

Think of the big ideas and important themes in what you have been learning.

- Write a headline for this topic or issue that summarizes and captures a key aspect that you feel is significant and important.

This routine naturally emerged from our own group's meetings at Harvard Project Zero. Many times when we were discussing an issue or wrapping up a discussion, we wanted to make sure we heard from everyone in the group in a very succinct way and without further discussion. The leader would simply ask everyone for a "headline" that would capture his or her thoughts, impressions, or key ideas about the topic being explored. The routine forced a quick synthesis by each group member and provided a read on where everyone in the group was at with regard to the topic. We adapted this basic idea for use in classrooms, as you'll read.

Purpose

The Headlines routine asks students to reflect and synthesize as they identify the essence or core of a situation or learning experience. Sometimes it is easy for the activity of the classroom to just continue on and on without the opportunity for learners to consider what is important or central in their learning. However, without capturing the significant essence, it can be difficult for learners to build understanding of big ideas and core principles. They may miss the forest for the trees. If students are not able to grasp the heart of what they are learning, they will find it difficult to make meaningful connections to these ideas in future learning.

By asking students to sum up their current notions of a lesson or concept using a headline, teachers send the message that taking notice of big ideas is critical to understanding. Documenting the group's headlines in some way helps students to consider a topic from multiple angles and create a rich mental picture of what is important to keep front and center in their thinking.

Selecting Appropriate Content

Since the Headlines routine calls for synthesis, it is often situated within an ongoing arc of learning to help students get a sense of what lies at the core of a topic that may have many layers or nuances. Simply asking students to write a headline for the definitions of the six types of simple machines might not yield anything compelling that captures ideas of central importance in physics. Students are likely to come up with catchy phrases for levers, pulleys, and wedges that might seem more "list oriented" than heart capturing. On the other hand, asking students to create a headline to express what they've come to understand regarding these simple machines—mechanical advantage—and how this all connects to some bigger idea might prove particularly insightful. In this case, the Headlines routine creates an opportunity to capture the essence of a few fundamental physics ideas. The Headlines routine can also be used after a single episode of learning, such as a field trip, reading of a book, watching a movie, or so on. In this context, the Headline helps students to identify what was important or stood out to them about the experience. Getting a better sense of what students see as important can be useful in planning future instruction.

Steps

1. *Set up.* After students have had some learning experiences, ask them to consider what they think some of the core ideas in what they've been learning seem to be.

2. *Write a headline.* Ask the students to "Write a headline for this topic or issue that captures an important aspect or core idea that we would want to remember." Students can do this individually or with partners, depending on what the teacher desires.

3. *Share the thinking.* Once students have an opportunity to draft a headline, ask them to share their headlines with students around them. It is important that students not only share their headlines but also the story and reasoning behind their choice, unpacking the headline for others. This step is not a competition for the best headline. The goal is to create a forum in which different perspectives and nuances are surfaced.

4. *Invite further sharing.* Once pairs or small groups have had the opportunity to share their headlines and tell the stories of their headlines with each other, you can create a class collection of the headlines that document the group's thinking. Working with a collection of headlines, you might encourage your class to search for common themes or elements among the headlines.

Uses and Variations

At Brighton Elementary in Tasmania, Julie Mitchell and her colleagues have found that Headlines is a great way of helping students deal with social conflicts on the playground. Julie felt the synthesizing move called for by Headlines would be useful for students experiencing social conflicts. She noticed that when conflicts arose, students often ran to the teacher to solve the conflict, tattle, or recount the entire episode of events. By asking students to stop and put the issue into headline form, Julie encouraged her sixth graders to think about what was the core issue at the heart of the conflict or event. This process forced students to calm down and think what it was that they were upset about. Julie and her colleagues found that the synthesizing, coupled with the act of listening to others, often minimized tensions and reduced the incidents in which teachers were playing referee. As students became familiar with this process, Julie introduced the idea of crafting a headline from the other student's perspective. By asking students to see the conflict from the other side, she was further able to defuse the situation and help students begin to resolve their own conflicts.

Clair Taglauer, a teacher at East Middle School in Traverse City, Michigan, used a modified version of the Headlines routine when exploring literary themes with her eighth grade language arts students. After her class had read *Touching Spirit Bear* by Ben Mikaelsen, Clair asked her students to nominate songs from their mp3 players that they felt would best capture a central theme from the novel. For each song selection, students were asked to explain and justify their choices. By keeping the focus on important literary themes, this activity created an opportunity for students to reflect upon all they had read. Their song choice acted like a headline to illuminate a central idea in the text worth remembering. Listening to the class's mix of song selections for *Touching Spirit Bear* was a memorable way to culminate their learning.

Eli Conde, a preschool teacher at the International School of Amsterdam, adapted the Headlines routine for her three- and four-year-olds by calling it "Story Titles." She introduced this into class sharing time after students told about what they had done over the weekend. After each child had told his or her story of weekend activity, Eli asked the class, "What title could we give to Carla's story?" After a response, she would push for more thinking by asking, "What else might we call it?" In this way, she introduced these young students to the idea of summarizing.

Assessment

Pay attention to each student's headline as well as the reasoning behind his or her choice. Has the student seen or noticed an idea that could have otherwise been missed? Has this student crafted a headline that highlights an issue that is worth the whole group's attention? Does the headline do its job in synthesizing and distilling the event or does it focus on tangential elements? What does this headline reveal about the student's current understanding of the topic?

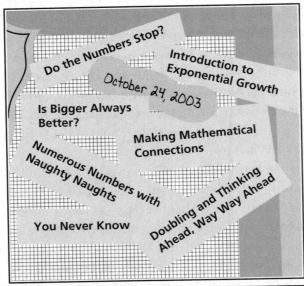

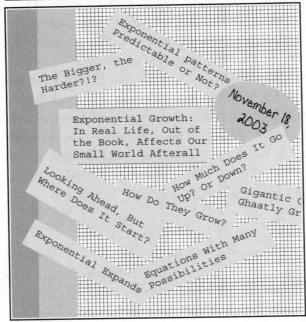

Of course, it would be unreasonable to expect that a single headline can sum up all the nuances and complexities of topics we teach. Therefore, you'll want to assess the class's entire collection of headlines to get a better sense of what big ideas are resonating with students. In addition, a class collection of headlines has the potential for revealing puzzles or questions that seem appropriate to explore next.

Tips

The Headlines routine seems straightforward enough. However, teachers have experienced a fine line between creating opportunities for students to put their thumbs on the pulse of a topic and students simply coming up with catchy slogans and titles. It is very useful for teachers to remember that this routine is not about students coming up with a superficial but catchy phrase. It is about inviting learners individually and as a group to gear their thinking toward core, central ideas and elements that are at the heart of a topic being studied.

For example, one student's headline, "Investigation of Exponential Growth," does not reveal exactly what he is understanding as much as another student's headline, "Exponential Patterns: Predictable or Not?" The former is merely a title of what the student is studying, whereas the latter captures more of the essence of what the student is beginning to understand about mathematical patterns of change and growth (see Figure 5.1). If students' headlines seem to be more catchy and clever than revealing, a teacher should not hesitate to probe the ideas a bit more with them to get a sense of what learners believe are the most important ideas of their study.

Since the Headlines routine asks students to summarize, teachers sometimes find it useful to ask for "words behind the headline" to understand why students made the choices they did if it is not evident from the headlines themselves. At times, it can be interesting to ask the class to first think what the "story" might be behind a student's headline before having that student supply a few more words to go along with what he or she has created.

A Picture of Practice

When Karrie Tufts, a fifth and sixth grade teacher for the Traverse City Area Public Schools in Michigan, first used the Headlines routine in her mathematics classes, she wanted to get a sense of what her students might come up with. After a mathematics investigation about fractions, Karrie asked her students, "So, what would you say would be a good headline for today's learning?" Though some student examples were straightforward and reported simple facts, others struck Karrie as having an intriguing bit of depth (see Figure 5.2).

As she gained a bit more familiarity with the Headlines routine, Karrie wanted to push her students' reflections and try to get more out of their headlines than surface knowledge. Karrie thought the headlines students were generating were good, but she was left to do a lot of the "interpreting" behind the headlines. Karrie wasn't clear about what theories or ideas her students were putting together about why something works the way it works in the different mathematics topics they were studying. Because of this, Karrie began asking students not only to come up with headlines for what they had been learning but also to share a few sentences on the back side of their papers that gave "a little more of the story." Karrie did not want this to become a laborious exercise for students to undertake, and she found that a few sentences that shared more behind their choice of headlines gave

Figure 5.2 Fifth and Sixth Grade Students' Headlines About Fractions

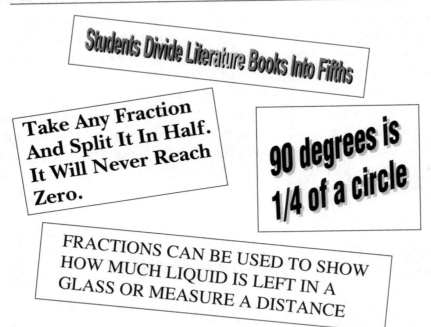

Students Divide Literature Books Into Fifths

Take Any Fraction And Split It In Half. It Will Never Reach Zero.

90 degrees is 1/4 of a circle

FRACTIONS CAN BE USED TO SHOW HOW MUCH LIQUID IS LEFT IN A GLASS OR MEASURE A DISTANCE

her significantly more insight into students' thinking. She also found this added explanation helped some students more clearly articulate ideas that they couldn't exactly capture in their headlines.

As the Headlines routine became more a part of the ongoing learning of Karrie's classes, she decided to vary the use of this routine. Whereas early on, Karrie asked students to come up with their own individual headlines, she later began asking them to partner up and collectively generate a few headlines to capture the big ideas behind what they had been studying. By pairing students up, Karrie noticed the power of students exchanging and discussing ideas. An important message she wanted students to receive was how learning can be very powerful when people kick ideas back and forth.

Once pairs of students had come up with a few tentative headlines that seemed to capture the core, Karrie pushed them further by asking them to choose just one to fine-tune and add to the class collection of headlines. Pairs then discussed which of their headlines seemed to be the most powerful. Karrie found it interesting to listen to their reasons for why a particular headline made the final cut while others did not. "These mini-conferences with each pair were very informative and useful for my own sense making of what my students were understanding and seeing as particularly important," reflected Karrie. Each pair then gave their final headline to Karrie for the classroom's display. Karrie wanted the group's thinking to be both visible and shared by all mathematics learners, even across class sections of students.

Karrie found that through Headlines she got a glimpse into how students were or were not connecting to ideas she thought to be particularly powerful in the topics they were studying. Becoming more aware of students' thinking, Karrie felt more informed in making decisions about how she would like her lessons to progress. "Knowing my students' headlines today helped me make decisions for my teaching tomorrow," recalls Karrie. She also found students' headlines revealed some misconceptions or overgeneralizations students had. Because she had created a safe learning environment, Karrie felt confident in addressing these misconceptions in ways that challenged and provoked learners' thinking rather than quickly resolving misconceptions for them.

Students in Karrie's mathematics classroom regularly engaged in hands-on activities. The use of thinking routines opened up ways for students to become more mindful of what they were learning through these active lessons rather than leaving it to chance. Karrie noticed that even struggling students were able to come up with headlines to capture some aspect of the topic at hand. Karrie also noticed students were making reference to each others' headlines when trying to express their own thinking, sometimes even days after the headlines had gone up on the classroom wall. In these ways, the curriculum became more accessible for all learners. Over time, all students felt comfortable enough to interact with the group's collective thinking via headlines.

Having worked to make her students' thinking visible in both fifth and sixth grades, Karrie wondered what students would take with them upon leaving her classroom. So a year after students had left her, Karrie arranged to meet her former students and asked them about what sorts of thinking they continued to make use of in their new classes. Several students made mention of the Headlines routine in particular, Karrie noted. Often this occurred in learning scenarios unprovoked by the teacher. For example, one former student mentioned that when he comes across a particularly challenging test question on a districtwide assessment, he often asks himself, "So what would a headline be for this topic?" to see if that helps him figure out a problem or response. Another student reported that when she listens to her soccer coach explain a new strategy or skill, she often considers, "What's the headline here?" to picture what is at the core of her coach's instructions. If something remains puzzling for her, this student reported that she uses the headline in her mind to frame the question to ask her coach.

◎ CSI: COLOR, SYMBOL, IMAGE

Think of the big ideas and important themes in what you have just read, seen, or heard.

- Choose a *color* that you think best represents the essence of that idea.
- Create a *symbol* that you think best represents the essence of that idea.
- Sketch an *image* that you think best captures the essence of that idea.

The CSI: Color, Symbol, Image routine emerged from our desire to make students' thinking visible in a way that didn't rely so heavily on the use of written or oral language. Having worked intensively with a number of international schools in which students are often learning in a new language, teachers shared with us the need for such routines. Similarly, teachers of young students felt that the lack of language facility sometimes made it difficult for their students to adequately express their thinking. The idea of using colors, symbols, and images taps into students' natural creativity and desire for expression. At the same time, it pushes students to make connections and think metaphorically.

Purpose

This routine asks students to identify and distill the essence of ideas—taken from their reading, viewing, or listening—in nonverbal ways by using a color, symbol, and image to represent the big ideas they have identified. In making these selections, students are pushed to think metaphorically. Metaphors are a major vehicle for developing our understanding of ideas as we connect something new to something we already know by identifying similarities and making comparisons. Put simply, a metaphor is a connection between one thing and another. "This is like that because . . . ," "This idea reminds me of or makes me think of this because . . ."

CSI can be a great way to enhance student comprehension and develop metaphorical thinking. However, there is no need to introduce the formal terminology of metaphors and similes, though this might be discussed with older students. Keep in mind that the connections students make are highly personal and need to be understood in terms of the individual's explanation. For example, one student may choose black to represent an idea because to them black represents possibility and the unknown, whereas another student may associate blue with the exact same idea because blue reminds him of the openness of the sky and infinite freedom and possibility.

Selecting Appropriate Content

Select a rich piece of content that has a variety of interpretations and meaning. Don't shy away from complexity, ambiguity, and nuance. There has to be something to interpret and discuss. The content might be a personal essay, a chapter from a piece of literature, a poem, a provocative speaker, radio essay, or short film. The content shouldn't be too long nor have too many competing ideas contained in it, however. Therefore, a single chapter in a book or even a passage is often preferable to the whole text. Select something that you want your students to interpret and think that their interpretations will give you insight into their understanding of that content.

Steps

1. *Set up.* After students have read a passage from a book, listened to a speaker, or viewed a video, have them think about the core ideas and make note of things that they find interesting, important, or insightful. They can do this individually or, if this is the first time introducing the routine, you might want to generate a class list of the various ideas people identified.

2. *Choose a color.* Each student selects a color that he or she feels represents the core ideas he or she has identified in the piece of content being explored. In most cases a single color should be chosen by each student. This color is recorded and, when age-appropriate, students explain and justify their choices in writing.

3. *Create a symbol.* Each student selects a symbol that he or she feels represents the core ideas he or she has identified in the piece of content being explored. A symbol is a thing that stands for something else. For instance, a dove stands for peace, the = sign stands for the concept of equality. If you look at your computer dock, you will see a variety of icons that stand for various programs or functions. The symbol is recorded and, when age-appropriate, students explain and justify their choices in writing.

4. *Sketch an image.* Each student selects an image that he or she feels represents the core ideas he or she has identified in the piece of content being explored. An image is like a photograph or drawing of a scene. Students need not worry about their drawing abilities, as they can simply complete a simple sketch that captures the idea of what is in the image. This sketch is recorded and, when age-appropriate, students explain and justify their choices in writing.

5. *Share the thinking.* Working with a partner or in a group, each student shares his or her color and tells why he or she made that choice. How did it connect to the passage or content the class is trying to understand? How does that color connect to the big ideas just read, heard, or seen? Repeat the sharing process until every member of the pair or group has shared his or her color, symbol, and image and explained the selections.

Uses and Variations

In her second grade classroom, Emma Furman at Bialik College decided to use CSI as a tool to help her students reflect on the upcoming school year. She asked them to think about what being a second grader meant to them and what color they might give "second grade." She then asked them to think of what kind of symbol they would pick to stand for being in second grade versus being in first grade or being in third grade. How was this year going to be different? Finally she asked them to draw pictures that for them represented their hopes about second grade.

As Joan in Hobart, Tasmania, began reading a new chapter book aloud to her fifth graders she made the decision to try the CSI routine as a whole class but to modify it to focus just on the choice of color. Using a class list, she created a table in which each student's name was assigned a row and twelve columns were created to correspond to the number of chapters in the book. After reading each chapter, the sheet was passed around the class and each student selected a color to fill in beside his or her name in the column corresponding to the chapter. Once the sheet was completed, a short class discussion ensued in which students were invited to explain and justify their choices to the rest of the class. The sheet was then posted on the bulletin board until it was needed again. What resulted was a patchwork display that provided a sense of the character of each chapter as well as the individuality of each student.

You can watch Melyssa Lenon using the CSI routine with her secondary chemistry students at Chesaning Union High School in Michigan on the DVD. Melyssa's students use the routine to capture the essence of the concept of stoichiometry, a branch of chemistry dealing with understanding and representing the quantitative relationship that exists among reactants and products in chemical reactions. Melyssa had spent a lot of time on the procedures involved in figuring out these relationships and used CSI to draw students' attention back to the broader concept.

Assessment

In students' selection of colors, symbols, and images, look for their ability to capture the essence of the stimulus from which they are working. Although this might be partially evident in their selection, it is their explanations of their choices that provide more insight. Why did a student choose that color or create that image? How does it connect with the big ideas of the stimulus? In helping to advance students' thinking, you will also want to look at the quality of the metaphors they are choosing. Initially, students may make very obvious choices, such as black for sadness, a sun for happiness, or a literal drawing of a scene from the story. You'll want to look for and ask students to provide metaphors that go beyond the obvious and that help us to understand the ideas on a deeper level. See Nathan Armstrong's example in the Picture of Practice following for an example of how this can be done.

Tips

Though the routine specifies color, symbol, and then image, it is not necessary to do them in that order. Depending on the content and the individual, some students may find it easier to start with the image while others may have a symbol that immediately comes to mind. Since the point of the routine is to encourage metaphorical thinking, making connections, and distilling the essence, don't place too much emphasis on the actual drawing of the image. While younger students might enjoy this diversion, it can be a distraction from the thinking if it is allowed to become the focus of the activity. Older students might even prefer to describe their images in words rather than draw them. Students can also complete the routine effectively on the computer by "filling" a box using the color palette, using the "Insert symbol" function as a source for symbols, and searching "Google images" to find a picture.

A Picture of Practice

As one of his and their first attempts at using a thinking routine, Nathan Armstrong decided to try out the CSI routine in his seventh grade English class at Wesley College in Melbourne. Nathan's students were reading Anne Frank's *Diary of a Young Girl* at the time. After beginning the book in class, the remainder of the book became assigned reading over the school holiday. To be sure that students were actively engaging with the text and that they would be prepared for a rich discussion when they returned to school, Nathan decided to use the CSI routine. He assigned students the task of doing the routine for five of Anne's diary entries.

Students would do the routine using a basic computer template of three boxes arranged across the sheet in landscape mode. Each box would hold a color, a symbol, or an image. Students would search for images on the Internet, use symbols from the "Insert symbols" function, and fill in the box with a color using "Fill color." Below each box students would write brief explanations to justify their choices (see Figure 5.3).

When students returned from the school holiday, the room was turned into a gallery of their work as students posted their five CSI routines. Students hung up their routines according to diary entry, so that the front wall became a visual representation of the entire text chronologically arranged. Since students made their own selection of which entries from Anne's diary to interpret, many of the diary entries had multiple CSI representations. Discussion quickly broke out regarding the various ways in which students interpreted the text, noting both similarities as well as differences in the colors, symbols, and images selected.

Nathan's goal for using CSI had been to give students a chance to develop a deeper understanding of the text. He felt the choices students made about their colors, symbols, and images along with their explanations accomplished this. At the same time, it provided him with a good sense of their understanding. Reflecting on students' work, Nathan noted that some of students' metaphorical choices were more sophisticated than others. This led to a class discussion about what makes a

Figure 5.3 Alexandra's CSI Routine for *The Diary of a Young Girl*

Color	Symbol	Image
Anne is unsure of what the future will hold for her and Peter. Black, like a chalkboard, represents all the different possibilities that could be drawn for their future.	In this diary entry Anne doubts she can keep her longing to reach Peter under control. She must wait until the silence breaks between them and they can act as their true selves.	Through this passage Anne talks about how she and Peter aren't really as different as they seem on the surface. Just like these apples, they look different but taste similar.

good metaphor. Students shared that some metaphors seem obvious and almost literal, like a road to symbolize a journey or a tree to stand for growth, while other metaphors were more complex, like a water droplet representing the idea of feeling simultaneous separation and integration since a water droplet has its own uniqueness but at the same time gets lost once it is combined with other droplets.

Based on these discussions about the degree of complexity and sophistication of metaphors, Nathan decided to push students' metaphoric thinking. Working with a subsequent text, Nathan drew a selection of random and varied objects and asked students to relate them to the text as possible images: "How might these drawings fit what we have just read as possible CSI images?" As students discussed and justified how the objects Nathan had drawn might connect to the text, they were developing their ability to create rich metaphors by connecting features of the text to features of the images.

With this initial experience using the CSI routine and thinking deeply about metaphors behind them, Nathan developed a scaling system for evaluating the quality of the metaphors students created. This "metaphoric level" was a continuum on a scale of 1 = low to 10 = high. Students used this scale to self- and peer assess as they continued to use the CSI routine throughout the year. During these sessions, Nathan continued to modify the routine to meet his needs and push students' thinking. Sometimes students were put in groups to do the CSI routine, thus requiring them to discuss and evaluate their choices of color, symbols, and images with their peers. To further extend students, Nathan sometimes asked for a quote from the text to be given to accompany students' choices. In this way, students were forced to justify the big ideas and themes they identified.

GENERATE-SORT-CONNECT-ELABORATE: CONCEPT MAPS

Select a topic, concept, or issue for which you want to map your understanding.

- *Generate* a list of ideas and initial thoughts that come to mind when you think about this topic or issue.
- *Sort* your ideas according to how central or tangential they are. Place central ideas near the center and more tangential ideas toward the outside of the page.
- *Connect* your ideas by drawing connecting lines between the ideas that have something in common. Explain and write on the line in a short sentence how the ideas are connected.
- *Elaborate* on any of the ideas or thoughts you have written so far by adding new ideas that expand, extend, or add to your initial ideas.

Over the years we have collectively looked at thousands of concept maps from students around the world. Regardless of the topic, one thing that we noticed was that, by and large, students don't make very good concept maps. This set us pondering over what kinds of thinking one needs to do in order to create a concept map that would both help one to organize one's thinking and ideas as well as to reveal how one understands a particular concept. The Generate-Sort-Connect-Elaborate (GSCE) routine was the result.

Purpose

Concept maps help uncover a learner's, mental models of a topic in a nonlinear way. Concept maps help us to activate our knowledge of a topic and then connect those ideas in a meaningful way. Learners often find that making a concept map helps them to organize their thinking and illuminate how ideas relate to one another. This can help to solidify one's thinking and understanding as well as to reveal that thinking to others. Of course, educators and researchers have long used concept maps for this purpose. However, for a concept map to be truly revealing of the mental model or conceptual understanding a person holds, it is helpful to structure the process of creating a concept map, not to constrain the thinking but to actively foster more and better thinking. This routine highlights the mental moves needed to create a rich and revealing concept map that makes full use of their graphical nature.

Selecting Appropriate Content

The topics or concepts selected for this routine are often of large scope: democracy, habitats, effective presentations, geometry, and so on. These topics have many parts and components to them and thus invite many and varied responses. When a big idea or goal is posed, students have an opportunity to generate a diverse list of ideas. The ensuing debate to determine the centrality of the ideas allows students to reveal the depth and breadth of their understanding. Concepts or ideas, such as freedom, power, and electricity, and processes, such as designing a science experiment, creating an animated film, or preparing for a debate, all lend themselves to this routine. The routine can be situated at the beginning of a unit to reveal what learners already know about a topic and spark discussion, or it can be used later in the unit to assess how students are making sense of ideas. Often students find that creating a concept map at the end of a unit is a good way to review what they have learned in preparation for a test or in planning to write a paper.

Steps

1. *Set up.* Check whether students know what a concept map is, and if not, explain that this is a way of showing one's thinking about a topic. If learners are already familiar with concept maps, the routine can be introduced with a brief introduction explaining that they will be creating concept maps in a structured way.

2. *Generate.* Ask students to generate a list of words, ideas, or aspects associated with the topic. Depending on the topic, this might mean you ask students to "make a list of key aspects or components of this topic" or "make a list of the various ingredients, processes, or needs associated with this goal/task." This step is designed to produce an initial list of ideas. Since it can be added to at any time, it is only important that students have a list of at least five or six items to use before beginning the next step.

3. *Sort.* Invite learners to sort their ideas according to how central or tangential they are, placing central ideas near the center and more peripheral ideas toward the outside. If desired, at this stage students can pair or form groups to do this sorting. This often results in rich debating of priorities.

4. *Connect.* Ask learners to connect their ideas by drawing lines between ideas that share a connection and to briefly explain this connection by writing it out on the line. For example, one idea might lead to another or two ideas might work in tandem.

5. *Elaborate.* Ask students to pick a few central ideas and elaborate upon them, creating subcategories that break the ideas into smaller parts.

6. *Share the thinking.* Have students pair up with another individual or group to share their concept maps. Focus discussion on the choices made in constructing the map and when there were debates or questions about placement or connections.

Uses and Variations

In sorting, one can choose classifications other than most-to-least important. For instance, one might group ideas according to those that appear first or need attending to first and those that come later or those ideas common to all versus common to some. Some students have devised a series of concentric circles to help in this grouping, creating inner and outer rings of influence.

Jenny Rossi used GSCE with a small group of third graders at Way Elementary in Bloomfield Hills, Michigan, to assess what they had learned through their geometry study. She asked students to collectively generate a list of all the things they had studied. As students came up with ideas, Jenny gave them index cards to write them on. Jenny then laid out the cards and asked her students to sort them, not by centrality, but just by those ideas that seemed to have something in common. This provided Jenny insights into the kinds of attributes students found significant. For instance, in grouping shapes, the students focused on the number of sides and put symmetry with lines and rays since they had talked about "lines of symmetry." Having the ideas on index cards meant that these groupings could be done flexibly and changed if need be. Jenny then asked the students to talk about how these groups were connected and she recorded this information on the connecting line. For "'Elaborate," Jenny told students they would be studying pyramids and prisms next, and after that study would come back to the concept map to add this new information.

When history teacher Sharonne Blum wanted her grade 9 students at Bialik College to study for exams, she decided to use the steps of Generate-Sort-Connect-Elaborate. At the start of the period, she kept all students outside the classroom, allowing only two to three of them in at a time. As the first group of students entered, they were asked to add an idea to the topic that had been written on the whiteboard, "Jewish Life in the Middle Ages," placing central and important ideas toward the center. Two or three at a time, students added their ideas, naming an event they knew about or expressing a theme, concept, or idea. As more groups entered, instructions were shifted, and the later entering students were asked to read what had been written and draw lines to show connections among events, concepts, or ideas. At this point, with all students in the room, the class was invited to add additional ideas, connections, or elaborations. Sharonne then used the concept map students had created as the basis for their review, asking if anything was missing or if there was any disagreement about placements. When students were asked what questions came up for them, an interesting discussion ensued. "Why do we always consider tragedy and disaster more important than happy peaceful times?" one student asked, having noticed that the tragic events were all placed much closer to the center. With that comment, students began to discuss how turning points in history are often triggered by disaster. They also spoke about human nature and how we tend to focus on the negatives in our lives and take for granted the positives.

Assessment

The concept maps created using GSCE contain a wealth of assessment information about what students know and how they see that knowledge related and connected to the whole. Notice the ideas generated and their placement on the map. Are students able to differentiate between key ideas and peripheral ones? Have they identified the most important ideas? The way the ideas are elaborated gives an indication of the depth of learners' understanding. What sort of connections are students making? Look for connections that are more than the obvious and show insights in the deep structure of the ideas. If the topic is a familiar one, GSCE can be done as an informal pre-assessment and again at the end of the unit to see how students' thinking has developed.

Tips

Creating a good concept map depends on generating a good list of ideas with which to work. To ensure this, you might want to have students generate initial lists individually and then work in pairs or small groups. This allows for combining lists to "Sort." Of course, although "Generate" exists as its own step, students can add additional ideas at any time. Practically speaking, it is useful to have large sheets of paper for students to write on. The size of the sheet will draw attention to placement and provide a greater range of possibilities. In addition, students will find it easier to write their connections and to elaborate ideas if the sheet is large enough to accommodate these moves.

A Picture of Practice

One of the assigned novels for Ravinder (Ravi) Grewal's grade 12 English classes at Bialik College, is Tim O'Brien's *In the Lake of the Woods*. The book's protagonist, John Wade, is a Vietnam veteran who is emotionally unstable. This complex book provides an opportunity to hone students' skill at character analysis, a skill that will be tested in their state exit exams.

After reading and discussing the text, Ravi wanted students to analyze the factors contributing to John Wade's mental breakdown. Rather than merely directing her students to write an analytic essay, Ravi decided to use the GSCE routine to help structure students' thoughts and begin their analysis. She also thought the routine would provoke lively discussion that would encourage her students to reexamine their own ideas. "I wanted a structure that would give students the freedom to air different viewpoints, make connections, and arrive at conclusions without fear of being incorrect. I also wanted them to be the main participants in the discussion and not allow it to become a teacher-directed one."

As this was the first time Ravi had used GSCE with her class, she was explicit with directions: "Individually, I would like you to generate some ideas. Think of all the factors that impacted on John Wade as an individual and compile a list of those." After giving her students time to do this, she gave the next instruction: "Place the ideas which you consider most important close to the center and those that are peripheral place further away from the center in descending order of importance." Ravi then went on to direct the students to draw connecting lines between factors that somehow complemented or influenced each other. Finally, she asked students to elaborate their ideas, adding details that would further their understanding. (See Figure 5.4 for an example of a student's GSCE concept map for the character of John Wade.)

After completing individual concept maps, students were placed in small groups and asked to make a collective concept map following the same steps. "They had to arrive at a consensus before placing an idea in a particular place during the 'Sort' stage. This encouraged a passionate discussion as each felt strongly that he or she had the most accurate 'spot.' That debate was exactly what I was looking for," Ravi commented.

In observing students in their groups, Ravi was impressed with the quality of the conversations: "The debate that occurred when they were creating the group concept map from their individual ones allowed the relative importance of each contributing factor to be discussed, further clarifying the ideas to the students. The 'Sort' stage was the most effective as it generated the most discussion. The 'Connect' stage was another one that opened up so many new ideas that the students themselves were surprised at the number of layers they had uncovered."

One particularly lively debate was that which focused on the question of whether it was Wade's experience in Vietnam that sent him over the brink or whether his breakdown was the result of his father's bullying during his childhood.

Figure 5.4 Tyrone's Concept Map for the Character John Wade from *In the Lake of the Woods*

GENERATE SORT CONNECT EXTEND - CONCEPT MAP

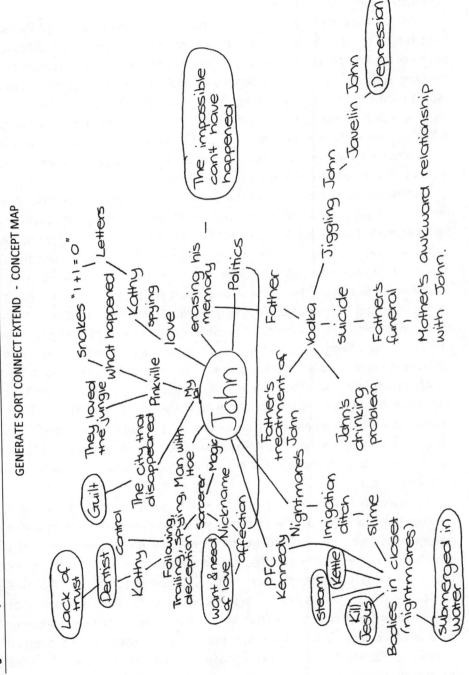

The students discussed the possibility that if his father hadn't bullied him and taken away his self-esteem as a child, would he have grown up strong enough to withstand the trauma of the Vietnam War? There was great conflict over this idea, with some students saying that no one could have experienced the trauma of the My Lai massacre and not have been traumatized.

In reflecting on students' understanding, Ravi observed, "Their final analysis was that all the factors were significant and Wade's response to each one was similar and in keeping with the strategy he had perfected in his childhood. This was exactly what I wanted them to understand. I did not want them to see Wade as either a damaged war veteran only or merely as a child affected by his abusive father. And they really got it! When they finally concluded that all individuals are capable of this evil given the circumstances, I knew they had understood the core issues here."

At the end of this 90-minute class, which you can see a portion of on the DVD, students were asked to write an essay discussing, "Is John Wade a monster or is his only fault the fact that he is a man?" The writing of the essay took place the next day. Ravi clearly saw how the structured process of the routine and the ensuing discussion were reflected in the students' essays. "Because they had explored so many factors, they realized that an individual is an outcome of a range of experiences and therefore one cannot form an opinion that condemns an individual as a monster. One must begin to understand that all humans are flawed and the flaws become apparent as a result of their experiences."

Reflecting on her students' first use of the routine, Ravi noted, "I found the students more willing to indulge in discussion, to listen, and to search for reasons that had led them to the decisions they had made when working individually. Thus they saw alternative viewpoints, but still had firm views of their own. What surprised me was the rational way in which they willingly engaged in debate but were willing to be convinced if they saw reason in the other person's viewpoint. I was really pleased at the structure provided by the routine, and the fact that the students saw that concept maps have a structure that reflects their mental moves—generating, sorting, connecting, elaborating!"

In reflecting more broadly on her use of routines, Ravi commented, "Thinking routines have enabled me to plan, keeping in mind the 'thinking' I want my students to do, given me structures and encouraged students to adopt these 'moves' in their approach to any form of literary analysis without directions from the teacher. They are moving toward independent thinking as they are now giving the appropriate 'signal' to their 'brain,' instructing it to 'connect' or 'sort' or explore the reason behind their conviction by asking themselves, 'What makes you say that?' "

⚙ CONNECT-EXTEND-CHALLENGE

Consider what you have just read, seen, or heard, then ask yourself:

- How are the ideas and information presented *connected* to what you already knew?
- What new ideas did you get that *extended* or broadened your thinking in new directions?
- What *challenges* or puzzles have come up in your mind from the ideas and information presented?

In puzzling over some of the challenges of teaching and learning, it struck our team that a common place at which learning breaks down, particularly in schools, is when students are given information but are never asked to do anything mentally with it. Listening, in and of itself, doesn't lead to learning. One cannot passively absorb information in a way that will make it useable in the future. And yet, one does learn a lot from reading, watching, and listening. By identifying what separates active listening from passive hearing, a new routine with wide applicability emerged: Connect-Extend-Challenge (CEC). Active processing of new information can be facilitated by connecting the new information to what one already knows, identifying the new ideas that extend our thinking, and looking for how these new ideas challenge us to think in new ways or to question assumptions.

Purpose

Students often receive pieces of information bit by bit in classrooms. This can cause them to view important ideas as isolated from one another. It is helpful to think of the Connect-Extend-Challenge routine as one that helps students fasten ideas together and that raises awareness of puzzles worth further attention. The use of this routine offers a structure and space in which new thinking around a topic, *as inspired by new learning experiences,* can be made visible.

In the routine, students connect new ideas they come across to those they already hold while reflecting upon how their thinking is being extended as a result of what they have just read, seen, or heard. By pressing for both connections and extensions, the teacher sends powerful messages to students that ideas and thoughts are dynamic, ever deepening and growing, and that a big part of learning is attending to the information we take in. Beyond the connections and extensions, this routine also asks students to articulate challenges and puzzles they believe to be particularly important to their efforts to explore an issue or concept. By taking notice of and expressing potentially complex conundrums within a topic, students become more aware of and sensitive to important ideas necessary to develop deep understanding.

Selecting Appropriate Content

This routine is designed to help students become active processors of information. Therefore, it is well positioned after information-rich sessions as a way of synthesizing that information. This might be at the end of a lesson, after a reading, or even after a whole unit of study. Our team frequently uses it as a way of reflecting at the end of a week-long institute. Because of its "linking" quality, a wide variety of content can easily work with this routine. Ask yourself, Are there connections to be made between this content and what the class has previously studied or already knows? Was new information presented that students can identify? Were puzzles and challenges raised from this information?

Steps

1. *Set up.* Before students begin listening to a story, reading a passage, viewing a video, visiting an exhibit, or participating in another information-rich activity, invite them to be mindful of how this new learning experience connects to what they already know. Ask them to think about how it pushes their thinking into new directions and to be aware of new challenges and puzzles that may surface as a result of what they hear, read, watch, or experience.

2. *Connect.* After the activity, have students take note of how what they've just experienced connects with ideas they have already explored or thought about. Ask, "How do the ideas and information you've just heard connect to ideas you already thought about or knew?" It is important to allow students time to write their connections individually before having any group discussion.

3. *Extend.* Now prompt students to identify how their ideas have broadened, deepened, or expanded in some way as a result of the new learning experience. Ask, "How has your thinking been extended in some way, taking it in new or further or deeper directions?" Again, have students individually record their responses.

4. *Challenge.* Finally, ask students to consider ideas that seem significantly challenging in the topic. "What challenges or puzzles have come up in your mind about this topic now that you've been presented with these new ideas and information?" These might be questions or issues that emerge.

5. *Share the thinking.* Once students have a chance to individually respond to the CEC prompts, have them share their thoughts with partners or in small groups. When sharing, it is important that students give their reasons or thoughts behind why they made their selections. A group could have this conversation in three parts so that each part of the routine is given due attention. Also, collecting the connections, extensions, and challenges from small groups to display on chart paper is a good way of making the whole class's new thinking more visible.

Uses and Variations

As part of their social studies curriculum, Jim Linsell's sixth grade students in Traverse City, Michigan, explored cultures of indigenous peoples across various geographic regions. To strengthen their understanding of the cultures they were studying, Jim's students viewed works of art created by members of an indigenous group that depicted the group's culture. Jim used CEC as a front-end organizer for students' looking, asking them to look closely at the art and share how what they were examining *connected* to what they had read previously about this group. He then asked how what they were examining seemed to *extend* their learning of this cultural group beyond what their textbook had offered. Finally, he invited them to voice interesting questions and wonderings the class might puzzle about as they continued in their study. Jim's students made use of their ongoing, documented connections, extensions, and puzzles as they went on to examine how climate and geography influence culture.

During a five-week mathematics unit on area and perimeter, Mark Church had his sixth graders at the International School of Amsterdam record the connections and extensions that surfaced for them following each investigation. Drawing from students' responses, Mark pulled together a dozen commonly expressed connections and extensions as well as a few unique, thought-provoking ideas and posted them investigation-by-investigation on a large classroom bulletin board. In doing so, Mark was building a display of his students' connections and extensions over the course of the entire unit. Mark hoped his students would see and experience the dynamic growth of mathematical ideas over time physically on the display as well as in the classroom discourse. As more connections and extensions were added to the bulletin board, Mark was able to have students look for common themes and important ideas worth remembering when considering area and perimeter relationships. On the DVD, you can watch how Mark's students also used the CEC routine to discuss a video on the archeological find of Lucy as part of their social studies unit on the origins of early man.

Assessment

Try to get a sense of how students are making sense of ongoing, collective ideas that matter to the understanding of a topic through the connections and extensions they share. Are students recognizing particular themes or nuances that tie ideas together, or are they viewing each learning experience as if it were a brand-new event with no interconnectedness to what has come before or what may lead on from here? Are students seeing how ideas and concepts explored in this topic are connected or have relevance to bigger ideas in other subjects or beyond school itself?

It is important to keep open to the connections and extensions students express. By being open, a teacher may see or hear something that might have otherwise remained invisible or overlooked. At the same time, it is likely that some connections or extensions will seem more powerful or deep than others. By making a list of the class's connections and extensions for all to see and share ownership of, a teacher can begin inviting students to consider which connections and extensions seem particularly strong. This kind of documentation, as well as the conversation it creates for a group, serves as a powerful model for what connection making, both to prior knowledge and toward new territory, looks like.

Tips

This routine often takes time to develop in a classroom, as students need to become familiar with the language. In addition, students need models of just what constitutes a meaningful connection, a rich extension, or a worthwhile challenge. In Chapter Seven, you can read more about how Mark Church developed this routine with his students and came to realize its power in directing learning.

Once familiar with the Connect-Extend-Challenge routine, a teacher will have a better sense of how to invite learners to share their responses. Sometimes it may seem appropriate to have students voice their connections and extensions together, with the teacher probing their reasoning. At other times, after individuals and small groups have shared their responses, a teacher may wish to stretch the class by asking them to nominate the top two or three connections and extensions they feel are most significant to the topic they're studying and ask them what makes them say that.

A teacher might also wish to have a class undertake the "Challenge" portion as a next step or follow on to an initial "Connections and Extensions" conversation. These challenges within a topic could even be expressed as a headline, capturing the essence of an important conceptual complexity. (See Headlines routine, p. 111.) It is important for a teacher not to feel obligated to answer or explain away all the challenges brought forth. He or she should use such puzzles as a way of drawing a group further into their sense making of a topic rather than solving all the puzzles for them.

Once this routine becomes familiar and students are comfortable with the language and have seen and heard examples of meaningful connections, extensions, and challenges, then a teacher could ask students to organize notes under the headings "Connections," "Extensions," and "Challenges." However, to do this before students are comfortable with the routine would probably not be effective.

A Picture of Practice

Josh Heisler, a teacher at Vanguard High School in New York City, saw a potentially good fit with thinking routines and his humanities curriculum. "One of the concepts our class explores in my humanities class is race and membership in society. Throughout the course we look closely at America's first forays into imperialism, how Americans have come to view foreigners at different points in history, and the encounters earlier Americans had with non-Americans, for example, in World's Fair exhibits. We even study complex and controversial topics such as the eugenics movement," Josh said. "In my mind, I saw many patterns within these topics—many connections linking these various units with one another. I became interested in creating ways for my students to begin recognizing and making these important connections." Josh set out to use the Connect-Extend-Challenge routine across many contexts and in various ways. As he did so, he followed the evolution of the routine as it played out with his students over time.

One of the first instances of using Connect-Extend-Challenge came when Josh's class was reading *Freedom Road*, a historical fiction work by Howard Fast, set in South Carolina during the period following the end of the American Civil War known as Reconstruction. The protagonist in the story, Gideon, is a former slave who purchases land in pursuit of autonomy and independence. This was perceived to be a radical idea for the times, and the powers that existed within society worked to crush Gideon's dreams. After they had read some of the novel, Josh distributed sheets to his students with "Connect-Extend-Challenge" written at the top and explained that he wanted them to do a little reflecting on the text with these headings in mind. "The kids actually came up with some intricate, interesting connections," said Josh. "It wasn't so much that I, myself, hadn't thought of these very same connections; rather, I didn't expect my students would make such strong connections that so clearly extended their thinking around the challenges that race and class pose in our society." Both surprised and pleased, Josh saw right from the start how CEC could help his students articulate how they were making sense of important ideas.

Some time later, Josh wondered what else he might do to scaffold rich thinking for his students. "I decided to put some sentence starters in with the Connect-Extend-Challenge steps. I wanted to support the connections they were making with evidence and rich thinking language." With this added scaffolding, Josh felt even more students began to make some fairly impressive connections (see Table 5.1).

Though Josh was pleased with his initial uses of Connect-Extend-Challenge, he knew that if he wanted his students to make deeper connections, then he would have to help them articulate just what these deeper connections might look like. Nearly two years after his first use of this thinking routine, Josh invited his students, some of whom had been with him in prior years, to begin looking closely at the connections they were making. "We had made use of this routine often enough over multiple school years that I thought they were ready to evaluate the quality of their thinking within this routine," said Josh. While reading *Tarzan of the Apes* and examining complex ideas related to the concept of Social Darwinism, Josh posted two pieces of chart paper in the front of the classroom: one titled "Examples of an O.K. Connection," and the other titled "Example of a Stronger Connection: One That Has Legs." Josh then invited students to look through their notes and find examples of each type of connection. Once his students had shared examples from their journals and Josh had written them on the paper under the appropriate headings, he asked them to describe the features distinguishing "O.K. Connections" from "Stronger Connections." Josh wanted his students to develop a shared sense of criteria for good connection making. His hope was that by deciding upon and examining these features together, his students would be more likely to develop deep connections in further studies (see Table 5.2).

Table 5.1 A High School Student's Connect-Extend-Challenge Reading Notes

Select at least four lines from the reading that you **connect** to, that **extend** your thinking, or that raise a **challenge or question**	Use one of the following sentence starters: For a **connection**: "This quote reminds me of…" For an **extension** of your thinking: "This quote is adding to my thinking because…" Or, "I used to think…Now I think…" For a **challenge**: "This quote makes me wonder…?"
"And if they declined to work the plantation the house must be vacated."	This reminds me of the Indian Removal Act—the Native Americans were either assimilated or kicked off their land.
"The sight of seeing African Americans with arms was a scary thing for the pro-slave Whites."	This reminds me of the Thomas Jefferson quote about holding a wolf by their ears because pro-slavery Whites fear Blacks coming together for rebellion.
"We have one master now, Jesus Christ, and he'll never come here to collect taxes or drive us off."	This quote reminds me of Nat Turner using his faith in God as the key to freedom.
"The ex-slaves desire for land and the presence of armed African American soldiers were an explosive combination."	This added to my thinking because I used to think that African Americans would be forced to leave the land, but now I realize that they weren't going to allow themselves to be forced off.
"Negroes on the land are armed and have announced their purpose was to allow no white man on it."	This surprises me because Gideon recruits Abner Lait (a White sharecropper) to assist him to buy land.

"In the past I tended to think that my students would take the easy way out and just give me something relatively shallow when I asked them to think deeply about a concept. Then I began thinking that perhaps they just didn't always know how to articulate something with more depth to it," said Josh. "That's why noticing and naming good connection making took on such importance for me together with my students. I wanted them to get much better with their connection making as the school year went on." Over time, Josh has come to appreciate the power of having his students evaluate and take ownership of their own thinking.

Table 5.2 High School Students' Criteria for Good Connection Making

Example of an O.K. Connection	Example of a Strong Connection (One That Has Legs)
Tarzan of the Apes reminds us of George of the Jungle because they both climbed trees. Tarzan reminds me of the "we & they."	Tarzan's learning separates himself from the Apes and the Africans—it is like the "we & they" relationship—this reinforces the idea of "we & they." Tarzan's teaching himself to read reminds me of Frederick Douglass—education equals power—he can outsmart people. Tarzan separates himself from a lot of people—sailors, African tribe. This is like Social Darwinism—the weak and the poor won't survive, but the rich will. Tarzan is an example of survival of the fittest, because Tarzan has noble heredity.
How we would describe the qualities or features of an O.K. Connection . . .	How we would describe the qualities or features of a Strong Connection . . .
Dry, stale, no details, simple, as if there is no explanation, just one statement—these aren't analyzed—these are shortcuts, more general Not much evidence, not many clues about what is going on—simple, cannot do anything with these, cannot push your thinking much further	These have deeper connections, details, ideas from the topic, considers multiple viewpoints—new and intriguing information, sets new ideas come out Makes you notice things, understand the situation better, and provokes new ideas, you can take an idea that will lead to another, draws attention and helps expand your ideas, these provoke the imagination

◎ THE 4C'S

After reading a text:

- *Connections:* What *connections* do you draw between the text and your own life or your other learning?
- *Challenge:* What ideas, positions, or assumptions do you want to *challenge* or argue with in the text?
- *Concepts:* What key *concepts* or ideas do you think are important and worth holding on to from the text?
- *Changes:* What *changes* in attitudes, thinking, or action are suggested by the text, either for you or others?

Nonfiction texts of varying sorts are used in all subject areas and across all age ranges. It can easily be taken for granted that these texts simply provide a source of content information. Although certainly nonfiction can be a very rich source of information, these texts can also provide a means to elicit vibrant discussions and further develop deep thinking. The 4C's routine provides a set of questions that encourage learners to grapple with the information provided in the text in a purposeful and structured way.

Purpose

This routine provides learners with a structure for a text-based discussion built around making connections, asking questions, identifying key ideas, and considering application. It encourages the reading and revisiting of texts in a focused, purposeful way that enables readers to delve beneath the surface and go beyond first impressions. Although originally designed for use with nonfiction texts, it can be applied to fiction as well with only minor changes.

Each step asks for different thinking moves that correspond to the kinds of active, thoughtful reading teachers want all readers to do. Although presented here in an order, and this order may be kept to facilitate discussion, each of these thinking moves is actually nonlinear in the practice of reading for comprehension. Asking the learner to make *connections* between the text and their own experiences personalizes the content while broadening it, as each new connection adds dimension to the text. Identifying *challenges* invites critical thinking and conveys to readers that one should raise questions of truth and veracity as one reads nonfiction texts. Recognizing key *concepts* requires learners to compare and prioritize ideas to uncover themes and messages. The idea of identifying possible *changes* to one's behavior or approach asks learners to think beyond information to consider its import and how it might be used. This calls for both analytical thinking and synthesis.

Selecting Appropriate Content

The 4C's routine works most effectively when utilized with texts that incorporate complex ideas and concepts that can be considered from more than one perspective and are "meaty" enough to encourage grappling with ideas and promote discussion and debate. Texts can come from a wide variety of sources and can include excerpts from opinion papers, newspaper articles, scientific reports, scholarly articles, personal essays, and so on. It is possible some textbooks may be appropriate; however, often textbooks try to not put forth any position or opinion overtly while spelling out key concepts in bold print. This tends to makes them less interesting sources for discussion. Although texts provide a vehicle for review, the routine can also be used with video or after listening to a provocative presentation such as a TED talk (www.ted.com).

Fiction can be a source of material as well if chosen with the steps in mind. Some simple modification on the wording would generally be appropriate. For instance, under "Challenges," you might ask students to focus on character actions with which they disagree. "Concepts" can be related to themes. "Changes" can focus on how the characters themselves changed and evolved over the course of the story and what caused those changes. However, with some stories it may be appropriate to ask, "How does the story *change* your thinking about things? What do you take away as a lesson or key learning?"

Steps

1. *Set up.* Invite learners to read the selected text either before the session if it is a lengthy text, or provide adequate reading time at the commencement of the session. After the routine has been learned, it is often useful for learners to know that the 4C's will be the framework for discussing the text. List the 4C's in a place clearly visible to all learners as a framework for the discussion.

2. *Make connections.* After reading the text, invite learners to find passages from the text that they can identify with, either from something that has happened to them or is somehow connected to other learning experiences. Begin group discussions by asking learners to read the passage from the text to which they are connecting. Ask them to explain the connection.

3. *Raise challenges.* Ask learners to find ideas or positions in the text that, as they read them, raised a red flag for one reason or another. These might be things that they did not agree with and want to challenge or simply feel they need more information before they can make a decision. With fiction, these might focus on a character's actions. Begin discussion by having students read from the text and then explain what questions came into their minds as they read those ideas.

4. *Note concepts.* Encourage readers to briefly review the text and note the key concepts, themes, or ideas. These are those elements that they might share with someone who hasn't read the text in discussing its main points and key ideas. These will not be text-based ideas as the previous moves have been; however, it is still appropriate to follow up student comments with, "What makes you say that?" to elicit the foundation for their ideas.

5. *Identify changes.* Ask learners to reflect on the overall text and think about its implications. If we take the text seriously, what does it suggest or encourage as actions or positions? Identify any changes of thinking or behavior that may have occurred for individuals as a result of the reading. For fiction, focus on the changes that occurred for the characters and the impetus for those changes. These ideas will not be specifically text based, but students should be asked to give reasons and justification for their responses.

6. *Share the thinking.* In the previous steps, learners have been sharing their thinking at each stage of the process. An alternative to this structure would be to provide time for the identification of all the 4C's at the outset and then commence discussion, working through each of the C's in turn. In either case, take a moment at the end of the discussion to debrief the conversation: How did the structure help learners to develop a deeper understanding of the text? Was it difficult to find material for any of the 4C's? Were there things that came up in the discussion that surprised them?

Uses and Variations

When Bialik College grade 1 teacher Roz Marks tried this routine for the first time, she asked a group of five students to read a fiction book during a guided reading session and then gave them a piece of paper divided into four equal sections. She explained the routine to them, clarifying and simplifying the vocabulary of the routine when appropriate. She asked the students to draw the connection they made, what they didn't agree with in the story, what was most important to them in the story, and whether they had learned something new or important from the story.

On another occasion, Roz used the 4C's routine informally for the group's discussion of the story "Feraj and the Lute" from the Junior Great Books program. Roz paraphrased the questions from the 4C's: "What connections do you make to the story from things that you know from your own life? Is there anything in the story that you want to challenge or don't agree with? What ideas do you think are the most important in the story and what makes you say that? Do you think after listening to this story that your thinking or ideas about things have changed?" As the group worked through each of the questions, Roz recorded students' responses on chart paper.

In the monthly professional meetings of the Ithaka Project, Julie Landvogt used the 4C's routine as a regular protocol for the discussion of professional readings. Before each meeting, attendees all knew the articles would be discussed in this way and prepared accordingly. Because the meetings had a tight time schedule, a rotating facilitator kept the discussion moving through each of the C's during the 40-minute session while a documenter recorded and later posted the group's conversation on a wiki. (You can read more about this group's use of the routine in Chapter Seven.)

Assessment

The choices learners make for their connections, challenges, concepts, and changes give insights into both their understanding of the text and their ability to see the themes within it in a wider context. Are their connections related only to personal experiences, or are students also connecting to the other learning they are doing in your class? Are they going beyond the obvious? What sort of questions are they posing when challenging ideas or concepts? Are they able to display a healthy skepticism, recognizing bias and overgeneralization in a text? Are they identifying universal themes or big ideas? Can they differentiate key concepts from those less important? As you ask students to explain the changes they are thinking about and the reasons behind them, look for the reasons they have for proposing those changes.

Tips

Although the routine has four steps and their ordering tends to be the most effective in terms of sequencing discussion, in the act of reading or even reflecting upon a text the steps are likely to be very nonlinear. The first time through the routine, you might want to work sequentially through the order as described above. However, once the routine is learned, students may be more comfortable taking notes or organizing for the discussion in a less sequential manner. The routine can be introduced before the text and learners can respond to it as they progress through the text, or alternatively, the questions can be posed at the conclusion of the reading. As students become familiar with the routine and its expectations, it can act as a protocol to structure student-directed discussions of the text.

The 4C's routine allows for a rich and fairly complete discussion of a text. Nonetheless, each step can be used as a stand-alone discussion. For example, at the end of a reading, you may ask, "In this reading, did you make any connections with anything we have done earlier this year? What changes are we noticing in these characters?" And so on.

This routine can be useful in training students in the process of a text-based discussion, which may or may not be something that they are used to doing. In a text-based discussion, explicit reference to the text is used as the starting point for discussion. This keeps a discussion centered and on track rather than veering down other paths. However, the teacher or facilitator will need to be vigilant in pushing learners to provide the textual reference. To set this up, provide time for learners to identify the places in the text they want to reference before discussion begins. In the discussion, ask speakers to first give the page and paragraph number in the text so that others can follow along as they read the passage.

A Picture of Practice

The grade 5 students in Saroj Singh's class at Bialik College were reading the novel *Holes* by Louis Sachar, a book that deals with many issues that Saroj considered important for her fifth grade students to think about. With this goal in mind, Saroj began to plan how she would introduce and proceed with the book study. She thought that incorporating the 4C's routine could lead to deeper understanding and extend her students' thinking. "I felt the plot of the story was rich enough for me to try my hand at a routine that I had never done before, and when I read the 4C's, even while reading it, I was mentally thinking where and at what juncture I could use this routine," Saroj stated.

This routine provided Saroj with a structure and a set of questions that she felt would be useful for debriefing the deeper meaning of the book once the class had finished reading. However, since it was a rather long text for fifth graders, she thought it would be better to introduce the routine before reading the book as a way of getting students to attend to issues beyond the plot.

Saroj discussed the 4C's of the routine, explaining that these were thinking moves that readers naturally engaged in as they read. She modeled her own reading of the morning newspaper and thought aloud for students so they could see how she was making connections, challenging ideas, identifying key concepts, and thinking about implications and challenges. She told students she wanted them to think of the 4C's while they were reading and to write their thoughts in the margins of their books as they progressed through the story.

Saroj noticed that the discussions following each chapter were becoming much more thoughtful. Students were finding similar situations in the wider world and making connections with issues such as apartheid, prejudices, racism, and more. The content of the discussions deepened and became more insightful as they drew closer to the end of the novel. Without Saroj's prompting, the children would begin the class keen to discuss a particular "C" that they thought fit closely with the text. She was heartened to see the students, who often were very reticent or would answer in only short utterances, join in the conversations and clearly state their stances or thinking.

On the day the class had finished reading the story, Saroj placed four large sheets of paper on the classroom walls. Each paper had one of the 4C words in large print at the top of the page. Saroj reminded her students of the thinking and documentation they had been doing throughout their reading and directed their attention to the four large sheets posted on the four walls of the classroom. "Now I want you to think about the book as a whole and what really stands out for you. What do you think the key concepts are? What connections are you making? What actions and events did you want to challenge? What changes have you noticed in the characters attitudes and behaviors?" Saroj then gave students sticky notes to record their thoughts about each question and place on the appropriate sheet (see Table 5.3 for a collection of students' responses).

Once students had finished posting their ideas for each of the 4C's, the class discussed each poster in turn. They carefully looked at each of the papers, discussing the ideas posted there, looking for commonalities in the responses, and identifying the big ideas that were arising. What was interesting to Saroj was the impact using the routine had on her personally. "My thinking was extended also," reflected Saroj. "As an adult with more life experiences, I may look at a character or situations differently to my students, but hearing their responses definitely gave me food for thought and challenged and broadened my thinking too."

Table 5.3 Fifth Grade Students' 4C's for the Book, *Holes*

Connections	Challenges
• I get blamed at home for things I do not do and I usually don't get to explain my side of the story. Like Stanley I am always in the wrong place at the wrong time! • I'm reading a book called *Reaching the Summit*. It is the story about Sir Edmund Hillary. It's about people surviving with very little resources while climbing Mt. Everest. Stanley and Zero too had to survive on just onions when they were up in the mountain. • It says in the book, "It felt good to blame someone." I too sometimes like blaming my brother for things that I do. • Text to Text—*Cherub* and *Holes*. In *Holes*, whenever they talked about the past incidents, the book had a different font. It was the same in *Cherub* too. • Mr. Pendanski said that Zero had nothing in his head. I too have been called "Stupid."	• Why did Stanley think he would be going to a fun camp when he was in trouble? • Everyone thought Zero was "Nothing," but he never got to show anyone who he really was except Stanley. • How did the people at Camp Green Lake assume that hard labor would build one's character? • Why was the reference made to "It's not a girl scouts camp" innumerable times? – Girls are not inferior!!!!!

Concepts	Changes
• Never give up trying! Try, try, try again, you'll succeed. • When you live your whole life in a hole, the only way you can go is up. • Friendship • Perseverance • Belief in oneself • Leadership • Determination • Give a friend a helping hand. • Bravery • What goes around, comes around. • Never judge a book by its cover.	• The story clearly states the prejudice people had back then (even now, maybe less) regarding colored people. • Kate used to be a wonderful woman, till Sam's death changed her completely. Certain incidents can change the way you think forever. • I thought that Stanley's father was silly to be doing stuff with sneakers but at the completion of the book I thought of him in a different way. • After Stanley caught the shoes "falling" from the sky, everything changed for him. He got arrested, taken to Camp Green Lake and had a tough time. Even then he thinks of what happened as "Lucky"!!! • Halfway through the book I realized that Zero was not a white person.

⚙ THE MICRO LAB PROTOCOL

Reflect individually on the issue or topic being examined, then working in triads:

- *Share:* The first person in the group shares for a set time (usually 1–2 minutes). The other members listen attentively without comment or interruption.
- *Pause* for 20–30 seconds of silence to take in what was said.
- *Repeat* for persons two and three, pausing for a moment of silence after each round.
- *Discuss* as a group (5–10 minutes), referencing the comments that have been made and making connections between the responses of the group.

The Micro Lab Protocol was originally developed by Julian Weissglass for the National Coalition for Equality in Education as a structure for discussion. What is presented here includes adaptations made by Tina Blythe. The Micro Lab is a simple structure for ensuring that all voices are heard and ideas attended to before the topic of focus is discussed. Though the Micro Lab isn't a thinking routine per se, that is, it doesn't prompt specific thinking moves, teachers have found it to be a valuable tool for making students' thinking visible and a useful structure for directing group conversation. Consequently, the Micro Lab has become a routine in many classrooms and staff rooms dedicated to creating cultures of thinking.

Purpose

Teachers often ask groups to discuss ideas in classrooms with more and less success. Often groups get sidetracked and/or a single person dominates while others sit back. The Micro Lab is designed to ensure equal participation and make sure everyone contributes. The rounds of sharing are timed by the teacher or facilitator. This keeps all groups on track and focused. The moments of silence provide time to think about what the last speaker said and a chance for the entire group to "recenter" itself. Groups of three provide for optimal interaction without asking people to be silent for long periods.

Once all ideas have been shared, an open discussion of the small groups occurs. Discussants now can make connections between ideas, ask clarifying questions, highlight themes, and further explore the topic. Teachers have found that regular use of this protocol helps students to be better listeners and to learn how to build on and connect to others' ideas. Some students learn how to present their ideas and talk from their own perspectives with greater confidence rather than relying on others.

Selecting Appropriate Content

As with any discussion, content matters. Meaningful discussions emerge from meaningful content. The possibility of differing perspectives also adds to the richness of discussion. The Micro Lab can be used to discuss and explore perspectives on current events and political issues, to reflect and share what one has learned thus far, to explore and process plans one has made, to discuss possible problem-solving strategies, and more. Other uses include reflecting on oneself as a learner: How are you becoming more accomplished as a reader or writer? Where do you want to see yourself improve? Whatever the case, if the discussion is to be more than sharing, you need to think how the discussion is likely to benefit the learning of the members of the group.

An important component of discussion preparation is reflecting beforehand. In some respects this preparation can be thought of as the content, as it is what students "bring to the table." If the members of the group don't bring something to the table, the banquet of discussion will be lacking. In helping students to bring something to the table, the Micro Lab can be combined with another thinking routine to structure students' reflection. For instance, after a field trip a teacher might have individual students reflect in writing using Connect-Extend-Challenge or the I Used to Think..., Now I Think... routine.

Steps

1. *Set up.* Inform learners of both what you want them to discuss and what you are hoping they get out of these discussions. Decide how long you will give learners to reflect (usually done in writing). Depending on the amount of material you are asking learners to synthesize, usually 5–10 minutes is sufficient. Explain the protocol, its purpose, guidelines, and how much time will be given for each round of sharing and silence. Form groups of three and have groups number off so that they will know who goes in which order. Inform the groups that you will act as timekeeper.

2. *Share.* Announce that Number 1s begin sharing for the assigned time (state a definite time between 1 and 2 minutes). No one speaks except the speaker. Other group members listen attentively and may take notes if they feel it will be useful. Call time by ringing a chime or bell if possible. Call for the groups to be silent.

3. *Call for silence.* Allow 20–30 seconds of silence for everyone to take in what was heard. Some people are uncomfortable with silence, but with time they come to appreciate its calming and centering effect. At the beginning, you may encourage people to just mentally review what they heard.

4. *Do rounds 2 and 3.* Repeat steps 2 and 3 above until each member of the group has shared his or her thinking. Note: If the speaker finishes before time is called, the group spends the rest of the time reflecting in silence.

5. *Commence discussion.* Announce that groups can now have an open discussion for the predetermined time (usually between 5–10 minutes). Encourage groups to begin by making connections between what others have said or asking questions of clarification. Call time by ringing the bell or chime.

6. *Share the thinking.* As a whole group, ask students to reflect on the protocol itself and how they felt it facilitated their thinking about the issue or topic.

Uses and Variations

One might not think a discussion protocol would find much play in a mathematics class, but Manuela Barden at Mentone Grammar and Linda Shardlow at Methodists Ladies College, both in the greater Melbourne area, have found multiple uses for it in their middle and high school classes respectively. Manuela found that the Micro Lab helped students to be more independent. After giving her seventh graders an investigative geometry task, she gave students 5 minutes to think about the task, review their texts, and write down any questions or issues that came up for them. Students then completed a Micro Lab with 1-minute rounds, 20 seconds of silence, and 5 minutes of discussion as a way of clarifying the task. Manuela found that her students accomplished the task with much less direction and more confidence than in previous years.

In Linda Shardlow's grade 12 class, she used the Micro Lab to structure more collective problem solving and better talk about mathematics. Having done the protocol once, when all students worked on the same problem, Linda thought the Micro Lab would be better if students were bringing different but related thinking to the table. Working in groups of three, each group was given a set of problems related to the topic of functions. Decisions were made about who would do which, and students worked for 10 minutes before entering the Micro Lab rounds. In the rounds, students explained what they did, why they did it, and where they got stuck or were confused. Silence was used for note taking. Linda found that the discussions that followed were rich and that students showed good insights into one another's problems and were making connections between them. Afterward, a senior girl commented, "I really had to think about what we were doing instead of just copying stuff down and, even though I didn't think I would have the confidence to explain to others how I did things, I did though. So, it made me feel really good about myself."

As instructional coaches and developers, we often use the Micro Lab to facilitate group reflection on the learning. One prompt we frequently use is, "How is your classroom changing as a result of your work with these ideas?" The prompt helps focus learners on the effect our professional development actions are having, and the discussions lead to lots of sharing, questioning, and clarification that helps to move us forward.

Assessment

The Micro Lab, existing as it does in a moment of time, presents both opportunities for and challenges of assessment. On the one hand, the individual sharing and subsequent conversations make thinking visible; on the other hand, it is only possible to hear snippets of these, especially when one is facilitating the rounds. Consequently, it may be useful to determine what you anticipate to be the outcome of the conversation, such as a plan, an increased level of understanding of the topic, a distillation of important ideas, or something else, and ask students to document this at the conclusion, much the way Alan Bliss did with his students in the Picture of Practice described following.

However, do try and listen in on groups as much as possible. You may want to target just one group to stand beside and listen to. This can give you a sense of the developing conversation and where and how ideas are being built. Are students able to make connections to what others have said? Do they ask probing questions of clarification where needed? Are students able to build on one another's ideas to deepen their own understanding? Can they spot ideas both different to and similar to their own?

Tips

Although the Micro Lab can be used by simply posing a question and giving students a bit of think time before talking, giving students adequate time to write and think before starting often ensures better contributions. This also creates a record that you can go back to later if you want to see what individuals were thinking. When learning the protocol, start with shorter times for talk, silence, and discussion, lengthening these as students become more practiced. Be consistent and deliberate in enforcing the rules of no interruptions and a brief period of silence. If these norms are broken, then the focus on listening and building on others' ideas will be lost as well. Finally, don't be afraid of the silence. As teachers we are so used to filling up all the airtime that we seldom have silence in our classrooms. Tell students the purpose of the silence is to take in what was just said and to recenter, getting ready to hear the next speaker with a pair of fresh ears, not merely to be quiet. Be sure to debrief with your students how the silent periods worked for them.

A Picture of Practice

At Melbourne Grammar School, Alan Bliss and his colleagues begin the school year teaching an interdisciplinary unit involving history, science, and geography to their eighth graders. The nine-week unit explores the idea of Atlantis. Specifically, asking the question, "Can the island of Santorini be Atlantis?" Alan explains the unit's organization. "We have a common, nondisciplinary specific introduction to the unit and then each of the three disciplines explores a different element of the puzzle. At the completion of the unit, students are asked to combine their learning across all three subjects to respond to the key question."

Although the unit has always been successful and engaging for students at the all-boys school, Alan noted that "over the last few years, we have noticed that one of the key issues arising for students is how the subjects link together." In addition, the teachers struggled with an issue common to all long-term, project-oriented work: "How can we most effectively enable a scenario where students' developing understanding can be made visible and thereby assessed?"

After Alan had worked with the Micro Lab as a learner himself in a professional development setting, he commented, "The Micro Lab protocol seems to be an ideal structure for enabling the boys to articulate their current understanding and so provide an opportunity for them to check on that understanding and misunderstandings. It also seemed a sound structure to enable students to share their thinking with their peers and to build their understanding and knowledge using each other as a resource, effectively increasing student talk in the learning process."

Using the Micro Lab also fit into a larger goal of Alan's to develop his middle school's facility at independent discussion. In an article entitled, "Enabling More Effective Discussion in the Classroom" (Bliss, 2010, p. 1), Allen wrote, "Over the last five years, I've begun to see more clearly that discussion in class can be a critical step for students in both developing and checking their understanding; and for me, as teacher, in checking on student understanding and misunderstanding."

Because he was interested in developing new thinking and gaining fresh perspectives, Alan decided to try the Micro Lab by combining two different classes. This would allow him to form groups of four students, two students from each class. However, this also meant the classes would need to meet in the library study area to facilitate the large group of sixty students. Alan began by giving his students 5 minutes to write individually about the question, "Can Santorini be Atlantis?" Each group member then presented his or her ideas and reasoning for 1 minute, followed by 20 seconds of silence. Once everyone had shared, there was a 5-minute period of discussion. Alan followed up the discussion period with another 5-minute period of reflective writing on the key question.

Because the group was so large and he was teaching the routine for the first time, Alan wasn't able to move around and listen to all the conversations as effectively as he would have liked. To gain a better sense of what students had taken from the conversations, he had students post their thoughts on the class wiki (see Table 5.4 for a short excerpt from this online conversation). In reading through these, Alan noted, "The wiki entries revealed that some students had developed appropriate disciplinary thinking in the three subjects that they were able to apply to their thinking about the topic. What was surprising was that some students were able to indicate that their thinking had been deepened through the sharing that took place within the protocol."

As a first round, Alan liked the way the protocol increased the level of participation among students. As a result, he continued to repeat this structure every two weeks of the unit, gradually increasing the time for writing and talk in the protocol as students were asked to integrate more and more ideas from their disciplinary studies.

In reflecting on the overall process, Alan remarked, "I have been pleased generally with the manner in which the protocol plays out in the classroom. Students have generally been cooperative, although the notion of students sticking to the *noninterruption* element of the individual talking section has proven a challenge. My anecdotal listening to the occasional discussion at the last stage of the protocol has indicated that it may be necessary to introduce some more structure to that aspect; to suggest some things which might be worth discussing as a natural outcome of the individual presentations, or to be a little more insistent on focusing on issues which arise or clarification questions."

The Micro Lab is just one of the routines Alan uses regularly in his classroom. "Using routines over the last few years seems to have led to student acceptance that on occasion they will be asked to think, consider, reason rather than be told. I would like to think also that they see the routines as a method of focusing thinking, even if they are not always able to articulate it. So, when a student says, "Are we using Micro Lab?" it might indicate that he recognizes that the process is of critical importance leading to understanding."

Table 5.4   Grade 8 Students' Wiki Conversation on Atlantis

__Carter__ said (at 11:28 am on May 19):   seriously Santorini CAN be Atlantis but that doesn't mean it is Atlantis.

__Eric__ said (at 11:30 am on May 19):   Yes, I think Santerini could be Atlantis becuase of many things

- Geographical Reference near Libya, Egypt
- There were a lot of other things on the list like Hot and Cold Water, Bulls, Sheltered from The North.
- And a very important one the circular shape of the island
- Volcanos Tsunamis and Earthquacks all happened

Thats why Santerini could be Atlantis

__Malcom__ said (at 11:31 am on May 19):   Can Santorini be Atlantis? Yes
Proof:

1) It is in a correct position in relation to possilbe pillars of Hercules location
2) Has a volacno in the middle that erupted at around the supposed time of Atlantis and so would support the theory that Atlantis was destroyed in an eruption. A volcano could also help support the theory that Atlantis had hot water plumbing: the water would be heated in natural springs then pumped down to where it was needed
3) It is in a correct location in relation to egypt and Lybia which was where the story came from and where elaphants that were mentioned in plato's dialogue could have originate
4) Is close to Athens supporting the fact that the Antheans could have possilby gone to war with the Atlanteans
5) The island is circular, slopes up to a peak and has a base rock that erodes quckly suggesting that the island was once much larger
6) Because of the volcano the soil would be very nutrutious allowing for food to be plentiful and for the civilisation to flourish
7) The dialogue mentions an impassable layer of mud: this could be the volcanic resedue after the volcano

__Chris__ said (at 11:31 am on May 19):   I don't think that Santorini can be Atlantis because the only thing that they have in common is being cicular. But think about it—if you only saw the top of Crete from a boat, it would look circular, wouldn't it?

Dr. __Alan Bliss__ said (at 2:43 pm on May 19):   I am impressed with Eric's and Malcom's considered responses, mostly because they have supported what they say with evidence. Doesn't mean that they are correct but their method of responding is logical.

__Deshi__ said (at 2:06 pm on May 24):   Eric, i think your right about Santorini fitting into Libya and Asia. But consider this option, how about if Libya and Asia were the size of Santorini. I know there not now, except maybe when Plato lived Libya and Asia could have been a lot smaller making them around the same size as Atlantis.

Note: Punctuation and spelling are reproduced as in the original.

Having students reflect at the end of a unit is a common occurrence in classrooms. However, much of the reflection students offer tends to focus on the activities they did and how they would rate their performance on those tasks. While asking students what they are proud of and what they would like to do better next time can be an interesting conversation, we wanted to create a reflective routine that would focus students' attention more on the thinking that class activities caused them to do rather than reporting on the activities themselves. We also wanted to focus attention on how the development of understanding is not just an accumulation of new information but often results in changes in thinking. This led us to create I Used to Think..., Now I Think...

Purpose

This routine helps students reflect on their thinking about a topic or issue and explore how and why that thinking has changed. It can be useful in consolidating new learning as students identify their new understandings, opinions, and beliefs. By examining and explaining how and why their thinking has changed, students develop their reasoning abilities and recognize cause-and-effect relationships. This routine also develops students' metacognitive skills, the ability to identify and talk about one's thinking itself.

Selecting Appropriate Content

This routine is applicable across a wide variety of subject areas whenever students' initial thoughts, opinions, or beliefs are likely to have changed as a result of instruction or experience. After reading new information, watching a film, listening to a speaker, experiencing something new, having a class discussion, or completing a unit of study are all potentially powerful times a teacher might make use of this routine. Greater depth and insights are likely when the object of reflection is conceptual or process oriented rather than merely an accumulation of new facts. Ask yourself, Have students had a chance to confront their misconceptions or to shift their thinking in fundamental ways based on the experiences they have had?

Steps

1. *Set up.* Explain to students that the purpose of this routine is to help them reflect on their thinking about the topic and to identify how their ideas have developed over time. It may be useful for students to have their journals on hand, class documentation available, and/or access to their learning portfolios where collections of their recent work reside.

2. *Encourage individual reflection.* Say to the students, "When we began this study, you all had some initial ideas about it and what it was all about. Take a minute to think back to when we started and remember what kind of ideas you once held. Write what it is that you used to think about our topic, starting off with the words, 'I used to think...'" Once students have had a chance to write their responses, say, "Now, I want you to think about how your ideas about our topic have changed as a result of what we've been studying, doing, and discussing in class. Write a few lines to capture where you are now in your thinking, starting with the phrase, 'Now, I think...'"

3. *Share the thinking.* Have students share and explain their shifts in thinking. Initially it may be worthwhile to do this as a whole group so that you can probe students' thinking and push them to explain. This also provides a model for students who are having difficulty. Once students become accustomed to explaining their thinking, you could have them share in small groups or pairs before soliciting a whole-group response.

Uses and Variations

After June Kamenetsky's first grade students at Bialik College completed their unit on communication, she brought the class together in a group and asked them to remember back when they first started exploring communication and to tell her what they used to think it was. June recorded students' responses on the whiteboard for all to see: *I used to think communication was a kind of message and sign language; another word for speaking; was talking on the phone and showing pictures; a long word; was being good and helpful.* June then asked them to tell her how their thinking had changed. Their responses to this prompt included: *Now I think communication means that when you don't know where to go, signs can communicate it to us; you can make a look on your face to show what you want; when somebody who cannot talk uses a computer, other people can read it; fossils and drawings communicate to people, too.*

The humanities teachers at Vanguard High School in New York City used the I Used to Think..., Now I Think... routine to help prepare their seniors for their exit exhibitions. Specifically, students were asked to explain how their thinking grew, shifted, and changed over time when considering the course throughlines: "What is democracy and why does it matter? What does it mean to be free, really?" Once students completed their reflections, the teachers asked them to put together a portfolio of artifacts from the most significant class activities they had experienced during the year that moved their thinking from what it was to where it is now regarding the concepts of democracy and freedom. By having students organize their portfolios around their thinking rather than around favorite projects or assignments with good grades, teachers thought the collection of artifacts represented the most momentous learning students experienced throughout their humanities course.

Assessment

This routine is fairly open-ended, so teachers must be flexible as to what information can be gleaned from their students' reflections. It is useful to note exactly what students recognize as having shifted in their minds about a topic from what they had initially conceived. This may unveil misconceptions about which the teacher was not previously aware. The responses are likely to be unique for each student. Nonetheless, looking for patterns of responses can be one way a teacher identifies key areas of the class's learning. Do students make mention of particular concepts that have changed for them, or do they reflect upon a new set of skills they've acquired? Do students mention shifts in their thinking about key ideas the teacher might expect them to have reconsidered, or do they mention other kinds of ideas that strike them as significant in ways unexpected to the teacher? Grouping students' reflections by possible themes might help a teacher get a sense of the story of learning that has taken place for students within the studied topic.

Tips

It is important that this routine carries with it the message that a teacher is genuinely curious about how his or her students' thinking has grown, deepened, shifted, or changed as a result of classroom endeavors. Sometimes there is a tendency for students to think this routine is about saying what they had "wrong" before and what they have "right" now. When students feel they need to be teacher-pleasing in their responses rather than introspective, genuine reflection on their thinking is compromised. The open-endedness of this routine can cause uneasiness for teachers looking for a specific response from students. By keeping open to whatever students reflect upon, teachers often get new ideas as to where to take their instruction next, even when student responses are not exactly what the teacher had initially imagined.

It sometimes strikes people as a good idea to do the I Used to Think... portion at the beginning of a unit, before instruction begins. However, one cannot possibly identify misconceptions and ingrained assumptions until they have been confronted. Consequently, this type of reflection can only effectively happen after new learning has occurred. With time, this routine develops students' disposition to be aware of their own thinking by keeping a clear emphasis on the cause-and-effect relationships of what students do and how their thinking changes. As a result it is not uncommon for students to suddenly become aware of new insights as they happen and to express these aloud as "I used to think..., but now I think..."

A Picture of Practice

The year before Erica Doyle began using thinking routines in her ninth grade Reading-Writing Workshop at Vanguard High School in New York City, she remembers a tense conference with a student about a memoir the student had just written. "I asked her about some of the details she'd written about. Whether she remembered what something looked like and what other details she might add to make her piece better," said Erica. The student seemed frustrated by Erica's questioning and finally said, "Why don't you just tell me what to write?" Erica was taken aback by this reaction. The student continued, "Well, there's obviously something you want me to write, so just tell me what to write!" Erica realized in that moment that her student had come to learn that school wasn't a place where her thinking mattered very much. School was a place that she came to repeat back the adult's thinking. "I never thought about this before. This young lady was the first person that was bold enough to call me on this game," remembers Erica. "It was then I became really curious as to how I could create a classroom culture where my students' thinking mattered. I started asking myself how I could make sure that our Reading-Writing Workshop was about our thinking, where all of our ideas could be validated and valued, not just mine."

Erica knows that many students come into her workshop not considering themselves good readers or writers. "It is as if they hold a fixed viewpoint that only some people have the ability to read and write well and most others don't, so I've wondered how I could help change that mindset. I've wondered how I could challenge their thinking about what it means to be a good reader and writer. Figuring out a way to help them become aware of their own growth seems key," believes Erica. "When I first encountered thinking routines, the I Used to Think . . . , Now I Think . . . routine seemed perfect to help students pay close attention to how their minds can grow over time throughout the school year."

Trying to keep the routine as open as possible, Erica started by asking her students to write for her what they used to think and what they're thinking now about their reading and writing at the end of the class period. "I soon realized the responses my students had written were a lot broader than just telling me what was happening with their reading and writing in my class," remembers Erica. The first time she used the routine, students said things like *I used to think I wouldn't like this book because I don't like this genre, but now I think I do like it*, or *I used to think I'd never do good in school because I didn't really do good in elementary and middle school, but now I think I will graduate*. These reflections weren't exactly what Erica was aiming for, but she quickly recognized that her students were genuinely telling her what was going on inside their minds. "At first I thought they didn't quite get the routine, then I realized that actually this was pretty amazing information about how my students were seeing themselves as learners. This was their thinking 'in the wild,' and that was a great place for me to start challenging their mindsets about what it means to be a capable learner," Erica said.

Rather than discarding the I Used to Think . . . , Now I Think . . . routine, Erica decided to use it even more. "I wanted to make this a regular part of how we make our thinking visible in this workshop," said Erica. "So I persisted in using this routine daily at the conclusion of each class session. Getting my students to open up about how they saw themselves socially, emotionally, and as learners helped create the kind of safe culture I wished for them to experience."

Eventually, Erica began to target her students' thinking a bit more toward what they were reading. "I said to them, 'Okay, as you do your I Used to Think . . . today, I want you to consider how your thinking has changed since we started reading Suzanne Collins's *The Hunger Games*. What have you been thinking about a particular character, or the plot, or the setting? Maybe there was a prediction you had that didn't come true? I want you to write to me with that kind of focus in mind today.' " Having familiarity with the routine and being gently prompted by Erica to focus their attention on the text, students wrote reflections such as:

- I used to think Katniss was a coward because she wouldn't speak up at the beginning of the games, but now I think she's not a coward because she shot an arrow at the judges.
- I used to think that Kat was going to let Prim fight because her personality wasn't big hearted, but now I know that she's thoughtful because she sacrificed herself.
- I used to think about coliseums as great heroic things because of "Gladiator," but now I think it's horrible because it's the same principles as the "Hunger Games."

Students who had previously told Erica that they were *not* readers and were *not* writers were beginning to share thoughtful insights with Erica and with others in the class the same way readers and writers would do. Erica was extremely pleased.

Along with helping students feel safe enough to make their thinking visible, Erica knew she had to communicate the value of her students' thinking. "I decided I needed to intentionally make use of their thinking in these 'I used to think . . . , now I think . . .' reflections," said Erica. "So I found myself starting class the following day saying, 'I noticed that a lot of people mentioned things about the main character, Katniss Everdeen, yesterday in your reflections, so why don't we talk about her a little more today?' or 'I noticed so many of you said things about characterization in your reflections, but I'm wondering what people have noticed about symbols and symbolization. What kinds of things are you picking up on there? What is shifting in your thinking?' " Erica did not want her students to feel their "I used to think . . . , but now I think . . ." reflections were just sitting on her desk never to be visited again; rather, she wanted to convey value for students' thinking by using it to guide where they would go next in their learning.

Erica believes that drawing her students' attention to how their thinking develops over time has had great impact on them on many levels. Over the course of a school year, Erica collects her students' reflections on their personal development as readers and writers and tries to sort them into categories so that she can learn from possible patterns that emerge (see Table 5.5). This provides her with valuable insight into the impact her class is having on students' development as independent, engaged learners.

Table 5.5   Erica Doyle's Categorization of Students' Reflections on Their Growth as Readers, Writers, and Learners

Self-Monitoring

I used to think I was able to multitask by talking and doing work but now I think I need to sit with people I don't like because I talk too much. (Andrea, 4/26/10)

I used to think that I couldn't do this because I was confused but now I think that I can do it. (Jose, 5/2010)

Emotional

I used to think I was a non-stressed person but now I think I'm not because so many things are on my mind as in: family, life, crushes, school. A lot of things are stressful because it requires a lot of time. I know this because something's always on my mind. (Nicholas, 10/26/09)

I used to think that I had a messed up personality because people say I'm bad and say pretty horrible things but now I think I'm all right because Catnip [main character's nickname from Hunger Games book we read together] is practical and that's me. (Aravis, 3/9/10)

Social

I used to think I would never get a long with nobody [sic] in this school because I barely got along with anybody in junior high school. But now I think I get along with a lot of people in high school because I have a lot of friends. (Dionna, 3/23/10)

What I learned today is that Salim is a good and smart friend. I used to think this project is lame because I didn't know how to do it. But now I think it's going good because Salim helped me. (Alexis, 4/22/10)

School—Grades

I used to think I wasn't gonna pass last semester because my grades were low. But now I think I passed it because I saw my grades and they were high[er] than I thought it would be. (Dionna, 3/22/10)

Writing Process—General

I used to think that writing was really boring because it seemed like you needed to take so much time and be creative, but now I think that it's fun because you can express anything you want in it and we don't get topics to write about, it's free write. (Pamela, 10/26/09)

I used to think writing could be two sentences because I didn't like writing because I was mad lazy. But now I think I can add so much details because writing opens up a whole another [sic] world. (Luis T., 10/26/09)

I used to think that writing was boring because it was a lot of work and confusion. But now I think it's fun because you learn a lot from your own writing. (Juan, 4/27/10)

I used to think that grammar wasn't really a big deal because I just went through school writing papers and having teachers check my work and not really teaching me about grammar. But now I see that grammar is really important and that I really need to work on it because it is important and I have to work better at getting what I'm saying through clearly. (Chekeshia, 5/2010)

I used to think that the hook is just a sentence that you write. And now I think that it would be something that would bring the reader in to read my essay because that's what makes the reader want to read. (Jessica, 4/2010)

I used to think that essays were just a summary of an object because I always wrote an essay on how the teacher told me. Now I think that essays are more complicated because it helps you understand grammar and also makes you a better reader. (Estiven, 4/27/10)

This evolving collection of students' responses provides valuable data that help Erica gain a sense of what seems particularly useful for her learners, or what might be missing from her instruction that could be revisited with students in following lessons. "This thinking routine has helped me get to know what is really inside my students' minds. Everything a student gives me, whatever he or she gives me, tells me something about the student. It is all good information that I can use to help them grow as readers, writers, and as human beings," says Erica. "I believe anything that makes their thinking visible is a prize to truly value."

CHAPTER 6

Routines for Digging Deeper into Ideas

⚙ WHAT MAKES YOU SAY THAT?

In follow-up to a statement, assertion, or opinion expressed by someone, ask:

- What makes you say that?

The What Makes You Say That? (WMYST?) routine appropriates and modifies a line of questioning from the Visual Thinking Strategies (VTS) developed by Housen and Yenawine (Housen, Yenawine, & Arenas, 1991). In VTS, students look at art and are asked open-ended questions like "What's going on in this painting?" Student responses are then followed up with "What do you see that makes you say that?" That question, modified slightly, becomes useful in a whole host of contexts both in and out of the classroom. WMYST? is as much a discourse routine as it is a thinking routine.

Purpose

The What Makes You Say That? routine helps students identify the basis for their thinking by asking them to elaborate on the thinking that lies behind their responses. Seemingly simple on the surface, this routine, when used as a regular part of classroom discourse, goes a long way toward fostering a disposition toward evidential reasoning. Students are asked to share their interpretations backed with evidence so that others have an opportunity to consider multiple viewpoints and perspectives on a topic or idea. In this way, discussions deepen and go past surface answers or mere opinions. Using this routine, the teacher doesn't present herself as the keeper of all answers but empowers the entire learning community to examine the reasons and evidence behind possible explanations to determine their worth. This helps convey a sense that the correctness of an answer doesn't lie in a lone outside authority but in evidence that supports it.

Selecting Appropriate Content

There are many occasions in life when it is useful to look closely at something and develop a personal theory. Students often have hidden ideas about the way things work, how something has come to be, or why something is the way it is. To make the thinking behind these theories visible, teachers need to help students identify the evidence and reasoning that give rise to those theories. It is only then that the nascent theories and ideas can be discussed, debated, challenged, and moved forward in a meaningful way. Consequently, WMYST? can be useful when looking at works of art or historical artifacts, in exploring poetry, making scientific observations and hypotheses, making predictions in reading, or investigating broader conceptual ideas such as racism or fairness. Because of its great flexibility, teachers have adapted WMYST? for use with almost any subject, especially for surfacing students' initial ideas when launching new topics but also throughout a unit of study to continually press for close observation, explanation building, and justifying with well-anchored evidence.

Teachers wishing to create a culture of thinking in their classrooms will find it of critical importance to uncover students' thinking in all kinds of situations. On the DVD, chemistry teacher Mylessa Lenon from Michigan talks about this shift in her own teaching. This overarching goal, more than looking for a fit with specific content, will help you find a natural place for asking, "What makes you say that?" Whenever you want to dig a little deeper and push students to give the reasons behind their responses, this routine will fit. With time, it will become a natural part of your classroom.

Steps

1. *Set up.* Unlike other routines, WMYST? doesn't need to be set up, as much as placed at the appropriate time. It naturally finds a place in response to students' explanatory or interpretive comments. Look for moments when students make assertions, give explanations, provide interpretations, or offer opinions.

2. *Push for elaboration with evidence.* As students share their ideas and explanations, it is important to follow up by asking the key question of this routine: "What makes you say that?" The goal here is to both elicit and support students' attempts at justification; therefore, it may be necessary to ask, "So what do you see that makes you say that?" or "So what do you know that makes you say that?"

3. *Share the thinking.* WMYST? exists mainly in the interchanges that teachers have with their students, so while documentation of students' thinking is an option, simply creating an opportunity for more learners to share what their thinking is when prompted by WMYST? is often enough to enrich a conversation.

Uses and Variations

At Lemshaga Akademi in Sweden, where we first began the Visible Thinking work, the teachers began referring to WMYST? as the "magic question" because they were always amazed at how much of students' thinking got revealed that previously lay hidden. They found that by using the question regularly in their interactions with students, thinking became much more visible. Other ways to convey the nuance of WMYST? include "What do you think you were basing that on?" Or "What evidence were you able to find to support that idea?"

This thinking routine works well in combination with any number of routines when students are sharing their thinking. On the DVD, you'll see Lisa Verkerk and Debbie O'Hara from the International School of Amsterdam using it with See-Think-Wonder and the Explanation Game respectively. Notice how the use of the question with Debbie's kindergarten class elicits much deeper responses and elaborations that in turn produce a greater level of student engagement. In these and other classroom episodes on the DVD, notice how teachers often use WMYST? in their interactions with students to move their thinking forward. As you watch the videos, consider how the use of the question helps to convey interest in students' ideas and create a culture of thinking within the classroom.

Assessment

As WMYST? becomes part of the regular pattern of discourse between teachers and students, as well as among students themselves, it is important to take notice of the students' responses to this question. More than calling for a procedural explanation or a short-answer response, WMYST? invites reasons based on what one has seen, noticed, or has drawn upon from prior experience or contextual evidence. The overall goal is to support students in their ability and disposition to create explanations, generate theories, and offer reasons that can be substantiated with proof. Over time, look for a deepening in students' responses. Are students going beyond a simple insistence that they are right or a reliance on an outside authority? Are students beginning to offer their reasons without prompting? Do students provide support for other people's assertions as a way of strengthening them?

Tips

The language of this routine's key question, "What makes you say that?" is intentional. When this question is asked with a genuine tone of respect, it has the potential to convey our interest in the other. The question shouldn't sound like a challenge or a test but convey a curiosity regarding how the learner is constructing understanding of a complex idea or perplexing phenomenon. If a teacher is not genuinely interested in how students are making sense of ideas, students will soon realize this and the responses offered will be reduced to short answer responses without elaboration. Therefore, it is important that this question, "What makes you say that?" gets asked in authentic contexts whereby student responses help drive the class's ongoing learning.

A Picture of Practice

"Prior to being introduced to thinking routines, I had been interested in my own questioning of students for a long time," said Mary Kay Archer, an elementary teacher and mathematics specialist in the Traverse City Area Public Schools in northern Michigan. "I'd always wanted to investigate the depth of understanding of my students using questioning as a key avenue, so the What Makes You Say That? routine immediately attracted me with its seemingly simple language yet profoundly complex nuance." Mary Kay had taught kindergarten children for more than twenty years when she first began using thinking routines in her classroom. While she saw at once the immediate possibilities of using thinking routines such as Think-Puzzle-Explore and See-Think-Wonder with her very young learners, the WMYST? routine seemed to resonate with her own professional interests in questioning and investigating as primary drivers of learning.

"I first experienced the power of What Makes You Say That? as a participant within a professional development setting offered within my school district," explained Mary Kay. "Though I can't exactly remember the context in which that question was posed to me, I do remember that such a simple question really pressed me to think and reason much deeper than before." From her personal experience with this thinking routine, Mary Kay decided that this question could become a good way for her to pursue making her young students' thinking and reasoning very visible in her classroom. "I was teaching kindergarten at the time, as I had for many years, and I was so excited—my young students really started to tell me what was going on inside their heads in ways I hadn't accessed before. Even when I began teaching fourth graders in the following years, I was amazed that such a simple question encouraged my students to justify their responses. They were clarifying ideas to me and to the rest of their peers as they explained and elaborated their thinking when provoked by WMYST?"

At first Mary Kay remembers that the very language of WMYST? didn't seem so natural. "I wanted it to feel blended in my teaching and connected to our classroom conversations," Mary Kay recalled. "When I first started to ask the question, I wasn't always sure where it would go, but since I had experienced the depth of thinking it caused within me as a professional learner, I persisted in making this question a part of my classroom interactions, and it didn't take long for it to take off with my students."

Mary Kay experienced many rich discussions with students. She was surprised and pleased that her fourth grade students would explain their thinking with such sophistication. "When visitors would come into our classroom, my students would impress them with their responses. Visitors would tell me that they never heard students discuss ideas with such depth. It really took the classroom discourse up a few notches." Mary Kay also noticed how this very simple question provided access for all students to participate, especially children who might have traditionally struggled in class. "They were engaged and willing to share their thinking as much as anyone in the classroom, especially when I posed the What Makes You Say That? question in a science experiment we'd conducted or a math investigation we were debriefing. My students were truly expressing their thoughts around complex ideas in ways I just didn't imagine possible."

When considering the benefits to her students that this thinking routine offered, Mary Kay said that a significant development was when students started asking "What makes you say that?" to one another, within the setting of group projects or pair interactions. "I began seeing some independence and responsibility for their own learning, which is challenging for young students. I had always wondered about how best to provide opportunities for the students I teach to be more independent and responsible, and here my students were using the language of WMYST? in the natural patterns of interactions they were having with one another. It was as if this question became a part of their natural abilities and inclinations to be curious about the topics we were exploring."

Regarding her own learning with using this thinking routine, Mary Kay remembers that at the beginning she felt perhaps she was overusing the routine. "Using it too many times seemed to weaken its impact. My students' responses, especially with my fourth graders, seemed to become shallow again as if they were verbally filling in a blank I had put before them. It was then that I became more aware of the placement of WMYST?" In time, though, Mary Kay felt that her teaching and use of the routine became more purposeful. "I began to understand what making students' thinking visible really means. My decisions within teaching moments became more centered on what kind of thinking I wished to elicit from my students. When reasoning with evidence was called for, WMYST? seemed appropriately placed, and that is when I became more aware of the depth of reasoning my students were capable of. I had been teaching for many years, but now I really strived to provide my students with opportunities to think about their thinking. I tried to create a classroom where their thinking was given visibility and value. I didn't want to just give my students activities to do; rather, I wanted to create opportunities for them to think, to talk about their thinking with one another, and to value each other's thinking within our classroom community. Striving to make children's thinking visible—especially with WMYST?—really brought our group together. It was powerful."

⚙ CIRCLE OF VIEWPOINTS

Identify the different perspectives that could be present in or affected by what you have just read, seen, or heard. Record these in a circle with the issue or event at the center. Choose one of these perspectives to explore further, using the following prompts as a starting place:

1. I am thinking of *[name the event/issue]* from the point of view of . . .

2. I think . . . *[describe the topic from your viewpoint. Be an actor—take on the character of your viewpoint]*. Because . . . *[explain your reasoning]*

3. A question/concern I have from this viewpoint is . . .

When you are seated in a circle, around a table, or in a theater, it is easy to grasp the idea that those sitting somewhere else in that circle will literally have a different view of the goings on. Using this physical model as a springboard, we developed the Circle of Viewpoints (COV) routine to help students with the process of identifying different perspectives and viewpoints on an issue, event, or topic that they might then explore further. We then set out a few prompts to begin this process of exploration.

Purpose

This routine focuses on perspective taking. Before one can develop skills at perspective taking, one must be able to identify the different perspectives present. It is all too easy to fall into the pattern of viewing things from one's own perspective and sometimes even being oblivious to alternate viewpoints. This routine helps learners to identify and consider these different and diverse perspectives involved in and around a topic, event, or issue. This process creates a greater awareness of how others may be thinking and feeling and reinforces that people can and do think differently about the same things. This routine also provides a structure to assist in the exploration of one of these viewpoints. The ultimate goal of this process is to gain a broader and more complete understanding of the topic, event, or issue through this process.

Selecting Appropriate Content

The effectiveness of this routine depends on having source material that invites exploration from many different viewpoints. Therefore, an image, story, issue, or topic that is rich with characters and/or possibilities lends itself immediately to considering the many and diverse viewpoints as opposed to something simplistic and obvious. Try to identify the different viewpoints yourself as you contemplate your selection. Whatever the case, the identification and exploration of viewpoints should help learners contextualize, problematize, and understand the topic, issue, or event being examined. As an introduction, a painting or other image can be useful, as it provides a chance to identify the perspectives within the image.

This basic idea of a circle of viewpoints can be introduced with a series of photos showing a building or landmark from many viewpoints, a still life set up with artists seated around it, or a series of YouTube video clips showing an event such as a home run in a baseball game from the perspective of the batter, the catcher, a fielder, and a spectator. Some of these clips show these different views side by side on the screen, emphasizing that this is all happening simultaneously. There are many examples, particularly from sports, that show the same event in slow motion or from different angles, which clearly highlight that there are many ways of seeing the same thing.

Steps

1. *Set up.* In introducing the source material—the image, story, issue, event, or topic—be sure and provide plenty of time for its examination. This may involve looking closely at the image or asking questions of clarification about an event. At the conclusion of this initial examination, identify and name the topic or topics that the class will be trying to understand better through the routine. Write the topic or issue on the board or on chart paper. (Note: You will need to decide if this will be an oral activity, one in which students make simple notes of their ideas, or a more formal written task. Keep in mind that younger students often produce less in writing than they can in an informal discussion due to the demands of writing.)

2. *Identify viewpoints.* Generate a list of viewpoints. The viewpoints don't need to be only people, though this is an obvious place to start. Students can also identify inanimate objects: parts from the setting, the tree at the side of the scene, the bird overhead, the grass underfoot, and so on. Students can identify actors and groups not immediately present in the story or image but affected by it. This can involve thinking forward to the future as well as in the present. Record these in a circle around the listed topic or issue.

3. *Select a viewpoint to explore.* Ask students to select a viewpoint that they want to explore. If students are working in small groups, you might ask that each select a different viewpoint to explore to create a richer and more complete exploration of the topic or issue. (Note: You may want to select one to do together as a whole class initially.)

4. *Respond to the "I think . . ." prompt.* Ask students to take on the character of their viewpoint and describe the topic from this new perspective. What does this person or character think about the event or situation? What is their take? Why do they think of this? Give students time to think about and imagine what this person or thing could be considering. This think time may involve taking notes or more formal recording of ideas or it may just be done mentally.

5. *Respond to the "A question I have from this viewpoint . . ." prompt.* Ask students to imagine what this person or thing might be puzzled or curious about and create a question from this viewpoint, as if the person or thing was asking this question aloud. Again, provide time to generate and/or record ideas.

6. *Share the thinking.* Decide whether sharing will happen in small group or as a whole class. Initially, a whole group will provide everyone with lots of models and give you a chance to assess everyone's efforts. Ask each person to introduce her or his viewpoint, state her or his thinking from that viewpoint and her or his questions. Document the main threads that permeate the discussion, particularly noting the differences in viewpoints.

Uses and Variations

This routine can be used at the beginning of a unit of study to help students brainstorm new perspectives about a topic and imagine the different characters, themes, and questions connected to it. Particularly, the routine can be useful when students are having a hard time seeing other perspectives or when things seem black and white. For example, after watching *Rabbit-Proof Fence*, Emma Furman asked her grade 5 students at Bialik College to consider the part of the film where Molly, Gracie, and Daisy were taken from their mothers. The class identified the trooper, Molly, the window of the truck, the fence that was run over, the mother, the truck driver, Gracie, and the grandmother as holding different perspectives. Students then sat in small groups and discussed their different viewpoints and raised new questions and insights, thus "complexifying" the situation.

Perspective taking helps to build greater empathy and understanding. When planning for school camps, David Reese asked his students at Bialik to identify and then take on the viewpoints of all the people involved in the camps. This experience helps them to understand the complexity of all the issues involved and why all their requests and ideas can't always be followed.

The prompts following the identification of viewpoints are just suggestions. They can be useful in helping students to actually take a different perspective than their own. However, you might want to add to or change these prompts to better fit your students and the content being explored. Another way of helping students to explore perspectives is to ask questions that help them determine who has similar and different perspectives. For instance, "If we were to rearrange the perspectives we have generated so that those having opposite perspectives were actually across the circle from each other, which positions would you place where? Which positions should be next to each other because they are similar? Who would you place yourself next to?"

Assessment

It can be difficult to look at issues from another perspective, especially if one is strongly attached to a particular point of view. Noticing how clearly students differentiate the viewpoints demonstrates an understanding that more than one viewpoint is possible and can indeed be valid. Typically this step is done in a group. However, once the routine has been learned and students have had some exposure to identifying multiple perspectives, you might consider asking students to do this individually before group sharing. These individual responses can inform you about students' ability to identify different perspectives.

When students take on a viewpoint and begin to think from that perspective, notice whether students are merely stating their own positions or they are expressing thoughts and ideas different from what they themselves hold. By the same token, take note whether students are imbuing their character with stereotypical or stock responses, for instance, ascribing evil intent to someone whose position differs from the student's own in a clownish or mockish way. In addition, attend to the complexity of the questions they pose from that perspective. Is it a simple clarifying question—"What is . . . ?"—or a more probing question with several layers? Notice whether the questions are broad and general, or are they honing in to the essence of the subject or identifying puzzles of particular significance? Are they surface questions or are they probing deeply?

Tips

With initial uses of this routine, the generated list of possible viewpoints is usually very predictable. Model other possible viewpoints, for example, with a newspaper photo of soldiers marching. Expected viewpoints could include those of the soldiers themselves, any onlookers, the photographer, and perhaps also the person reading the newspaper. Other viewpoints that could be modeled or suggested could include the earth on which the soldiers are standing—what is it thinking, what questions would it ask? Or perhaps that of the battle-worn boots or the nearby trees that have witnessed many troops of soldiers marching past. It does not take long for students to suggest many different viewpoints once they know that this is encouraged and valued.

Likewise, you may need to draw attention to and/or model what it would mean to "think" or "ask questions" that go beneath the surface of the topic in order to encourage more thought-provoking insights and intriguing questions. Don't expect this to occur right away. However, students are always trying to figure out "what we want from them." If they get the impression a superficial or comical response will do, they will give us more of the same. Continue to push students' thinking. If you teach multiple classes, you might type up students' responses from one class (without attribution) and give them to another class to sort according to the level of thoughtfulness and insight the responses reveal about the character whose viewpoint is being examined.

Rather than have each student stand and read, you might have one student share and then ask others who have that same viewpoint to add to that response until the class has built up a good understanding of that viewpoint. Then invite someone "on the opposite side of the circle of viewpoints," that is, who has a markedly different perspective, to present his or her ideas. Next, invite someone to speak from a position more in between those two perspectives. This will encourage more active listening and processing of the information rather than students just waiting their turn.

A Picture of Practice

Nicky Dorevitch was exploring the topic of poverty with a group of grade 5 students at Bialik College in her creative writing seminar. While the discussion was lively and interesting, Nicky was concerned that the children were not really delving into the issues. "After overhearing a heated discussion about the phrase 'Make Poverty History,' I realized that after listening to the children, many of their views of poverty were basically clichés, and I felt that this could be a really interesting and valuable topic," Nicky commented.

She decided to use the Circle of Viewpoints routine in order to ascertain exactly what the students knew about poverty and encourage them to think more broadly and from other perspectives about this topic. Nicky shared her thinking about the choice of COV: "I chose this routine to explore the children's perspectives of poverty.... I feel that this routine will help the children consider different and diverse perspectives and that it will also encourage them to confront this topic with sensitivity and humility." None of the students had done this routine before, and each was intrigued with the idea of choosing a viewpoint.

As the stimulus for this exploration, Nicky chose a photo of a Mongolian family crammed into the front seat of a bright blue, but battered, old jeep that looks more handmade than factory produced. On the roof what appear to be household items are stacked precariously, blankets draping over the edge and partially covering the side windows. Seven family members, all with the same jet-black hair, are visible in the picture, some with faces nearly pressed to the front glass. A shirtless man, perhaps the father, drives. A girl in a red shirt in the center of the photograph smiles at the woman (the mother?) behind her, dressed in bright plaid and grinning broadly. The vehicle sits in a barren, flat landscape devoid of trees or buildings. Only the smallest tufts of short grass can be seen to one side of the frame. It is impossible to tell if the jeep is on a road or traveling cross country. In the background, a darkening sky turning a purplish pink caps the scene. The image isn't particularly sad or depressing and, while it shows a certain level of hardship, it avoids some stereotypes about poverty. Not wanting to lead students to think in certain ways, Nicky choose not to share any information about the photo with her students. Time was given for the students to look carefully at the photo. Then students named and noticed what they observed before identifying the various perspectives. Students were then asked to each choose the viewpoint of someone or something in this photo and respond to the question prompts of the routine from the viewpoint that they had selected.

One student chose the mother's perspective, writing, "Oh my husband is so good, trying to keep the kids so calm when all of us are scared. With not even butterflies in our stomachs, they're more like leeches. I wonder when the fuel is going to run out. I hope we have enough to last at least the night. I think by then we will be able to get to the little village. I really hope that we'll also have enough food because I have a whole family to feed and I can't bear to see them suffer. If one of us is hungry I really hope it's not the children. Oh no, the enemy is catching up. I must make sure the children don't look back. I see my husband's face as he bashes down the accelerator and now I know it's bad." This was followed by a briefer response concerning possible questions: "What will happen to us if the fuel runs out?"

Several other students took the perspective of inanimate objects in the picture, such as the car, the blankets on top, the road, the wheels, and so on. Perhaps these students felt this choice would allow them to be more creative and free in their writing.

Writing from the car's viewpoint, a student responded to the prompts with "I'm an old battered car. I think my bonnet will blow any second, and the wheels are on the verge of falling off. Why oh why did they cram seven people into me? I'm nearly out of fuel. There is a long road ahead, and there has been no fuel point for 210 miles. My lights have no globes and my steering wheel is dysfunctional. And to make matters worse, they have dumped about 20 kilos of tents and rugs on my roof. It's hot and squishy inside, but it's late afternoon and cool outside. My tires are barely holding up, and I desperately need a repair. A question I have from this viewpoint is: Will I survive?"

The students became deeply engaged in their choices. They took on the persona of the new viewpoint very seriously, and Nicky felt that their writing was evocative and powerful in response to the "think" prompt, perhaps less so with the "questions." The students were interested and excited to hear each student read his or her response, and this triggered new questions and further discussion. The structure of the routine enabled the students to approach the image in a way that asked them to take more than a cursory look at it, took them out from their everyday lives, and enabled them to make new and different connections about the concept of poverty.

⚙ STEP INSIDE

Think about a person or an object that is a part of or connected to the event or situation you are examining. Place yourself within the event or situation to see things from this point of view. Some questions to consider:

- What can this person or thing see, observe, or notice?
- What might the person or thing know, understand, hold true, or believe?
- What might the person or thing care deeply about?
- What might the person or thing wonder about or question?

The idea of stepping inside or embodying a character or historical figure is one that teachers have long made use of. Sometimes students do this in a way that deepens their understanding and appreciation of the character and events, and other times it may be more superficial. By adding just a few guidelines to the process of stepping inside a character, as this routine does, we can structure students' thinking and, we hope, deepen their understanding.

Purpose

From a very early age, children's games often involve role play and imagining being someone else. Like Circle of Viewpoints, this routine focuses on perspective taking. However, it seeks to provide a structure to take this thinking to another level and to develop an even greater empathetic response. By asking the learner to hypothesize what this person or thing observes, understands, believes, cares about, and questions, this routine helps students to delve even more deeply into the person or thing. It takes the learner outside himself or herself to understand that one's perspective often shapes how events are understood. As such, the Step Inside routine can be an effective way for students to push their thinking further than what they might do in Circle of Viewpoints.

Selecting Appropriate Content

To develop an empathic response that shows a deeper awareness and appreciation of the other's perspective, it is important that students have good source material with which to work. Material that evokes an emotional response and/or embodies some sort of dilemma or question having multiple perspectives often works well. With such material, different takes on the situation can be expressed and supported with evidence and/or logical explanations or theories. The idea is for the students not to be fanciful when stepping inside, but to try to see things from a different perspective based on evidence. This is one of the reasons this routine begins by noticing and observing from the person or object's perspective. These observations become the basis for the stances, opinions, and ideas that follow.

A potential provocation for Step Inside might be an event depicted in a work of art, a social issue that has been in the news, a story or novel that the class has read, a photograph from the newspaper, or a proposed policy. Often it is helpful first to identify all of the possible viewpoints, including the inanimate ones, that are present in the event or situation. For this reason, the Circle of Viewpoints routine is often linked to Step Inside. However, there can be occasions when you will want students to explore a particular viewpoint that you assign, and that is okay.

Steps

1. *Set up.* After the image, video, audio, story, issue, or question has been introduced, provide time for learners to think about the players and observers (both animate and inanimate) in this scenario and either ask them to select a person or thing to Step Inside (Note: You may want to use Circle of Viewpoints as part of the set-up), or, if it suits the learning, assign class or group perspectives. Decide whether you will do the routine as a whole class (this works well the first time through the routine), in groups, or individually.

2. Ask, *"What can this person or thing see, observe, or notice?"* Ask students to imagine themselves as the person or thing they have selected and describe what they could now see, observe, or notice. This can be done as a simple list of items generated by individuals in writing or by the class aloud and documented by the teacher.

3. *Ask, "What might the person or thing know about, understand, or believe?"* Ask students to respond to this prompt from the chosen perspective. Make a list of these ideas. This kind of thinking may be a bit of a stretch initially, but very soon students immerse themselves into this new viewpoint and either write or speak about the new knowledge and beliefs. If done as a whole class, you might follow up students' responses with "What makes you say that?" to focus on the evidentiary basis for these statements.

4. *Ask, "What might the person or thing care about?"* Ask students to respond to this prompt from the chosen perspective. Record these ideas. Encourage students not only

to state this but also to provide information as to why this person or thing would or might care about these matters.

5. *Ask, "What might this person or thing wonder about or question?"* Ask students to respond to this prompt from the chosen perspective. Make a list of these ideas. Again, you may ask for the reasons and justification behind these.

6. *Share the thinking.* If the routine has been done as a whole class and documented, then the group's thinking has been visible throughout the process and there is a record of all responses. Looking at the documentation, ask the class to articulate what image of the character is emerging. If the routine was done individually, group students together in one or more ways: One option is to form groups with each person in the group having chosen a different perspective. Another option is to ask students who have chosen the same perspective to compare their Step Insides. Another alternative is to discuss the issue or dilemma at hand as a whole class, inviting students to introduce their thinking from different viewpoints as a stimulus for class discussion.

Uses and Variations

Saroj Singh, a grade 4 teacher at Bialik, introduced this routine at the beginning of the year to assist with issues relating to friendship, bullying, and acceptance within and outside the class. Saroj read several books and poems on accepting differences. One of the poems dealt with the impact of gossip and described how a comment that had started as a joke caused the character in the poem, David, to be so unhappy as to leave the school he had just started. The children were asked to step inside David's shoes. Students commented that, as David, they *knew,* "I am sad, that people laugh at my accent, that I am invisible," and that David *cared about* "what people think, having friends, and being accepted," among other responses. Both Saroj and her students found the impact of this routine in this situation both humbling and powerful.

Another fourth grade teacher, Jan Zimba at List Elementary in Frankenmuth, Michigan, used Step Inside when her students were studying about electricity. She asked her students to think about what they had learned about circuits and the various circuits they had explored, such as lights and doorbells. Students then selected one aspect of a circuit: the wire, the electrons, the light bulb filament, and so on, to Step Inside. After students had written their responses to the question prompts, the class played a game in which a student read his or her responses without revealing the chosen perspective, and the rest of the class tried to guess the viewpoint they had chosen.

When studying texts at senior levels, Bialik English teacher Sharon Berenholtz found that her students tended to focus primarily on the main characters. Sharon found that by asking her students to follow the steps of this routine and Step Inside some of the minor characters, ones often overlooked, the routine gave students deeper insights into the text, helped them understand different perspectives, and gave them a greater appreciation for the complexity of the crafting of a powerful narrative. Similarly, elementary art teacher Barbara Jaffe, also at Bialik, found that asking her students to Step Inside works of art gave students new insights into the works. Depending on her purpose, Barbara would ask her students to Step Inside the buildings, the artist, the people in the painting, or an inanimate part of the picture. This led to many vibrant discussions with students comparing the different stories created when looking through "different eyes."

Assessment

In students' responses, take note to see if they are merely stating the obvious and the most clearly defined and widely known aspects of the topic—which is a fine place to start—or if they are able to infer and hypothesize what might be happening. Are they aware of the complexities of what someone may feel or care about? Or, are they unable to move beyond their own positions, feelings, and questions? Are students' responses calling for inference still based on evidence and reason? Can they build a plausible case for the positions they advocate?

Sometimes teachers use Step Inside as a precursor to more elaborated writing, as is shown in Sharonne Blum's Picture of Practice following. In these situations, look to see how students are able to use the routine as a starting place for their writing rather than merely an end in itself. Are they able to create a rich and full sense of a character using the ideas generated from the routine?

Tips

The terminology is worth thinking about when introducing this routine. Notice the use of the word *might* in the second, third, and fourth questions in the routine. By asking "What might the person or object wonder?" rather than "What does the person or object wonder?" the teacher implicitly sends the message to students that the idea is not to find a single definitive answer but generate reasonable possibilities and alternatives. We can never know exactly what a river, a dog or, for that matter, a historical figure is thinking, feeling, wondering, or caring about, and the use of this conditional language opens the way for thinking broadly, hypothesizing, and raising possibilities.

Be adventurous with the use of this routine; it can lead to some of the most creative and insightful thinking. Encourage students to take the perspective of the unexpected. We have seen examples of five-year-olds "stepping inside" the curtains in a room where a celebration is occurring and providing carefully considered thoughts and observations about the events taking place, or teachers discussing a newspaper photo of soldiers in Iran through very different perspectives ranging from the soldiers' shoes to the butts of the rifles, and students "stepping inside" countries and cities and even their own classrooms.

Teachers of young children may feel that perspective taking is difficult for young children, yet role play and fantasy are a large part of their world. Perspective taking is a skill that can and should be further developed through many and different opportunities. One strategy Emma Furman, a grade 2 teacher at Bialik, created was making the Step Inside routine more concrete by providing cutouts of pairs of shoes for the children to step into when changing viewpoints. This proved most effective and popular, with the children enjoying the novelty. In a very short time the students would visualize the stepping inside process and no longer chose to use the cutout shoes.

To avoid this routine becoming just a fun activity, think about what you hope students will learn through the process of stepping inside. Do you want them to have a better understanding of the complexity of a problem or issue? Do you want them to understand a particular character better and eventually be able to produce writing that will demonstrate their understanding?

A Picture of Practice

Grade 7 students at Bialik College were studying ancient Egyptian history. Their teacher, Sharonne Blum, was concerned that her students were not fully understanding the significance of the Nile River in ancient Egypt. Sharonne selected the Step Inside routine to help her students flesh out the role of the Nile in the lives of the ancient Egyptians. Conscious of how hard it can be for teenagers to relate to the past, Sharonne thought that if her students made an emotional connection they could better understand the importance of the Nile, both spiritually and agriculturally.

To help her students begin to make that emotional connection with the Nile and understand a little of its past, Sharonne began by setting the scene. She asked students to close their eyes while she dramatically read an ancient Egyptian prayer honoring and worshiping the Nile. She then asked them to imagine that they were the Nile, flowing down through Egypt, seeing farmers checking on flood levels and babies bathing. Sharonne encouraged her students to visualize what else might be in front of them and happening around them and gave them time to silently envision the events in their minds' eye. The students became completely immersed in their thoughts.

Sharonne then asked them to open their eyes and to capture on paper what they had seen and felt and individually write those words. To assist this process, Sharonne shared the questions of the Step Inside routine with her students, asking them what, as the Nile, were they seeing before and around them? What did they know about, believe, and understand? What did they care about and wonder? Students used these prompts to record their thoughts and ideas, some making lists, others writing in more complete sentences.

Once students had their ideas before them, Sharonne asked students to use their list of words and thoughts to each compose a poem or work of prose writing from the perspective of the Nile. One student's poem is reproduced here:

I am the Nile River
By Jemima

I can see the farmer with his animals.
Boy with his friends playing on my bank.
I can see a woman washing her clothes in the water.
I can feel the sunlight trickle down on me. I know that I am helping all the people.
So I continue to flow.
I flow past the boy and the farmer and past the woman.
Now it's just me. I am solitary and I grow quieter.
Soon I see an old man drink from me. I smile to myself and am glad that I could help him.
The animals drink and swim as I splash through the rocks and roots.
I stare as far as I can and I see the place they call the Red Lands. They are long and dry and I am glad I give the people what they need.

Another student's work of prose appears following.

Step Inside: I am the Nile River ...
By Davina

As the Nile River, I tend to travel constantly through Egypt, as if I am a whirlpool and there's no way of stopping myself. As I pass I spot women and children greeting me and using me to wash their clothes, or to collect water. Animals indulge in my waters, and I support boats and others who swim in me. Farms, people, animals and plants live off me. People use me for fishing and I am surrounded by vegetation. If I look into the distance I can see the Red Lands. Plants of food grow because of me and people with weapons fight over me. People are living because of me. Children play on the banks.

I feel powerful because I am a source of life. I feel used, exploited because I am open to everyone. I feel that I am the centre of gravity. I give fruit water and nourishment. At times I feel terrible because of the vegetation, people take my molecules of water – they are considered my friends. I am humbled because I notice the impact that I have. However, I want to help the Red Lands. It is very dry there. I feel disrespected, because if I am considered holy, then why do people dirty me?

I feel I am helping the environment and people, and I have the ability to save people. I tend to feel guilty at times for starting wars, because people fight over me. I feel special because I watch and am a part of sacrifices. I feel proud and happy.

Sharonne was surprised by the quality and detail of the writing. "Before I have asked students to pretend they were someone or something else, but there was never the detail that I saw in these poems and prose. By deconstructing the information in the steps of the routine, it's like you are looking at a building, but not just seeing its shape, but really noticing the individual bricks. There are things you can't see if you don't take some of the bricks apart. Step Inside enables people to 'see' things that they might otherwise have missed if all they saw was the whole building—the overarching theme."

Reflecting on students' learning as evidenced in both the poems and prose written after doing Step Inside, Sharonne observed, "It provides opportunities to pay attention to details and intricacies and slows the process down so there are fewer pat answers and the students notice things they wouldn't always notice. If I had asked them to pretend to be the Nile, they would have fallen back on clichés. A peaceful atmosphere was created, it was calmer with thoughts flowing and time to document."

In our research into the development of thinking dispositions, we identified a key place where dispositions falter: the spotting of occasions for application. People often have the thinking skill, but they fail to use that skill because they didn't spot occasions for its use. This led our colleague David Perkins to develop the Red Light, Yellow Light (RLYL) routine that focused specifically on the spotting of occasions to be skeptical and ask questions. Spotting these occasions would cause students to be more active listeners and readers, to have their skepticism antennae up if you will. Using the metaphor of a traffic light, students are encouraged to think in terms of green lights giving them the freedom to continue, yellow lights as slowing them down, and red lights as stopping them.

Purpose

Red Light, Yellow Light is about becoming more aware of specific moments that hold signs of possible puzzles of truth. Sweeping generalizations, blatant self-interests, oversimplified conclusions, unexpressed bias, hidden motives, and so on can easily come off as incontestable or perhaps even invisible. If students are to develop deep understanding of a topic, they have to learn to see the potential falsehoods and to handle them in ways that aren't dismissive, overlooked, or debilitating. Red Light, Yellow Light should be used often in deliberately different ways to build sensitivity to spotting potential puzzles of truth within claims, ideas, conclusions, generalizations, and so on.

Selecting Appropriate Content

The most suitable content for Red Light, Yellow Light would be source material that presents particular stances, claims, conclusions, or generalizations. Opinion articles in a magazine, mysteries that have yet to be solved, mathematical proofs that might have some weaknesses present are all possible good fits for students to do some Red Light, Yellow Light thinking. Situations outside of school could also prove to be useful content for this routine: regulations for potentially risky behaviors, playground arguments, proposals for fundraising for a class trip, and the like.

One thing to keep in mind with Red Light, Yellow Light is to make sure the issue, problem, conflict, or controversy is large enough so that a variety of red lights and yellow lights can be identified. If the source is too small, there isn't likely to be rich conversation about potential problems of truth to be alert to. Likewise, if the red and yellow lights all stem from the same source or force a global attribution, for example, "This newspaper is always biased so I would never believe anything," then discussions will be less useful in helping students to identify different sources and reasons for red and yellow lights. Examining chapters in a book or keeping track of a current media debate over a few days can help students stay alert to puzzles of truth in sustained ways.

Steps

1. *Set up.* Briefly introduce the source material that will be used. You don't want to say anything that will prejudice the reading. In some instances you may not want to even disclose the source. Tell students you want them to dig below the surface of the ideas, issues, or findings that may be present in the material.

2. *Look for red lights and yellow lights.* Ask students working individually, in pairs, or even in small groups to search the source for specific moments and signs of possible puzzles of truth. Using the stoplight metaphor, red lights could be framed as glaring, halting places. Yellow lights are places to proceed with a little care and caution. Everything else is an implicit green light. You might even want to give students red and yellow markers for this purpose.

3. *Collect students' observations and reasons.* Make a list of specific points marked *R* for red or *Y* for yellow as students offer them to the group. Also note specific "zones" that students identify as mostly red or yellow. Ask students to provide their reasons as to why they've categorized a particular point or zone as red or yellow. Document these reasons as well.

4. *Share the thinking.* Once a collected list of red lights and yellow lights has been created, have the class stand back and look at the documentation. Ask, "What have we learned about particular signs that indicate there could be a problem or puzzle of truth? What have we learned about zones to watch out for?" Allow students to share their thoughts and reasons.

Uses and Variations

In his facilitation of professional learning communities in the Traverse City Area Public Schools in Michigan, Mark Church regularly makes use of the Red Light, Yellow Light routine. When teachers share their classroom efforts, student work, or reflections around professional readings, Mark uses Red Light, Yellow Light to move their conversation beyond merely agreeing or disagreeing with one another's ideas. "By creating an actual space for people to voice what possible red lights come up for them and what yellow lights seem to emerge, I notice that teachers listen more closely to each other and build on each others' thinking. Before it was more likely they would remain silent when a particular point was made that didn't sit particularly well with a group member," said Mark. "Red lights and yellow lights create a sense of safety to navigate difficult ideas instead of coming up against roadblocks as soon as conversations become difficult. Red lights and yellow lights are not hard and fast judgments; rather, they identify potential zones to keep our eyes on."

Another professional use of RLYL can occur around the discussion of action plans. School principals and department heads have made use of Red Light, Yellow Light when bringing forth proposals or plans of action to larger groups of stakeholders. Asking for the red lights and yellow lights that come up for those in the group helps leaders to convey a message that there will be natural points of dispute in any proposal that need working through. However, noticing these points collectively helps a group to tackle issues head on rather than become flustered by them.

Tony Cavell, a sixth grade teacher at Bialik, found the metaphor of red lights and yellow lights could be useful to students in monitoring their reading comprehension. When students read independently, he asked them to identify any passages in the text that slowed them down slightly as readers and those passages that seemed to stop them completely, for whatever reason. In discussing the text the next day, students would then share their red and yellow light passages and discuss what it was that caused them to slow down or stop. As a class, they were then able to talk about how readers deal with such red lights and yellow lights.

Assessment

When using the Red Light, Yellow Light routine to get underneath the surface of ideas, there are several things a teacher may wish to pay attention to. What are you noticing about how readily students are identifying places of potential puzzles in what they read, hear, watch, or experience? As students identify various red lights or yellow lights, what are you noticing about their reasons for making such choices? It is important for a teacher to develop a sense for how his or her students are developing as critical consumers of information. Also, taking note of the quality of assertions students themselves may offer in classroom discussions is important. Do you see them scrutinizing their own arguments, ideas, theories, and generalizations with red lights and yellow lights to catch their own overgeneralizations or weak arguments?

Tips

It is easy for students to get into an "It's all red!" or "It's all yellow!" frame of mind once the search for red lights and yellow lights begins. Once this happens, rich classroom conversation is difficult to guide; students begin to see the issue as either one way or another—all black or white. This can happen when the source material starts with a red light, coloring everything that follows. When this is the case, a teacher should pull students back to identifying just one red light and one yellow light and reboot the conversation from there. This helps to redirect the class's attention and keep the focus on teasing apart various nuances and complexities presented within puzzles of truth rather than moving quickly into an "all or nothing" judgment.

Teachers have also found it useful to acknowledge implicit green lights in sources their students are exploring. Helping students identify places where the claim is solid can be just as powerful as examining why other claims seem to make us stop and question. Many teachers have figured out ways to track red lights and yellow lights over time together with students, particularly when a topic is rich and covers a lot of territory. By keeping documentation of red and yellow lights visible and public, students begin to see Red Light, Yellow Light less as an isolated activity and more as a metaphor for a type of thinking they can bring to new learning situations. This ongoing practice helps foster an inclination to spot occasions when an idea presented as truth needs to be questioned more thoughtfully.

A Picture of Practice

Tammy Lantz, a fifth grade teacher at Long Lake Elementary School in Traverse City, Michigan, has used thinking routines with her students for a number of years. She recalls that her initial use of thinking routines was as more of a stand-alone activity, not necessarily connected to any particular lesson. "I realize now that I needed to have that experience just to see where my kids' thinking would go. It really was engaging for them, I remember. I also remember having multiple *ah-hah* moments as my kids were sharing with me what thoughts were actually inside their heads.''

Recently, Tammy introduced Red Light, Yellow Light to her students, eager to see how it would aid their thinking. ''Red Light, Yellow Light is a new routine for me,'' said Tammy. ''It feels a bit like going back to the beginning in terms of my feeling comfortable with its steps—unlike other routines that flow quite naturally. I can already see, though, how this routine is going to start dropping into my conversations with students more and more.''

Tammy decided to make use of a routine they were already familiar with and build upon it as a way of introducing the Red Light, Yellow Light routine. ''I displayed some Claim-Support-Question samples I had kept from previous years when former students had expressed generalizations about the slave trade and the Middle Passage. Because my current students had already studied this topic and already knew the Claim-Support-Question routine, I thought this would be the perfect place to launch Red Light, Yellow Light.''

Tammy asked her current students to review claims offered by former students and to think about the strength of some of these claims. A few of the claims they looked at included:

- The Middle Passage took a long time.
- West Africans lived in freedom.
- West Africans feared a horrible trip across the Middle Passage.
- All slaves would rather die than suffer the voyage to America.

Tammy then explained the metaphor of a traffic light. She explained to her class, ''Red lights make you stop and say, 'Hey, wait a minute!' and yellow lights sort of make you pause and say, 'I see your point, but...''' She then asked her students to start making some mental notes of where red lights and yellow lights could possibly be in these claims. Tammy also pressed her students to not just point out red lights or yellow lights but to share with the class what makes them say that. She purposely put a range of samples up on the wall so her students would have some interesting things to talk about.

The students didn't have much difficulty jumping right into this thinking routine. ''It was a spirited conversation right from the beginning,'' said Tammy. ''It required them to remember back to some things they themselves had already studied and then challenge some of the claims I had posted on the board.'' For example, many students took issue with the vagueness of a claim, such as ''The Middle Passage took a long time.'' While they didn't argue with the basic premise of that claim, Tammy's students felt it was a bit yellow light, noting that ''a long time'' seemed too open and not concrete enough. Tammy's students also critiqued the actual language of the posted claims, identifying potential red lights any time the words *all*, *never*, or *always* were used. Tammy felt the language of Red Light, Yellow Light helped her students examine these claims not only with a sense of healthy skepticism but also a sense of precision and veracity that pleased her.

Some days after introducing RLYL to her students, Tammy asked them to look through their social studies journals and find one of their own Claim-Support-Question entries to scrutinize using red lights and yellow lights. In doing so, Tammy wanted to draw students' attention to being self-critical in their own claim making. Tammy had students join together with partners to look at each other's selections, again asking them to watch for red lights and yellow lights as a way to help each other refine their claims and make them more solid. ''I noticed how much better their own claims became when they interacted with each other in this way. They talked about each other's ideas with one another and did not simply say, 'Right or wrong,''' Tammy reported. ''They offered each other valuable feedback using red and yellow lights. Everyone seemed really into it.''

Tammy believes that before too long, the language of this thinking routine will become a common phrase in the culture of her classroom: *What are our red lights here? Where are we seeing yellow lights in this material?* She believes this will become a natural routine to draw upon when the class encounters moments of disagreement or controversy. ''Even though I've just started using this thinking routine, I see how red lights give students an opportunity to challenge a particular viewpoint with thoughtful reasoning. And when red lights seem a little harsh, yellow lights give students an opportunity to simply keep some ideas up for skepticism,'' Tammy said. ''I can already see that the scaffolding that Red Light, Yellow Light provides will truly promote conversations, feedback, and self-reflection that will be richer for my students.''

⚙ CLAIM-SUPPORT-QUESTION

Drawing on your investigation, experience, prior knowledge, or reading:

- Make a *claim* about the topic, issue, or idea being explored. A claim is an explanation or interpretation of some aspect of what is being examined.
- Identify *support* for your claim. What things do you see, feel, or know that lend evidence to your claim?
- Raise a *question* related to your claim. What may make you doubt the claim? What seems left hanging? What isn't fully explained? What further ideas or issues does your claim raise?

For students to be more critical consumers of information, they need to become better at spotting and analyzing "truth claims." These may be ideas and opinions that are being presented by the speaker or writer as facts but in actuality might be better thought of as generalizations, conjectures, hypotheses, or propositions. A collective way of referring to these is as *claims*. These claims need to be evaluated in terms of their supporting evidence as well as those things that make us question the validity of the claim. The Claim-Support-Question (CSQ) routine evolved from these steps.

Purpose

Teachers and students come across declarations of fact or belief all the time. Claim-Support-Question is a thinking routine designed both to identify and to probe these claims. Identification of claims calls on students to look for patterns, spot generalizations, and identify assertions. Sometimes these come from others, but we can also put forth our own claims about what is going on based on our analysis of events or investigation of phenomena.

In classrooms in which explanations or interpretations are identified and discussed, conversations frequently tilt toward getting students to say whether they agree or disagree with a particular claim. Often this happens in a casual manner, without much depth or challenge. However, rarely are claims entirely black and white. One purpose of CSQ is to help students take notice of the claims presented, either as truths or as potential truths, and hold them up to thoughtful scrutiny. This thinking routine focuses students on evidence as the arbiter of the truth or validity of a claim: What support can we muster for it? What makes us question it? Offering supporting or conflicting evidence for a claim provides students a rich opportunity to make their thinking visible beyond merely offering their opinions, reactions, or feelings about a particular matter.

Selecting Appropriate Content

Inundated with scientific research debating the existence of global warming and politicians persuading constituents with oversimplistic arguments to support a policy, a thoughtful member of society must be able to cipher through what is true and what is questionable. The public forum thus provides many sources for potential claims. These can be found in newspapers, magazines, television debates, even political cartoons.

While big societal truth claims certainly are interesting to explore, no less important and more frequently occurring in classrooms are the theories, ideas, generalizations, and interpretations students themselves are encouraged to make as they perform and analyze experiments, read texts, solve open-ended mathematical problems, and so on. Mathematics is an area in which you can find or generate a rich variety of claims, generalizations, and conjectures as to what is going on or what is likely to happen—that is, if students are encouraged to explore mathematical events, games, and problems and then speculate and generalize from them. A teacher should listen closely to what students come up with during such investigations, as it is easy to overhear claims that could be interesting for a class to explore further.

Claim-Support-Question fits with any content in which various interpretations or explanations are solicited that might then be worth further exploration and justification. By being primed to recognize claims, interpretations, and generalizations, teachers can use Claim-Support-Question as an "in the moment" tool to press for evidence *in support of* or *in opposition to* claims that students frequently espouse.

Steps

1. *Set up.* The idea of a claim needs to be introduced to the class. The word *claim* was chosen for this routine because it encompasses a lot: conjectures, speculations, generalizations, assertions, statements of fact, theories, hypotheses, and so on. A very loose definition could be, A claim is a statement about "what's going on here." Present the situation to be examined to the class and tell students the group's goal is to figure out "What's going on here?" At the end of the lesson, the class will have a better understanding of the truth and reality of this situation.

2. *Identify claims.* Prior to launching a topic, a teacher might ask her students, "What claims, explanations, or interpretations might you have already about this topic?" Or, after a class has spent some time on a topic, a teacher could invite his class to make or locate claims by asking "Now that we've been studying this topic for some time, what claims can you come up with that offer us an explanation or an interpretation of our topic?" However they are generated, claims should be documented for the entire class to see, leaving room to add more thinking at a later time or in subsequent lessons. Some teachers like to write the claims in the center of the page or board, adding supports on one side and questions on the other.

3. *Identify support.* Ask students, "Now that we have these claims to consider, what can we see, notice, know, or find that might give support to them?" Students might be encouraged to seek out this support through additional experimentation, research, or fact finding in some instances or to draw on previous knowledge in other cases. Have students articulate the supporting evidence for each claim. This should be written near the original claims for all to see and collectively consider. This step is really about asking students to consider the reasons why anyone might stand behind a given claim.

4. *Raise questions.* In this step, a teacher asks students to be healthy skeptics of the claims being examined. Invite students to think beyond the support already offered for the claims and consider what might make one hesitant about the truth or accuracy of a claim. One way of asking this is, "Now that we've given some support for these claims, is there evidence on the other side? What questions do we need to raise about these claims in order to truly examine their credibility? What more might we need to examine or explain?"

5. *Share the thinking.* Documenting the routine as it evolves makes students' thinking visible throughout the process and allows students to build on as well as challenge others' thinking. Having fully examined a set of claims, it would be appropriate to ask students to take a stance toward them. You might have students rank the claims on a line of confidence, from "still questioning" to "definitely believe." If CSQ has been used to explore a particular issue, students can be asked to give their positions regarding the issue.

Uses and Variations

Claim-Support-Question can easily become a valuable pattern of thinking for students to develop. Caitlin Faiman, a mathematics specialist at Bialik, has integrated CSQ as an ongoing part of her dialogue with both primary and middle school students. Caitlin often introduces a mathematics problem, one that can be explored from a variety of perspectives with multiple strategies and for which there isn't an obvious, single solution, and then gives her students time to work on it. After ten minutes or so, Caitlin will bring the group together and ask what sort of findings they have so far, what ideas have come up, and what generalizations seem to be emerging. Caitlin documents these initial and tentative claims on chart paper. She then asks students to continue working on the problem, keeping their eyes, ears, and minds open for evidence that seems to support the initial claims as well as evidence that seems to refute or disprove them. Making use of CSQ in this way, Caitlin not only addresses specific mathematics content but also frames the enterprise of mathematics as being about speculation, generalization, analysis, and proof.

A secondary history teacher in Saginaw, Michigan, in the 2010 election cycle used CSQ to help his students better understand the issues being debated. He identified several claims being made by various candidates around issues ranging from unemployment, job creation, Social Security, health care, Don't Ask Don't Tell policy, and immigration issues without assigning the claims to any particular candidate or party. For instance, the claim that people would be better off if social security were abolished and they controlled and invested their own money for retirement. The class then looked at the supports for the claims as well as what would make them question the claims. After the class discussion, students were given the task to pick a candidate, which could be one they supported or not, and research where that candidate stood on the claims the class had discussed. Many students were quite surprised by what they discovered.

Assessment

When Claim-Support-Question becomes an ongoing pattern of thinking in classrooms, it is useful to notice how often and in what contexts students are spotting and making claims. Do they recognize when suggestions have been made or explanations have been given that seem too broad-stroked to go unchallenged? Are they looking for the generalizations and conjectures that get to the truth of an event? This is an indicator that they are processing information analytically and with a sense of healthy skepticism.

Pay attention to the strategies students are adopting for assessing the validity of claims. When students offer support for a given claim, does it seem anchored in solid, well-grounded evidence versus opinion or personal experience? When students seek to make sense of a given claim, do they recognize what questions might be worth asking of the claim in order to fully comprehend its complexities? For instance, do they recognize special cases that need to be investigated? Within a discipline, do students understand the weight of various kinds of evidence? For instance, finding that something works once or even twice in mathematics is supporting evidence but not proof.

Tips

It can be useful to think of CSQ as an overarching structure for the examination of ideas and the generation of new understanding. However, it is easy for this kind of thinking and learning to be shortchanged or even nonexistent in classrooms. This is often true when the focus is on students taking in rather than examining information. Claim-Support-Question is ultimately about creating opportunities for learners to reason through complex issues from various angles and perspectives with substantial evidence. Using Claim-Support-Question regularly can be a powerful way to convey messages to learners that anything really worth understanding is worth finding support for and scrutinizing with a thoughtful eye.

Keep in mind that CSQ is not necessarily about getting all students to agree or disagree about a particular topic. It is not always about drawing a hard-and-fast line in the sand on a given issue, though in some instances it might be. However, if students suspect that at the end of the lesson you will tell them what is right and what is wrong, they will find the routine pointless. Keep returning to the evidence. If students have missed something important, raise questions for their future exploration rather than tell them.

A Picture of Practice

Upon entering Mary Beth Schmitt's seventh and eighth grade mathematics classroom in Traverse City, Michigan, one is immediately impressed by the mathematical activity of students. Large pieces of chart paper with all sorts of graphs and equations cover the walls, exhibiting small groups of students' attempts to reason with real data. Colorful strips of tagboard on the windows display students' reflections of big mathematical ideas they've studied. Student theories and strategies are posted throughout, giving the impression that Mary Beth values students' mathematical thinking. Mary Beth had always believed in active learning. However, it was not until she went beyond simply creating hands-on lessons for students and began listening more closely to the generalizations, conjectures, and ideas they put forth that she began to notice a powerful shift in the culture of her classroom.

"I already believed that mathematics learning would be powerful for my students if they backed up their ideas with evidence," remembers Mary Beth, "so that's why I was initially drawn to Claim-Support-Question. I suppose I had always done a version of this routine, but it was more like 'claim and support' without much questioning. By that, I mean students would say something like, 'My claim is that x = 7 because that is what I found when I did the equation.' They didn't offer much more than that and I didn't ask them to do so." Mary Beth was only asking her students to give solutions and justify them by the procedure used—a relatively narrow conversation. "Though I asked them to explain their solutions, I really wasn't asking them to seek evidence to support or disprove theories, ideas, or conjectures."

Mary Beth wanted the Claim-Support-Question routine to be broader in scope than analyzing any one particular problem or procedural steps. She decided to ask her students to make initial claims about a big mathematical idea that could be looked at over time from multiple entry points. "I began with a question, a deeper question, a bigger question," said Mary Beth. Asking students, "How do we ever know whether two expressions are equivalent or not?" After providing some think time, she began documenting students' initial ideas (see Table 6.1), regardless of whether they were right or wrong. "Knowing some misconceptions would come up was part of the fun in this for me. I figured then we would have something authentic to investigate and prove," Mary Beth commented.

After collecting students' initial ideas, Mary Beth told students she would like them to keep these "claims on trial" just as if they were judges in a court of law. "Some of these claims seem true, others perhaps not so much. In either case, we've got some claims that we'll need to get to the bottom of over the next few weeks."

Table 6.1   Eighth Grade Students' Initial Claims About Equivalent Expressions

How do we ever know whether two expressions are equivalent or not?

- Two expressions are equivalent when they have the same solution.
- You can decide if they create the same table and graph. (And can be modeled the same way sometimes.)
- They are equal when the values are the same. They can be written in different formats, but the value is the same.
- You can decide by using the distributive property to find equations in their simplest form, then compare.
- You can put in the same number for x in both equations and if you get the same sum then they are equivalent.

As her class worked through a variety of mathematical investigations that examined aspects of equivalence, Mary Beth frequently directed her students back to the courtroom of "claims on trial." She asked students to offer supports from their mathematics work that would give credence to some of their initial ideas. She also asked them to suggest questions that needed to be raised regarding some of the claims now that they had gained a little more insight into the topic of equivalence. "I wanted our claims to have purpose and a life beyond any one problem or any one lesson," said Mary Beth. "I wanted my students to build upon their initial ideas and consider how our lessons were leading us to examining more questions, more strategies, and more perspectives for making sense of this big mathematical idea of equivalence than they had originally thought."

Near the end of their unit, Mary Beth asked her students to individually choose one of the initial claims and address the court in their journals: supporting the claim, questioning it, or tweaking it in some way so that it could become a more solid mathematical claim grounded in evidence. The open-ended nature of this opportunity allowed Mary Beth to see what students were understanding about equivalency (see Figure 6.1).

Mary Beth was surprised by the depth of her students' responses. She felt that the routine, with its emphasis on generating claims and searching for supporting evidence, caused her students to engage in deeper thinking about connections, strategies, and processes and not just verbalize specific procedures. "They really seem to own the ideas that they suggest and even own the claims their classmates come up with. They'll actually name the claims of their peers with phrases like, 'Remember the other day when Joe claimed that . . .' or 'You know how Alex claimed such-and-such? Well, I looked that up and . . .' They seem more engaged with each other's ideas now than ever before. I have really been enjoying this shift in how they interact with one another around their mathematical claims and reasoning."

Mary Beth believes that her regular use of CSQ has significantly changed her teaching. "I've found that my own classroom language has changed. The kinds of questions I ask and the kinds of things I listen for as my students share their ideas has gone deeper than simply listening for their solutions and steps," said Mary Beth. "I'm also thinking much more about the connections between mathematical ideas and concepts throughout the year. It seems that I am starting to notice where ideas get revisited and built upon over time now that my students and I are regularly seeking out claims, generalizations, and theories instead of just covering individual skills lesson by lesson."

Figure 6.1 Eighth Grade Students' Evaluations of Equivalency Claims

You can put in the same # for x in both equations and if you get the same sum then they are equivalent.

If this works for 3 different x's

---

* You can put in the ~~same~~ *any* # for x in both equations and if you get the same ~~sum~~ *answer* then they are equivalent. I agree with this statement *for more than 1 x.* because I know that if 2 expressions are equivalent, they will always have the same y for x.

Example

$y = 3x + 100$ $y = 100 + 3x$

If x was 7, they for both would be 106. If x was 3, both y's would be 109. We know the equations are equivalent because they got the same y.

You can put in the same # for x in both equations and if you *always* get the same ~~sum~~ *solution* then they are equivalent.

I changed this statement a little bit. I crossed off sum and wrote solution because 'sum' implies addition and in equations there are some multiplication problems you have to do. I also added 'always' in between 'you' and 'get' because if you only try one x value and the solutions are the same, it could just be where the two lines cross

---

⚙ TUG-OF-WAR

Place a line across the middle of your desk or table to represent a tug-of-war rope. Working with a dilemma that can be considered from multiple perspectives or stances:

- Identify and frame the two opposing sides of the dilemma you are exploring. Use these to label each end of your tug-of-war rope.
- Generate as many "tugs," or reasons that "pull you toward," that is, support each side of the dilemma as you can. Write these on individual sticky notes.
- Determine the strength of each tug and place it on your tug-of-war rope, placing the strongest tugs at the farthest ends of the rope and the weaker tugs more toward the center.
- Capture any "What if . . . ?" questions that arise in the process. Write these on sticky notes and place them above the tug-of-war rope.

When we thought about the challenges of decision making, a metaphor that came to mind was that of a game of tug-of-war. You have one group of factors, reasons, or influences pulling one way and another group pulling the opposite. However, in a tug-of-war, not all pulls are of equal strength. The anchor positions on the rope are generally the strongest, whereas those closer to the center are the weakest and most likely to be pulled over the line. The Tug-of-War routine uses this metaphor to explore issues and ideas.

Purpose

Taking a stance on an issue and supporting that stance with sound reasoning is an important skill. However, taking a stance on issues too quickly and rushing to defend that stance before examining the complexity of the issue can lead to narrow thinking and an oversimplification of the problem. The Tug-of-War routine is designed to help students understand the complex forces that "tug" at opposing sides in various dilemmas, issues, and problems. It encourages students initially to suspend taking a side and think carefully about the multiple pulls or reasons in support of both sides of the dilemma. By inviting students to explore the arguments for both sides of a dilemma, Tug-of-War strives to develop appreciation for the deeper complexities inherent to authentic dilemmas and reach beyond what may appear to be black and white on the surface.

Selecting Appropriate Content

Tug-of-War is best suited to situations involving dilemmas, issues, or problems in which two obvious, contrasting stances or ways of resolving an issue can be clearly identified. (Note: Adaptations can be made for more than two pulls, but plan to start using just two.) These dilemmas can come from school subjects, current events, or everyday occurrences. For example, considering the advancement of a growing population upon protected land, examining tensions between government taxation and provided services, deciding upon what is best regulated and what is best left untouched, the choices a character in a novel faces, ethical dilemmas of students, and so on. It is important to remember that the generation and exploration of multiple supporting ideas, rather than the quick selection of a preferred stance, as in a debate, is key to developing deeper understanding of complex dilemmas.

Steps

1. *Set up.* Identify and frame a particular dilemma for the class to examine. This may grow out of their current studies or be embedded in new material, such as a reading or a video. Alternatively, a teacher may wish to ask students to identify the issues or dilemmas: "Just what seems to be the issue here?" or "What is this issue really about?" Once the dilemma has been clearly defined for the class, draw a line on the whiteboard or chart paper representing the tug-of-war rope. Ask students to name the two ends of the rope. What are the two opposing viewpoints or stances in the defined dilemma. Label these.

2. *Consider the "tugs."* Ask the students, "On this side of the dilemma, what are the 'tugs' or reasons that support this position?" Have students generate as many tugs as possible, whether or not you personally agree with their reasoning. Students can generate tugs individually, in small groups pooling individual ideas, or as a whole class. Have students record their reasons/tugs on individual sticky notes so that they can be moved around later. Ask students to do the same thing for the other side of the dilemma, generating as many reasons as they can. (Note: It is not always necessary to do the two sides separately, but initially this may make the process easier for some.)

3. *Place the "tugs."* Have students, either in small groups or as a whole class, discuss the placement of the tugs on the line. Although consensus is important, the focus should

be on the reasons and justification for each placement and how the tugs compare with one another in strength.

4. *Ask What if? What about? questions.* As students are discussing placement, questions might arise. For instance, sometimes students say, "Well that depends on whether or not that would be legal." These "it depends" issues can be framed as questions, written on a different color sticky note, and placed above the line. Once placement is complete, stand back and generate additional "What if. . . ?" questions. These questions capture issues, factors, or concerns that might need further exploration.

5. *Share the thinking.* If this routine has been done in small groups, take time to look at each group's finished tug-of-war line. Ask students what new ideas emerged for them about the dilemma that they didn't have at the outset. Do they still feel the same way about the dilemma? If not, what changed their mind or added to their thinking? How might they summarize the complexity of this issue for someone else?

Uses and Variations

This routine works well and facilitates lively discussions among groups of students, particularly around the placement of the "tugs." Teachers often find the power of this routine is that it can easily be referenced to elicit reasoning around dilemmas without always doing the full routine. For instance, teachers can merely ask, "What are the tugs pulling us in favor of lengthening the school day?" to begin to generate a discussion. Of course, not all dilemmas or issues have just two sides. There are, in fact, three-way and four-way tugs-of-war in which multiple ropes come together at a common point. If an issue has more than two tugs, this metaphor might be introduced to explore the issue.

As a part of this routine, teachers sometimes spend time on the identification and framing of an issue. This can be an important skill, since the way we frame a problem will shape the solutions we try to find. For example, in a high school social studies class in Massachusetts, students read a news report about a local food service for the homeless being shut down because it didn't meet health standards for food preparation and storage due to its context of providing food on the street. After reading the article, students had to frame what they saw as the issue. Many emerged: health safety, government regulation of charities, the moral dilemma of the service provider to break the law or not, moving the site of the food service, and so on. Each group then did a tug-of-war based on how they framed the issue.

During a discussion about conservation during Earth Week, a year 1 student at Trinity Grammar in Melbourne raised the issue of car pollution. Another student suggested that one way to improve the environment would be stop driving cars altogether. Rather than dismissing this idea, the teacher decided to engage students in a Tug-of-War around the issue. Each student generated a "tug" and wrote it on a piece of paper. Students then physically arranged themselves on a line drawn on the floor according to how strong they thought their tugs were. Starting from the center, students then read off their tugs, alternating between each side of the rope.

Assessment

The Tug-of-War routine provides multiple points of assessment: How does the class perceive or frame the issues? Are students able to capture the essence of complex dilemmas? How do they frame the opposing sides in a dilemma? Do they go back and forth between both sides of the dilemma, offering "Yeah but on the other hand..."? Students' responses to these tasks provide insight in to how they are navigating the complexity of issues.

While students are identifying tugs, note the supports students are able to articulate as significant for both sides. Are they able to step outside their own positions to consider the other side? Pay careful attention to the discussions around the placement of ideas. What do you notice regarding the reasoning and justification given for the placements? Are students putting forth qualifiers for their tugs and generating questions around them? What do students' "What if...?" questions reveal about what they see as key to advancing their understanding of the dilemma? At the end of the routine, are students able to articulate a richer understanding of the dilemma?

Tips

Be sure to identify a dilemma that is generative enough to foster student engagement and layered enough to generate multiple arguments. If students are not connected to or engaged with the dilemma, it will be difficult for them to do good thinking. At the same time, suspending quick judgment is vital to students' ability to look at the dilemma from opposing viewpoints and generate a variety of reasons that lend support to each side. A teacher may very well want to create a time and place for students to convey their sense of advocacy or share their stances on the dilemma, but it is important to hold off on that kind of conversation until a variety of viewpoints with supporting reasoning can be articulated, examined, and used to produce further questions to explore. Using the "I Used to Think...Now I Think..." routine after the Tug-of-War could be a useful way to return to original positions.

One advantage of using sticky notes for this routine is that "tugs" can be rearranged easily. If many of the students' tugs are similar, multiple reasons can be grouped together and relevant categories or themes for reasons become more apparent. This process can also be done on an interactive whiteboard and then printed out for future discussions. For instance, after the class's collective response has been documented, students could be invited individually to find a "tug" placement they disagree with and then discuss why.

A Picture of Practice

"This entire idea of making thinking visible attracted me right away," remarked Clair Taglauer from Traverse City, Michigan. "I really wanted to see what was going on in their minds," she said. The Tug-of-War thinking routine was a good fit for her middle school language art classes. It appealed to her desire to have students look at issues from multiple perspectives. Clair noticed that students often came to a conclusion quickly in their reading. Once that occurred, it was difficult for students to make further inferences from the text. Clair wanted students to be able to be more flexible in their thinking, add to it, expand it, and move it around. She wanted her students to tease apart some of the complexities embedded within issues they were reading about.

"I was drawn to the Tug-of-War routine because it seemed to be a tool for my students to work through a thought process. It seemed safe enough by not immediately requiring them to defend a particular stance. My students could change their thoughts and ideas around, give them shape, and keep open-minded about possibly conflicting perspectives," said Clair.

When her eighth graders began reading Lois Lowry's novel, *The Giver*, Clair thought it would be the perfect opportunity to make use of the Tug-of-War routine. The novel follows the main character, Jonas, through his twelfth year of life in a futuristic society that is at first presented as a utopian ideal and gradually appears more and more dystopian. This society seems to have achieved perfection by adopting a plan for "sameness" in which diversity and emotional depth have been eliminated. Clair recognized a dilemma that seemed to capture the attention of the middle school students: humankind's fascination with eternal happiness and an ideal, utopian society.

After her students had read much of Lowry's book, Clair drew a horizontal line across the length of her whiteboard and told her students they were going to have a tug-of-war. She drew upon earlier conversations she'd had with her students about this theme in *The Giver* and posed the question, both orally and in writing above the line she'd drawn on the whiteboard, "What would help achieve an ideal world?" Clair reminded students that Lois Lowry's text gives us ways of thinking about one side of this complex question and wrote on one side of the line, "If we were all the same . . ." Clair then said that, of course, there are others who would argue the opposing side and wrote at the other end of her line, "If we were all different . . ." Next Clair mentioned she did not want her students to pick one side or the other, but in small groups, generate possible reasons or "tugs" that would support both sides of this complex question. Clair suggested they come up with as many ideas as they could for each side, writing each reason on a different sticky note.

Once students had generated several reasons for each side of this debate, Clair invited her students to arrange their sticky notes according to their strongest reasons. "Just like you have an anchor person in a real tug-of-war, I want your group to place your reasons in the order that seems to be the best line-up, that makes the most sense in terms of strength of reasons."

As students conversed about the placement of their reasons, Clair listened in. She was both pleased and surprised to find herself becoming more aware of how students were interacting with the themes of the novel (see Figure 6.2). "I really got a glimpse into their own lives more than I expected," said Clair. "I started to see my kids' beliefs, fears, and anxieties so clearly as they discussed all that they had been reading and thinking about with their friends. For example, when students mentioned that 'sameness' like Lowry had written about could be ideal, they mentioned reasons such as that there would no longer be any teasing or people being bullied. It was such a natural way for students to bring their personal lives into our language arts classroom." Clair was also surprised by how well her students debated among themselves. Some agreed pretty quickly to disagree while others really changed their thinking based on what their classmates shared with them. "The Tug-of-War allowed them to articulate their thinking and rationale about a pretty complex concept, but it also kept them open to others' ideas that didn't exactly mirror their own. I was really pleased with that," said Clair.

Figure 6.2 Eighth Grade Tug-of-War About the Makings of an Ideal Society

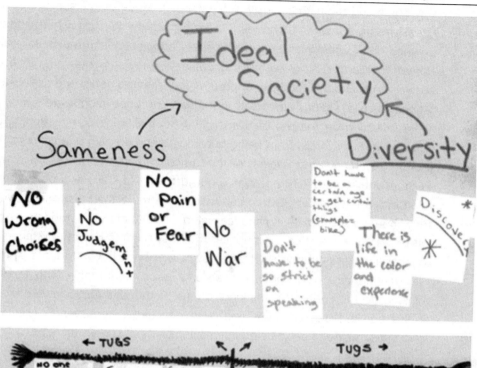

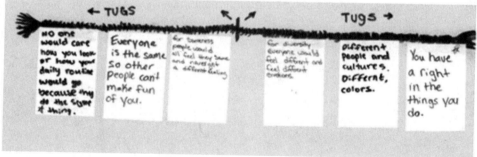

Clair has continued to make use of the Tug-of-War thinking routine on a variety of occasions. "Tug-of-War works so well in the language arts classroom. We're currently reading historical fiction and studying some concepts about slavery in conjunction with what my eighth graders are learning in their social studies class. I'm using Tug-of-War to structure conversation around the choices a young man at that time might have faced about whether he would join the Army and fight or stay home and protect his family. Also, stepping inside the perspective of a slave, I'm asking my students to consider, 'What would tug me to stay here and remain "owned" and what might tug me to flee along the Underground Railroad with Harriet Tubman?' It's not so much about having my students come to a correct answer as it's about creating an opportunity for them to notice and understand the rationale behind various viewpoints individuals or groups might have."

In reflecting on the use of this thinking routine, Clair commented, "For me, Tug-of-War has evolved from being one cool thing I do with one novel to filtering itself into so many other aspects of my curriculum and even across the curriculum to other subject areas. Tug-of-War is not just a set of steps or a procedure; it's a mindset—a real process. It transcends so much more than just one activity—it's truly about perspective taking and reasoning." Now that Clair's students are familiar with the thinking process, Clair notices that they seem to be better listeners to one another and can better articulate their own thinking with comfort and confidence. Clair mentioned, "You know, I've become more comfortable with this kind of thinking, too, by using this thinking routine. Some of the issues we come across at this age are big, complex, and even difficult...like slavery...like war. I've found this routine to be so helpful in making sense of sticky situations."

⚙ SENTENCE-PHRASE-WORD

In your discussion group, review the text that you have read and each select your own:

- *Sentence* that was meaningful to you, that you felt captures a core idea of the text
- *Phrase* that moved, engaged, or provoked you
- *Word* that captured your attention or struck you as powerful

As a group, *discuss* and *record* your choices. Begin by each sharing your words, then phrases, then sentences. Explain why you made the selections you did. Looking at your group's collective choices of words, phrases, and sentences, reflect on the conversation by identifying:

- What themes emerge?
- What implications or predications can be drawn?
- Were there aspects of the text not captured in your choices?

This routine is an adaption of the Text Rendering Experience developed by educators affiliated with the National School Reform Faculty. Having used this protocol—that is, a structure for a conversation—for discussing readings with other adults, we felt it had wide applicability for use in the classroom as both a discourse and a thinking routine. We liked the fact that something as simple as one's choice of a single word, phrase, and sentence forced one to think about big ideas and often led to rich discussions. Because we like to name routines by their thinking moves whenever we can, we changed the name to Sentence-Phrase-Word (SPW).

Purpose

Sentence-Phrase-Word helps learners to engage with and make meaning from text with a particular focus on capturing the essence of the text or "what speaks to you." It fosters enhanced discussion while drawing attention to the power of language. However, the power and promise of this routine lies in the discussion of why a particular word, a single phrase, and a sentence stood out for each individual in the group as the catalyst for rich discussion. It is in these discussions that learners must justify their choices and explain what it was that spoke to them in each of their choices. In doing so, individuals are often struck by how a single word can have the power of conveying the essence of a whole text. The discussion of sentence, phrase, and word choices sets the stage for considering themes, implications, predictions, and lessons to be drawn.

Selecting Appropriate Content

Choose a text that is rich in content, with ideas and concepts that invite interpretation and discussion. This can be fiction or nonfiction, but strictly informational texts may be difficult to discuss. The length of the text chosen is important in this routine. If it is too long, students will be more likely to skim it and not have the patience to read it carefully. An engaging chapter in a book, a professional reading that discusses problems of practice, a newspaper article, a poem, or a scene from a play can be used effectively with this routine.

Steps

1. *Set up.* Give learners time to read the selected text in advance of the discussion unless the text is short and can be read on the spot. Encourage active reading and highlighting of the text. However, it is not necessary to read with Sentence-Phrase-Word in mind.

2. *Select a sentence-phrase-word.* Ask learners to identify a sentence that is meaningful to them and helped them gain a deeper understanding of the text; a phrase that moved, engaged, provoked, or was in some way meaningful to them; and a word that has either captured their attention or struck them as powerful. It's important to be aware that each learner's experience will be reflected in the choice of words, phrases, and sentences. There are no correct answers.

3. *Share Selections.* In groups of four to six people, ask learners to each share and record their choices, explaining why they selected them. Sharing and discussion should occur in rounds, so that discussion is facilitated. The first participant shares her sentence and explains why she chose it, inviting others to comment and discuss. The sentence is recorded and then the next person shares, records, and discusses until everyone has shared his or her sentence. Then the group moves to phrases and finally words. This keeps the discussion flowing and deepening.

4. *Invite reflection on the conversation.* Each group looks at its documented responses. They identify the common themes that emerge from these responses and then the implications and/or predictions they suggested. Finally, the group identifies any aspects of the text that were not represented in their choice of sentences, phrases, and words.

5. *Share the thinking.* Post the documentation from all the groups. Provide time to look at the sentences, phrases, and words chosen and the themes and implications drawn. Invite each group member to reflect briefly on his or her current understanding of the text and how using the routine contributed to his or her understanding of it.

Uses and Variations

Teachers have found some surprising uses for SPW, from capturing the essence of a text students are studying for a test to developing language fluency in early childhood. In these adaptations, teachers sometimes focus on just a portion of the routine, combine small groups with whole-class use, or even use the "identify a part to stand for the whole" aspect of the routine for use with stimuli other than text. Adaptations can also be made in synthesizing the conversations. Although it is natural to pull out themes, you could also identify morals and messages or make predictions depending on the text. This diversity of uses is captured in the following brief examples from teachers at Bialik College and elsewhere.

- After reading articles in history classes, teacher Sharonne Blum finds that the sentences, phrases, and words her grades 9 and 10 students choose provide wonderful springboards for discussion as they search for commonalities and discuss the differences and the interpretations they have made for each.

- When Josie Singer wants her grade 8 English classes to review novels they have recently read, she groups the students in pairs, allocates a chapter to each pair, and asks them to complete a Sentence-Phrase-Word. Josie then goes around the class, commencing with the pair who reviewed the first chapter. Each pair gives a quick recap of the chapter using the sentence, phrase, and word they have selected and the reasons for their choices.

- Although we thought this routine was strictly text based, preschool teacher Lindsay Miller adapted Sentence-Phrase-Word for her pre-readers using individual pages in picture storybooks and asking her four-year-old students to look carefully at the page, choose one thing on the page that they thought was really important and then one small section of the page, and explain how and why they made those choices.

- Also working with young children, a first grade teacher in Merrill, Michigan, has his students collectively nominate sentences, phrases, and words after read-alouds. He records this collection to read back to students at a later date, asking them to guess which story the responses are from.

Assessment

The individual sentence, phrase, and word choice usually will not tell you much about how students are making sense of the text. However, the explanations learners provide for their selection of sentences, phrases, and words can say a lot about what they are taking from the text and what struck them as important. Is the reasoning behind these choices showing that learners have been able to capture the essence of the text? Are learners identifying significant concepts and issues or are they staying peripheral? What kinds of personal connections lie behind the choices?

In the discussions, look for students to make connections with others' responses rather than merely focusing on their own contributions. Are learners able to use the sentences, phrases, and words as springboards for discussion? Do these discussions go back to the text to deepen and enrich the discussion?

Tips

While this routine asks for three specific choices, it is not always essential to complete all three steps to achieve the purpose. Particularly with younger children, as shown in Lindsay's example, the use of the two steps—sentence and word—can be very effective. It is also fine to reverse the order of the routine, starting with the selection of a word, then a phrase, then a sentence. In fact, some teachers have found that discussions that begin with word choices and then move to phrases and sentences build more naturally. You may want to try it both ways and see what you notice.

To aid discussion, it is important to document the evolving conversation. A simple three-column division of a large piece of chart paper works well for this purpose. Underneath those three columns you can draw three horizontal rows for groups to identify themes, implications, and what was in the text that was not represented in learners' choices. However, don't let the recording of responses distract the group from conversing about the choices and ideas. When an individual shares his or her selection, he or she should reference the page and paragraph from which it came so that others can find and read it in context. Having the group's sentences, phrases, and words in front of them captures the conversation and makes it easier to discern themes, implications, and what might be missing.

A Picture of Practice

When Lisa Verkerk wanted her fifth graders at the International School of Amsterdam to better understand the human impact of the slave trade, she selected the book *From Slave Ship to Freedom Road,* written by Julius Lester with paintings by Rod Brown, as the vehicle. "This is a very interesting book," commented Lisa. "The paintings were first created by Rod Brown, and when Julius Lester saw them exhibited, he asked if he could write a story to accompany them. However, the text, though only a single page for each image, is rather challenging for my students."

To deal with both the richness of the images and the complexity of the text, Lisa decided to separate the book into a selection of individual images with their accompanying text. This would allow small groups of students to look at the images, help each other in reading the text, and then fully discuss a section of the book. Following this small-group work, Lisa planned to call the class together to share their sections and collaboratively build an understanding of the story.

To begin, Lisa shows the class one of the paintings, and together they use the See-Think-Wonder routine to begin to make sense of it. Lisa tells the class, "We've used See-Think-Wonder many times, and I want you to begin to look at the image your group has using that. Really examine it and discuss it. They are beautiful pictures, and they tell their own stories. I think you will see why Julius Lester was so captivated by them. And then, once you're done with that, you can read the text together. We're going to use a new routine to explore the text. It is Sentence-Phrase-Word."

Although Lisa had first experienced this routine as Word-Phrase-Sentence, she realized that her students in past years seemed to find it easier to select one important sentence that summed up the big idea, then a phrase that supported it, and last one important word. She explains to students, "After you have read, and you may need to read it more than once, I want each person in the group to select one sentence. It will be a sentence that you feel really captures a big idea in the text. What is it that you think Julius Lester wants you to take away? And then, you will select a phrase. Now the phrase shouldn't be part of the sentence. Try to find a new one. One that helps you gain a deeper understanding of the text. And then finally, choose your word. A word that strikes you as powerful or important."

Because this book study is situated within a larger unit called "Different People, Different Lives," Lisa wants her students to focus on the themes and implications from the text. "Our unit is contemporary," Lisa adds, "and I want to see if students can make connections between a story that happened a long time ago and some of the issues that are present in our world today."

Lisa assigns groups and hands out the individual pages of the book. What follows is a period of intense and purposeful discussion, each group completely absorbed in their pages. Students make careful observations, discussing what they see. Stopping in at a group, Lisa encourages students to ask each other, "What makes you say that?" as they begin to interpret the paintings.

Once Lisa feels that individual groups have thoroughly looked at the images, she encourages them to read the text aloud to each other. It is not long before students are heard deliberating over their choices of sentences, phrases, and words and justifying their choices to their peers. After each student's response has been recorded, the groups move to discuss the themes and implications, making connections to present-day world events. Students have spent close to 90 minutes working, and Lisa collects the pages of the book and students' documentation for the day. You can watch this initial exploration of the book using these two routines on the DVD. As you watch, pay attention to the level of engagement the combination of rich content and the facilitative structure of the routines enables.

The next day, students are eager to share their thinking with the rest of the class. Lisa displays each picture on the interactive whiteboard so that everyone can take a few minutes to look carefully before the groups present. Lisa then asks the group to give a one-sentence summary of what is happening at this stage of the story before sharing their sentences, phrases, and words. Lisa documents these on chart paper for everyone to see. The class and teacher question individuals, asking them why they thought a sentence was so important or why they chose that word. Last, the group shares the themes and implications that they found significant, which are also documented on separate charts. Page by page, the students jointly build their understanding of the story, distilling the essence of the story through the sentences, phrases, and words; recognizing the important themes that the artist and author wanted their audience to think about; and finally making a connection from the past to the present.

Reflecting on the learning, Lisa comments, "Students are often filled with awe at what they achieve. They feel, and quite rightly, that they have made some important discoveries. They have developed a much more comprehensive understanding of the story of the slave trade than if I had just read the book to them. And, they are connecting to the contemporary issues they have heard about on the news or at the dinner table."

At the end of the week, the class returns to the Themes and Implications charts Lisa has left on the wall of the classroom. She reads through all of the ideas that surfaced, discussing them some more. Lisa asks her students to consider which themes or implications stand out for them; which are personally significant, powerful, or important; and which they would like to reflect upon in their painted reflection journals, another routine Lisa has established in her classroom (read more about this in Chapter Seven).

Lisa puts on acoustic music and students quickly get to work. At the end of the painting session the students roam around looking carefully at each other's paintings and reading the written reflections that accompany them. They comment on things they like, similarities of ideas or significant differences, what surprises them, and so on. Often something precious and previously private has been revealed, leading the class to a sense of deep personal sharing. Lisa believes that in these moments of collaboration, self-discovery, honesty, and openness, the relationships that will sustain a culture of thinking in a classroom are developed and nurtured. "One of the reasons I find the routines so effective is that they help the students to find their own voices and to value and respect the voices of others."

PART THREE

BRINGING THE POWER OF VISIBLE THINKING TO LIFE

CHAPTER 7

Creating a Place Where Thinking Is Valued, Visible, and Actively Promoted

As you read through the thinking routines presented in Part Two of this book, we hope you got a good sense of how they can be used to support understanding and make thinking visible across a variety of circumstances, groupings, and content areas. At the same time, the Picture of Practice accompanying each routine likely extended your thinking about how to situate thinking routines into the fabric of effective instruction so that they are much more than just activities. From these stories of how a routine played out over time for a teacher and his or her students, you may have gotten a sense that for any thinking routine to take hold and be a vehicle for promoting the development of students as thinkers and learners, something more than just having a go and trying out the routine is required. Indeed, although any of the routines presented may play well as a stand-alone activity *once*, their continued use and development as patterns of behavior takes some ongoing effort by teachers and group leaders. It is no accident that many of the Pictures of Practice come from classrooms at Bialik College and other schools where we have been working extensively over several years to both understand and build a powerful culture of thinking. It is in such environments that thinking routines and other visible thinking strategies truly flourish. In this chapter, the process of developing patterns of thinking is explored and the broader context of creating a culture of thinking examined.

In the Cultures of Thinking project, we define *cultures of thinking* as "places where a group's collective as well as individual thinking is valued, visible, and actively promoted as part of the regular, day-to-day experience of all group members." It is worthwhile to point out several aspects of this definition to gain a clearer sense of what exactly it captures and delineates. First, you may have noticed the use of the word *places* rather than *classrooms*. Any time a group of people come together where learning and intellectual growth are identified as part of the group's mission, there is the opportunity to create a culture of thinking. This can be in a classroom or a boardroom, a book club or a museum tour, a committee meeting or a study group.

Creating a Place Where Thinking Is Valued, Visible, and Actively Promoted **219**

Next, the definition mentions "a group's collective as well as individual thinking." Thinking is generally considered an individual endeavor that takes place within the mystery of the individual's mind. However, without the benefit of others, our thinking would be severely curtailed. Our individual thinking benefits from being challenged, from the need to articulate ideas clearly and concisely to others, from the presentation of alternative perspectives and insights through others' presentation of logic, the raising of questions, and so on. Furthermore, what we are able to achieve as a group by way of problem solving, decision making, and understanding is usually far greater than what can be achieved by the individual alone. To be sure, there are many inspiring examples of individual achievements that demonstrate the heights of accomplishment; however, throughout history the human race has relied on the efforts of groups more frequently and directly to conquer its challenges. As creativity expert Sir Ken Robinson (2010) says, "Most great learning happens in groups. Collaboration is the stuff of growth. If we atomize people and separate them and judge them separately we form a kind of disjunction between them and their natural learning environment." Therefore, within a culture of thinking we want to harness the power of the group to advance general thinking while recognizing the contributions and growth of each individual.

The subsequent part of the cultures of thinking definition states that thinking must be "valued, visible, and actively promoted." One would be hard-pressed to find an educational enterprise that says it does *not* value thinking. It is a bit like mothers and apple pie; everyone feels obligated to be in support. However, for something to be truly valued it has to be well articulated and identifiable. As was mentioned in Chapter One, *thinking* as a word is so widely used and encompasses so many different cognitive activities that its meaning isn't always clear. To value thinking, one has to unpack it and identify what it entails in any given situation. One must then lay claim to those kinds of thinking one deems valuable and worth promoting. Rather than say, "We value thinking here," leaders of any group need to articulate the kinds of thinking that they value. Only then can efforts be employed to make that thinking visible. Throughout this book, practices that support visibility have been presented, such as questioning, listening, documenting, and using thinking routines. This visibility gives us a window into how students are making sense of ideas. As we are not content merely to gaze through this window, visibility also gives us the toehold from which we can support and promote that thinking, advancing it and, with it, students' understanding.

"As part of the regular, day-to-day experience." This part of the definition of a culture of thinking echoes Vygotsky's (1978) idea that "children grow into the intellectual life around them" (p. 88). If we want to promote a culture of thinking, we must surround students with thinking, not as a one-off activity that we engage in on special occasions but in the day-in, day-out, ordinariness of the classroom. A darker side to Vygotsky's quote is offered by Robert L. Fried (2005) in his book *The Game of School,* in which he both recognizes and criticizes the fact that too often and in too many places students don't so much learn as they learn to play the game of school. Often this is a game that requires mastering techniques for committing ideas to short-term memory but very little real thinking. These sentiments are a recurring theme in the aptly titled 2010 documentary *Race to Nowhere,* directed by Vicki Abeles and Jessica Congdon, in which the voices of students from across the United States who feel they are working for grades and not learning at their schools are chronicled. If we want to reverse this situation and develop students as thinkers and learners, then the expectations for thinking must be present on a daily basis.

Finally, in closing out this examination of the cultures of thinking definition, one must take notice of the fact that it concludes with "of all group members." Too often thinking has been seen as the exclusive domain of gifted or advanced students. How often have we heard teachers utter, or ourselves express, the notion that until students have the basics they can't be expected to think, to learn, to achieve, to excel? However, this notion is fundamentally flawed, as it assumes that one is not always a thinker or that by neglecting thinking and engaging students in mindless rote memorization a teacher will somehow produce students who will be able to think at some later date. In fact the opposite is true: when teachers lament the fact that their students are not thinking, it is often precisely because they have been taught not to think or told, often implicitly through the kinds of work they have been assigned, that they cannot think. During the past ten years in our work with teachers in the Visible Thinking and Cultures of Thinking projects, one consistent observation has occurred at every school where our team has worked: when thinking becomes part of the daily practice of the classroom and teachers show an interest in and respect for students' thinking, then students who had not previously been seen as academically strong begin to shine. When school is no longer about the quick right answer but focuses on the expression of one's ideas, questions, and observations, then a new playing field is created for all students. Does this upset those good at the game of school? At first it may, but with time those students too learn a new game that is much more engaging and worthwhile to play.

This definition of a culture of thinking as places where a group's collective as well as individual thinking is valued, visible, and actively promoted as part of the regular, day-to-day experience of all group members stands as a goal for educators to work toward rather than a state that is ever perfectly achieved. Even after six years of work at Bialik College, the development of a culture of thinking is still seen as an ongoing goal that must be revisited every year with each change in school personnel and shift in leadership. It continually must be built up and nurtured. It is never something that can be taken for granted, as the creation of any group culture is ongoing and evolving in nature, constructed over time with the active participation and input of those in the group.

To understand this process and how we might more directly affect it, three cases of group learning are presented here for exploration: the first from Lisa Verkerk's classroom at the International School of Amsterdam; the second a cross-school group of teachers from the Ithaka Project in Melbourne, Australia, directed by Julie Landvogt; and the third a museum tour conducted by Dara Cohen at the Museum of Modern Art in New York City. A fourth case of a professional learning group at Bialik College can be found on the DVD. While each of these cases makes use of thinking routines and other efforts to support the visibility of thinking, they also illuminate the much larger surround that must be leveraged to foster engaged, active, and independent learners and thinkers. Taken together, these cases provide readers with a feel for how a thinking culture can be effectively built. Following the presentation of these case studies, the significant forces that shape all cultures of thinking are identified and discussed.

Case Study: Making Room for Reflection
(written with Lisa Verkerk)

In 2001, Lisa Verkerk joined thirty-nine other international educators from Europe for a week at the Harvard Graduate School of Education in Cambridge, Massachusetts, to explore what it means to teach for understanding. Throughout the week the teachers read, discussed, and planned units that focused on developing students' understanding using the Teaching for Understanding framework (Blythe & Associates, 1998). While these activities engaged Lisa as a new teacher and forced her to think differently about her unit planning, one experience from the week stood out for her in particular. Every day, when the group of teachers arrived to the workshop setting, they were asked to reflect on their own developing understanding of understanding. Starting rather than ending the day with reflection was certainly novel, but it was the means of reflection that caught Lisa's attention and engaged her as a learner. At the beginning of the week, each participant was given an artist's sketchbook and was asked to create a visual metaphor that represented what understanding meant to her or him. In a quiet atmosphere punctuated only by the sounds of classical music, participants were provided with a collection of colored pencils, watercolors, crayons, pastels, and collage materials and a half-hour to create their visual metaphors.

This initial exploration into visual reflections and metaphorical thinking was certainly engaging for Lisa, but it was the opportunity to revisit the central idea of understanding each day, to reflect anew and integrate current thinking and puzzles, to allow oneself to think through art, and to create abstract metaphors with deep personal meaning that had the deepest impact on Lisa as a learner. Lisa was struck by how powerful this nonwritten form of reflection could be. Although the use of writing and words weren't forbidden, they tended to be useful in amplifying the visual rather than replacing it. Furthermore, the open-ended use of materials had a unique way of allowing ideas to flow in ways they didn't always seem to do in purely written reflections. With the visual, there wasn't necessarily a beginning or end. The thinking was nonlinear. By the end of the week, Lisa knew that she wanted this same kind of experience for her fifth grade students. "I had so enjoyed the experience of using the painted reflection journals, but I was also aware that some colleagues had not particularly liked the experience, feeling that they could not draw or paint, so I was aware that it might be difficult for my students at the start," Lisa observed.

Back in Amsterdam, Lisa requisitioned a set of art sketchbooks for each of her students for the new school year and began the process of building up a collection of art materials. Lisa knew that setting aside time each day for painted reflections wasn't even remotely feasible with her schedule. At the same time, she knew that if she didn't make a regular commitment to the reflection process, then her students would be unlikely to experience the power of thinking through art that she had. Her compromise was to set aside 45 minutes each week for the painted reflections. "This meant that it was honored and given time," Lisa remarked.

In that first session, Lisa began the reflection period by telling her students the story of her own learning through reflection and her plan to use the painted reflection journals throughout the year as a way of regularly reflecting on their learning. She also laid down some ground rules, telling students that this would be a quiet time and that she would put on some music to help them concentrate. She explained that the reflections would be private if students didn't want to share them. However, after the reflection time, students who were willing to share could simply leave their books open and the class would have the opportunity to walk around and see one another's painted reflections. For this initial launch, Lisa chose the topic of "friendship" for students' reflection. At an international school, where often as many as 30 percent of students could be new in any given year, the topic of making and being friends was always close to the surface. She asked her students to think about "What does it mean to be a good friend and why do friends matter?" and then to reflect upon those ideas in their painted reflections. Lisa joined her students, this day and in subsequent times, in painting her own reflections.

"The students responded really well," Lisa noted. "I have a lot of non-native speakers of English and I know they appreciated the fact that they could begin to express their ideas without having to use English." Over time, Lisa noticed how these students seemed to blossom during the painted reflection time. "These students love the freedom of this activity, that there are no rights or wrongs, words are for once less important than artistic creativity. After a while they find the words too, but at the start it is the experience of painting that helps them to make the connections, even if we cannot talk about it together."

Lisa continued the regular reflection time each week. Slowly she noticed a change in students' paintings. "In the beginning, some students wanted to represent their ideas in literal pictures, drawing stick people, houses, cars and whatever," Lisa observed. "If they couldn't draw very well then they became blocked. Some of these students then found it difficult to express their ideas in writing after painting, giving only a simple or superficial reflection." To address this issue, Lisa pointed out that this was not about being a good painter or drawer or creating nice pictures but rather a time to express ideas in a different way using materials. She emphasized that she herself was not an artist but found that when she didn't have to try and draw things but could use lines, symbols, and colors to represent her thinking that it freed her in trying to express herself. "I encouraged everyone to try making an abstract painted reflection, so that they wouldn't get restricted by trying to draw literal images. Still, I noticed that it was difficult for some students. I would see common themes of colors and patterns in the table groups," Lisa noted.

Eager to try and advance students' reflective thinking, Lisa decided to formally introduce her students to the idea of metaphors, the idea that one thing could stand for something else or one thing could be used to illuminate another. "I told them that I sometimes feel like my life is a merry-go-round and asked them to think about why I might make that comparison," Lisa explained. The class then talked about the features of the merry-go-round—that it goes around, that things go up and down, there are lights and music, that at first it seems fun but sometimes it goes too fast, you get dizzy and eventually you want to get off, and so on—and made connections to these literal aspects of a merry-go-round and life. Lisa then took the idea of metaphor a bit further: "I explained about visual metaphors, which are in many ways much easier to paint, as the colors, textures, lines, shapes, and movements tell the story in the mind of the artist." She also talked about how color might represent a feeling or emotion or how even a shape might not represent something directly but might stand for some idea. "Again, I asked my students to just try making an abstract painting," Lisa commented.

Over the years, Lisa has come to recognize this movement from the literal to the abstract as a normal transition period for her students. One that she takes note of and actively seeks to advance but at the same time is perfectly natural and expected. "Now I find every year that we reach the six-week point and miraculously every painting is unique. Everyone now understands how this works; they have their own ideas to paint about and their own way of doing that. Students start to thoroughly enjoy the process and to share more of their ideas and themselves in the written reflection."

Drawing on her own experience, Lisa was aware that the power of any reflective experience is largely dependent on the object of reflection. She had spent a week at Harvard reading, discussing, and exploring what it means to teach and learn for understanding and time reflecting was an opportunity to synthesize and consolidate what she was learning. To make the reflection journals something that would really push students' thinking and advance their understanding, Lisa recognized that she couldn't just ask students to reflect and then give them some paints and expect great things to happen. She had to think carefully about what she wanted students to think about and how these intense moments of reflection would connect to the opportunities she provided for in-depth study. Consequently, Lisa began to look for those learning moments that might benefit from reflecting through art. She found natural opportunities in the class's reading, often reflecting on the core themes of a book. One example of this was presented as a Picture of Practice for Sentence-Phrase-Word in Chapter Six. Lisa also found opportunities in the class's study of poetry, expressing through painting the meaning of a poem the class had studied.

Lisa also found the essential questions and central ideas from her social studies units were rich topics for sustained reflection. For instance, at the start of a unit on migration, she asks students to reflect on the following questions: "What does home mean to you? How does it feel? What do you value about it?" Midway through the unit, the class reads various stories about forced migration and studies the plight of refugees. At the end of this unit, students reflect on a set of questions to consolidate their learning: "What were the most significant things that you learned about in our migration unit? What will you take away and remember as important?" (See Figure 7.1.)

As the first-year experiment with painted reflections progressed in Lisa's room, so did the students' engagement with the process. It became an important part of the week and one to which students looked forward. "If we had to miss it due to a special event, such as sports day, my students would ask that we still find the time by missing out on something else, which we often did," Lisa stated. At the same time, Lisa observed how important the modeling of both reflection and the use of metaphors were to students' development. "After each session we walk around looking at the paintings and reading the written reflections. Students ask each other questions and afterward point out things that they like or are interested in. It is in this way that they develop the confidence to let their

Figure 7.1 Student's Painted Reflection on Migration

minds run all over the topic, to make connections to their own lives, to express their feelings, beliefs, and values," Lisa shared. "Each week they write more and more to explain their paintings. Sometimes we share very personal things that we would have no reason to discuss in other situations. We make an agreement that what we share in our reflection journals is personal, so to make that safe we should not speak about another person's reflections outside of the classroom. Students find it fascinating to see the different perspectives people have about the same topic or theme, and gradually they begin to trust and value their own perspectives."

Lisa also recognized the important role that her own modeling plays in students' valuing of reflection. "The important word here is *honesty*. My students see me sitting very quietly, often with my eyes closed. I become completely absorbed and excited about the materials and how the picture is unfolding and then I write, sometimes all over the picture or at odd angles. So my exploring encourages them to be more adventurous too. I am totally honest, and although I am writing from an adult perspective, my reflection still connects to what we have been exploring together in class. So I trust them with my honesty. Maybe that gives them the courage to be vulnerable too? I talk about how this activity helps me to focus in on what really matters to me, and they see how much I really enjoy doing it. We take our time to share and discuss each reflection, so valuing the rich thinking, and learning from each other's perspectives. This sends a clear message, that I think pausing in our busy day and taking time to reflect matters."

By the end of the school year, Lisa's students came to value this weekly time so much that many remarked they would continue the process of painting their reflections on their own at home. Most students felt it really added to the development of their understanding and learning. Danniyal commented on his process of reflecting through painting by saying, "When I am painting my reflections, sometimes I just go on and then when I am in the flow then I start saying, yeah I can put this down which represents this and I can put this down that connects to that." Several other students also recognized the notion of flow and how the act of painting could advance and promote thinking. Henny observed of himself, "Usually I don't think deep enough or understand it totally but when you start painting or drawing it helps. You write a bit and you draw, and you think much deeper." Alex echoed these sentiments, saying, "You get a deeper understanding of what you are painting, and you can make more connections and then you can paint about that."

Leor Zmigrod, a non-native English speaker, shared how painting helped her express her thinking: "It is much easier to paint than to speak the words out for your ideas. And then I can look at it and see more things that I have learned and what I know." She even painted her understanding of how her limited proficiency with English was often a barrier to her expression and understanding. Her representation of a brick wall holding back a world of ideas is shown in Figure 7.2.

Now, several years along the path of doing painted reflections with her students, Lisa reflects on what this routine has come to mean to both her and her students. "The time we share doing this is very special. We all enjoy the process: the soft music, the lovely materials. It is as if we are stealing a little time for ourselves in what can often be a hectic day, moving around to different classrooms all over the school. The activity asks us to engage with the emotional self, a part of us that we often keep hidden. The sharing of that self bonds us together, we develop a deeper level of respect and understanding. In this activity there is no competition; no one is

Figure 7.2 Leor's "Brick Wall" Painting

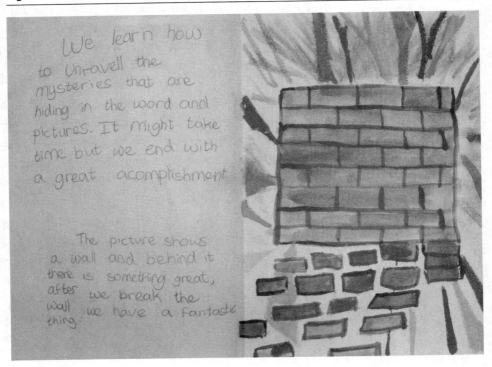

more correct; no one scores higher. We are all equal." Lisa feels the time she spends developing this pattern of behavior in her classroom each year helps students to be better thinkers as well. "Learning to truly listen to another, to try to understand their point of view, however different to your own, is an essential part of creating an effective culture of thinking. If we can do that then we can truly think and learn collaboratively. I have a favorite instructional throughline that I use each year, 'Why is thinking together more powerful than thinking alone?' It may take a few months, but eventually a student each year will eventually quote that back to me—it's a moment that always makes me smile."

Case Study: Making Time for Our Own Learning
(written with Julie Landvogt)

It's 7:00 A.M. on a dark winter's morning halfway through the Australian school year. Coffee is brewing and the croissants are warm as teachers, arriving from their homes across the city, greet one another and exchange news of the last month. This is a chance to reconnect with teachers from other schools whom they have not seen since the last meeting prior to the official start of the workday. The choice of the beginning of the day—or really, prior to the beginning of the day—has been critical to the group's success. People are not yet caught up in the demands of the day; they have made a commitment to set this time for looking beyond the urgent to better understand the bigger issues competing for their attention.

The context of these meetings is the latest phase, and sixth year, of the Ithaka Project, a loose network of teachers from eight Melbourne-area schools interested in improving learning by thinking about pedagogy, curriculum, and assessment. Central to the group's explorations has been the lure of the concept of intellectual character (Ritchhart, 2001, 2002). While not everyone attending the Breakfast Group has been part of the Ithaka Project for its duration, there is nonetheless a common set of understandings and behaviors. Most important, the group has attracted teachers who understand that there are no simple recipes for effective learning and teaching, and that there is always more to learn.

It's 7:30, and everyone has found his or her group and settled in, coffee or tea in hand. There is no need for announcements, preliminaries, or admonitions from the group's convener, Julie Landvogt. This is the fourth meeting. By now the format is familiar and an easy rhythm sets in. There is a buzz of discussion as groups of six delve into the ideas found in this month's reading, "When Good People Turn Bad," an interview with the psychologist Philip Zimbardo, designer of the Stanford Prison Experiment. Each of these small discussion groups consists of six people and is constant for each meeting. Everyone, including Julie, belongs to two groups for the year. The first group, "In Conversation," is concerned with big ideas, and the second group is for more school-based dialogue, which this year is underpinned by sharing of practices and readings about formative assessment.

Each group's consistency means relationships are developed with a number of people, nurturing a sense of commitment to the group. One's absence is both noticed and felt as there is a sense that the diverse perspectives represented in each group—teachers, administrators, mathematicians, artists, and so on—are vital to the group's exploration of ideas in full. This bond didn't just happen by chance, however; it was part of Julie's deliberate planning. "My intention was that this group would function as a think tank, a critical friends network, and a forum for an open and tentative trying out of ideas. I knew this could only be possible if we came to know one another through the common shared experience of the sessions." Julie believed this required people to make and sustain a commitment to the group, something she understood could sometimes be an uphill battle in schools, what with last-minute meetings and emergencies. Still, she made her intent unmistakable to the prospective members of the group at the outset. In her letter of invitation, she was clear that community and continuity were vital and wrote, "Please do not commit to this group if you know you will have to leave 15 minutes early, or if you know you will not be able to attend all sessions."

7:45. The groups' discussions are moving ahead at a lively pace and on a level at which any teacher or facilitator would be envious. Discussion is often punctuated by the sound of typing of the group's documenter, a rotating role within the group. One factor at work here is that a pattern of behavior and interaction has been cultivated through the use of routines. Conversation is guided by the 4C's routine (see Chapter Five) in which the group is asked to identify Connections, key Concepts, points to Challenge or debate, and suggested actions or Changes of behavior that they find in and take from the reading. The routine adds a structure to the conversations that is known in advance and provides each reader with various points of entry into the conversation. To make sure all 4C's get their airtime, each group has a facilitator, a role that rotates each session.

Today's reading promotes connections to the behavior of the guards at Abu Ghraib prison in Iraq and discussions of group behavior, norms, and peer pressure. These connections segue into life at schools and the effects of the peer pressure students feel as well as the norms that get established among teachers. The key concepts of culture, expectations, values, and interactions are discussed, which leads to an exploration of the challenge of living one's values and the changes educators might make. As one teacher put it, "If we don't have structures in place to support our values, then we won't get the best out of students. Too often schools concentrate on fixing behaviors rather than putting in place strategies that might prevent them from occurring in the first place." Another voice in the group picks up this theme: "As teachers, our identity is often formed by the institutions we work at. They sway what we do and cause us to take certain things for granted as just the acceptable way of doing things. We can get lulled into group behavior as well."

It is a lively and far-reaching discussion lasting just 30 minutes and informed by more than the reading for today. The group has a history, a common base of reading and talking, of shared ideas and roles that all surface. Consequently, it is not surprising that the group makes connections to the building of culture even though the reading didn't directly address this issue. The group's conversation often refers back to previous thinking and forward to the future in this way. In prior sessions, the groups have considered ideas such as Julian Savulescu's work *Stronger, Smarter, Nicer Humans* or Matt Ridley's *What Makes Us Human?* What is unusual here is that these readings do not connect directly to the working life of schools, but as with all big ideas, associations appear—to surprise, challenge, and delight—as conversation progresses.

It's 8:00, and there is an opportunity to refill cups with the caffeine of choice and take a second croissant. As people take their seats at their second group for the morning, Mary and Angela come forward for the "In My School, We..." section of the morning. It is their turn today to share what is happening in their school: a 10-minute snapshot of current thinking and progress in formative assessment practices and professional learning, with a focus on successes and challenges. They invite feedback, which is given openly and honestly, as was their story of practice. This is not a "show and tell" or a "look at me" exercise but a chance to think aloud with peers, get ideas, and share disappointments as well as triumphs. Suggestions given by colleagues are noticeable for their conditional language—"You might try...," "What I'm hearing is...," "I wonder if..."—rather than an opportunity

Creating a Place Where Thinking Is Valued, Visible, and Actively Promoted   **231** to start a story about one's own work. As such, there is a sense that the group is learning with and from one another. This makes sharing the challenges and out-and-out failures much easier, as there is no judgment, just another opportunity to learn. Over the year, each of the eight schools participating in the network takes a turn to reflect on the connection between the readings and their lives in school, their stories bridging the theoretical and practical.

It's 8:15, and the second discussion of the morning begins. Its format is the same as for the first: constant group for the year, rotating and pre-decided facilitators and scribes, pre-reading and a routine to structure the discourse; this time Connection-Extend-Challenge (CEC). Today's discussion is stimulated by a choice of related readings on the nature of feedback, from which participants have chosen a practical article from Susan Brookhart entitled "Feedback That Fits"; a more psychologically based article on "The Promise and Perils of Praise" by Carol Dweck; or "The Goals of Differentiation" by Carol Ann Tomlinson, focusing on big picture issues. Although everyone in the group won't have read the exact same article, the diversity of stimulus readings encourages connection making, comparison, and further questions. The facilitator uses the CEC protocol to keep debate moving between the findings of research and the particulars of the daily life of classrooms while avoiding the temptation teachers often have to simply tell others, "The way I do it is..."

Almost immediately the connections are flying. People reading Brookhart's article on effective feedback immediately acknowledge that they often are guilty of feedback that simply summarizes rather than moves the learning forward. Those reading Dweck make a connection to students they are teaching now who seem to view themselves as incremental or entity learners. "You can see it in how they respond to difficulties. Those that see intelligence as fixed are so quick to say they just aren't good at it, whatever it is." Alan Bliss, head of history in the middle school at Melbourne Grammar, makes a connection between Brookhart's article and the pressures that senior school teachers feel in preparing students for the Victorian Certificate of Education (VCE) exam, postulating, "We might learn something from them about how they give targeted and formative feedback to students."

As discussion continues, the group's facilitator moves them to think about extensions to their thinking and an interesting observation arises spontaneously from the group. Linda Shardlow, head of mathematics at Methodist Ladies College (MLC), begins talking about the power of awareness and noticing. Soon others are chiming in, "To give good feedback, you have to take time and notice. You have to be more deliberate." Alan adds, "And students have to be aware of themselves as learners too and know how the brain is malleable." Warrick Wynne, director of learning at MLC, then brings up the challenge of report writing and puts out the question, "How might reports better reflect the learning we value? It seems that if we involve students in learning we value and then involve them in reflecting on their own learning, progress might be more beneficial in the long term."

The articles certainly provide good content for discussion and ample opportunities for teachers to think about connections to the classroom. This accounts for some of the liveliness in these discussions. At the same time, the conversations are not a free-for-all. The Connect-Extend-Challenge routine provides both a structure and a sense of freedom. It dictates focus. It gives permission to linger yet still demands moving on. Thus, each conversation has a sense of direction both individually and collectively.

At 8:45 the gathering comes together briefly to share notices of coming events of interest and to hear the focus for the next meeting. Ten minutes remain for discussion in school groups—to share perspectives, consider how the morning's discussion illuminates or challenges or extends the issues facing their particular context. Many of these conversations will continue on the drive or walk back to school or be picked up in the coming weeks in various administrative and department meetings. By 9:00 A.M. people are off, most able to be in their schools by the beginning of the second period of the day. So much has happened in this brief 90 minutes. As outside observers, we are both exhausted and energized. In much professional learning there is less expected of teachers in terms of contribution and behavior than they would expect from students in their classes, but this is not the case at the Breakfast Group. The group takes seriously the importance of being learners and thinkers. At the same time, there is recognition of what the group offers and the rarity of these kinds of professionally rich conversations.

Alma Tooke, head of visual arts at MLC, acknowledges and laments this fact. "It is unfortunate that we don't have research time in schools. We seem to do so many 'busy' things that have no effect on teaching and learning. . . . I hope we can retain this group going forward. I love education and this is the only time we really spend on trying to improve our practice." Kate Rice, a grade 6 teacher at Westbourne Grammar, agrees and says she really values "the opportunity to stop, think, reflect and discuss ideas that are central to everything I do each day as well as the challenge of being critical of what I do and how I do it." Kate acknowledges that the discussions of the Breakfast Group create some confusion at times, but they also force her "to consider what is worth keeping and what needs discarding in my personal practice and also on a wider scale in our school."

As the convener, if not leader, of the group, Julie can't help but smile at these reflections. The Breakfast Group was a bit of a calculated risk. She wanted to create a stimulating atmosphere for her own and others' professional learning that didn't put her constantly in the center. "The core idea underpinning this group is that in order for schools to be places of thinking for children, they must also be places of thinking for adults: something Ron Ritchhart talks a lot about. The goal has been to support people leading constructive dialogue in schools by providing them opportunities to engage with key issues current in education, share what is happening in different schools for constructive feedback, and read, think, and talk about ideas current in wider society. Of course one has to be realistic about what we can consider in 90 minutes. These sessions are a kind of 'taster' of key issues current in education; there is some theory, some stories of application, and some bigger picture ideas to keep our eyes on the horizon." She even named the group to reflect this sentiment, calling it the BFG network after Roald Dahl's book in which a Big Friendly Giant captures good dreams and blows them into the windows of sleeping children. Although not peddling in dreams, Julie recognizes that good ideas and rich professional discussions are out there and just need a little help to blow them into the lives of teachers and schools.

Case Study: The Making of an Elaborated Conversation

54th Street is alive with the honking of horns in midtown traffic as an iconic yellow school bus turns off Sixth Avenue and pulls up alongside the Museum of Modern Art (MoMA) in Manhattan. A group of seventh and eighth graders tumble out of the metal hulk of a vehicle and onto the sidewalk. It's time away from school, and the students' energy and talkativeness is an indication that they are clearly savoring the freedom a field trip offers from the classroom. Museum educators such as Dara Cohen are well aware that both students and teachers often focus on this motivational aspect of museum tours (Anderson, Kisiel, & Storksdieck, 2006).

When students come to the museum it is often a novelty. For some it will be their first, and possibly only, visit to MoMA. This freshness of experience can be both a blessing and curse for educators like Dara. On the one hand, she wants to capitalize on students' interest, excitement, and desire to take it all in. On the other hand, she knows from her own experience as a lover of art that "wall cruising" and grand tours of the collection offer little of lasting educational value. Furthermore, museum school visits, just like those of the millions of tourists who descend on the museum each year, are notoriously brief. Given the wealth of opportunity afforded by the museum itself and the time constraints of its visitors, how does a thoughtful museum educator like Dara structure students' visits? Answer: By focusing on a big, generative idea that will both frame their time at the museum and transcend it.

"We're going to be thinking about one thing today: identity... We're going to think about how artists communicate ideas about identity, either their own or someone else's... We're going to see four works of art and then use these ideas and what we have learned to do some printmaking about your identity." Dara presents the focus—identity—and signals that students' thinking will center on the methods of portraying that identity. For this particular tour, the topic of identity was chosen in conjunction with the students' teacher and has wide appeal to a group of adolescents. It also connects to the coming-of-age novels they have been reading in their English class. The printmaking experience to follow draws on the studio expertise the museum has at hand. It is part of a program designed to allow students the opportunity to create art in a socioeconomic climate in which many schools' arts programs have been gutted.

With her few introductory words, Dara has framed the museum experience for students, set expectations for the learning, and established a clear purpose. However, this isn't her tour; it is the students', and for them to learn they need to engage with the ideas and activate their own thinking so that a series of conversations can begin to develop: conversations between Dara and the students and among the students themselves, a conversation with the works of art, and a conversation with oneself that can lead to creative expression. "What is identity, anyway?" Dara asks to launch the first conversational volley. "How you define yourself," a young woman in a green T-shirt courageously offers—much to the relief of her peers who seem a bit hesitant to speak. It is a useful definition that Dara can easily build on to uncover more ideas. "What are some of the major characteristics or ways we define ourselves?" Dara asks.

The open-endedness of the question seems to have enlivened the group of twenty-four students, and they begin shouting out attributes: character, culture, looks, style, personality, your environment, language, beliefs, and ideals. Dara records each of these comments in red on a sheet of large white construction paper she has brought for this purpose. It's a simple yet effective way of capturing students' responses and signaling to them that their ideas matter. Before putting the paper back into her bag and starting the tour, she holds it up and tells students, "We'll come back to this and see what other things we can add after we've looked at some of the art today." With some quick words about staying with the group—the museum will officially open to other visitors in a few minutes and the galleries will fill quickly, Dara notes—and then a mention to students about avoiding leaning up against the white walls when they stop to look at the art (the walls scuff easily, it seems), the group is off, up the escalators and into the midcentury painting and sculpture gallery on the fourth floor.

Having selected "identity" as the focus for the tour, Dara took time to consider which works of art might provide students the opportunity to investigate both the issue of identity as well as the different ways in which artists convey aspects of identity. Of course, MoMA offers an embarrassment of riches, and consequently many decisions have to be made: Which works might speak best to adolescents? Which are accessible but still complex enough to pull viewers in and provoke conversation? How should the viewing best be sequenced to constantly extend and push the emerging conversation? (Note: Readers can view the artworks mentioned here by searching for them by artist or title on the MoMA website: www.moma.org.) Dara felt that one particularly rich opportunity for students' thinking was afforded by the museum's placement of Rosenquist's *Marilyn Monroe, 1* adjacent to Warhol's *Gold Marilyn Monroe*. As students spill into the space, Dara asks them to sit in the space in between the two paintings. She then asks them to think about the differences they notice in the two pieces and how they each convey different aspects of the subject's identity. Students remark on the isolation of the image in the Warhol print versus the disembodied nature of the face in Rosenquist's painting. They comment on the difference in focus between the works: "Here [Rosenquist] it highlights the lips, but in this one [Warhol] I'm drawn to the eyes." Dara directs students' attention to the lettering in the Rosenquist work, and a discussion ensues about celebrity, icons, and pop references, with one student noting, "Coke is bubbly and explosive. Maybe that was like her personality." Before moving on, Dara takes advantage of one more opportunity the Warhol provides, the chance to talk about printmaking, the activity students will do after the tour, pointing out how that medium might also say something about identity.

From start to finish the discussion lasts just over 15 minutes, quite an extended amount of time in a museum setting. However, Dara knows that thinking requires time. Without the time to engage properly with an object or idea, an opportunity for thinking can feel hollow. It is only through extended inquiry that conjectures can be made, perspectives examined, theories weighed, and new understandings developed. Even in unstructured museum visits, time correlates highly with interactions and subsequent recall (Cone & Kendall, 1978). Dara knows this and so has made the decision to look at only a few works of art and push for conversation and connections around them. Even so, the pressure of time is always felt. It can be a challenge to give students time to look closely at a work of art before being asked to discuss it. The silence that sustained looking of more than a few seconds invokes, and the potential for discipline problems and outbursts, make many museum educators more than a bit uncomfortable. In addition, knowing what one still has to cover and get through creates another kind of pressure.

Feeling this pressure of time, Dara has students on their feet and walking briskly upstairs to the late nineteenth- and early twentieth-century painting and sculpture gallery. Stools are available here, and students unfold them before Picasso's 1932 modernist classic, *Girl Before the Mirror*. Standing in front of the artwork's wall tag, Dara opens the discussion by asking, "Does anyone want to take a guess at what's going on in this painting?" A student offers a broad overview of the work: "It is a lady looking in a mirror." Dara follows up by asking the group a deceptively simple and open question: "What else do you notice?" The question focuses on observation and is invitational in nature. The conversation deepens:

STUDENT: The woman's face is split. Maybe it is showing that you have two sides to your personality.

DARA: Okay, where are you looking? [Student points]

DARA: Anyone else want to elaborate on that idea?

STUDENT: Maybe she is looking into herself in the mirror.

DARA: Okay. Since you brought up that idea, let's talk about how these two sides are different.

STUDENT: One is light and one is dark.

DARA:	Say more.
STUDENT:	The two faces. It looks like night and day. One has a sun on it.
STUDENT:	One is more abstract
DARA:	Abstract. What makes you say that? Can you explain?
STUDENT:	There are more shapes on the darker side.

Dara's questioning begins with interpretation and then moves to noticing of supporting evidence and details (Housen & Yenawine, 2001), a slight variation from the See-Think-Wonder routine. It is a routine she uses frequently to get viewers into a work of art and beyond their obvious first impressions. The routine focuses on the learner's own interpretation and analysis without the addition of information by the tour guide, a stance that is not without controversy in museum education (Dobbs & Eisner, 1990). In this context, Dara has had to think about whether she wants students to learn *about* the painting or to learn *through* the painting. In the arc of learning she is trying to create for these middle school students, her intent is to raise issues of identity and focus on the methods and techniques artists use to portray that identity—methods that students might appropriate in their own printmaking experiences later in the day. Within this arc of learning, information about the artwork becomes secondary. It is not withheld, but it is not the focus of the learning at this time.

As conversation about the painting deepens, students bring up the idea that the model in the painting is seeing into herself, perhaps noticing qualities no one else sees. "Maybe she thinks she is not a good person or has done something wrong," one student offers. When Dara asks, "What makes you say that?" the student again mentions the darkness of the image in the mirror and that it seems less friendly and pretty than the lighter image. Before leaving the Picasso, Dara recognizes a chance to connect with students' earlier ideas about identity, and she reaches for the sheet of white construction paper she has kept folded in her bag. Unfurling it, she asks, "Which of our characteristics about identity would you say are internal and which external?" Looking at the list, students remark that most of the qualities that they have listed are external. "Maybe beliefs is more internal," one student offers. This apparent deficit in their list sparks students to add new attributes such as feelings, emotions, how you think about yourself, your dreams, and self-esteem. Dara records these on her sheet. By documenting students' thinking and keeping it visible as needed throughout the tour, Dara is creating her own moveable classroom environment.

Moving away from representational artwork, Dara escorts students back downstairs to the contemporary gallery to look at Mona Hatoum's + and −. Students gather around the 4-meter-wide pit of sand bound inside an aluminum circle, watching as a toothed metal arm makes perfectly spaced grooves in the sand, only to be wiped smooth a few seconds later by the flat blade that is the other half of the kinetic sculpture's motorized arm. At first the students are mesmerized by the hypnotic motion of the sculpture but also puzzled by its meaning. Dara provides some background on the artist but doesn't explain the work itself. She mentions that Hatoum is Palestinian, born in Lebanon, and now a British citizen. With nothing more than that, Dara asks students to form small groups of three or four to talk about the work and discuss how it conveys identity. There is a quiet buzz as students talk about birth and death, a clean slate, building and destroying, old patterns of behavior and new ones, the traditions of the past being lost in a new generation, the constancy of change, and so on. This discussion might not have worked earlier in the tour, but at this point students have built up an extended conversation around art and identity on which they can now elaborate and expand. In addition, Dara has nurtured the conversational process throughout her tour, moving from whole-group discussion to pairs and finally now to small groups. This notion of conversational elaboration (Leinhardt & Crowley, 1998) adds depth and dimension to students' museum experience, moving it well beyond a tour of the collection.

It's been just 90 minutes since students first stepped off the yellow bus onto 54th Street. Students' exploration of identity isn't over yet, but Dara says good-bye to the group as she leads them down the escalator to their basement classroom. As students pile into the space and into seats, Dara takes a spot at the front of the room. Retrieving her white sheet of construction paper with red marker writing, she posts it on the whiteboard. Quickly, she recaps students' ideas about identity using many of their own words and snippets of their conversation from the galleries. Closing, she adds, "Identity has so many sides and facets to it. We're all complicated people. Artists don't try to capture all of those aspects of identity, but make choices about what might be illuminating and interesting, what seems central or core to the person. When you start your printmaking, think about that for yourself. What aspect of your identity, be it external or internal, do you most want to highlight?"

THE FORCES THAT SHAPE CULTURE

Although people tend to think of culture with a big *C*, the fact is that our lives take us in and out of any number of micro-cultures on a regular basis. These micro-cultures develop in all kinds of group settings and across a variety of enterprises. The three cases presented here demonstrate some of this diversity in educational settings: from the year-long goings on of the traditional classroom, to a monthly meeting of teachers, to a single-visit museum experience. As each of these cases demonstrates, group culture is a dynamic enterprise continually under construction. Unexamined, these cultures may seem mercurial in nature. However, analysis reveals that there are a set of clearly identifiable forces at work: expectations, opportunities, time, modeling, language, environment, interactions, and, of course, routines. These forces provide the leverage points for creating a culture of thinking and can help us to understand the context in which the use of thinking routines and other efforts to make thinking visible can flourish.

Expectations

In creating a culture of thinking, setting expectations for learning and the types of thinking required is key. In Lisa's classroom, establishing the goal of reflecting on learning was crucial to ensure that the activity of painting didn't overwhelm students' efforts to examine their evolving understanding. Lisa continually kept this intent at the forefront of students' experience, just as Dara did with the middle schoolers visiting MoMA when she said, "We're going to be thinking about one thing today: Identity." Likewise, Julie set her expectations for the Breakfast Group in her initial letter of invitation. This included not only behavioral norms—Don't duck out early or miss meetings—but more important an emphasis on openness, listening, and questioning.

Expectations include the goals and purpose of the group, outlining the nature of the learning enterprise itself while signaling the kinds of thinking that will be necessary to that enterprise. Traditionally, teaching has focused on setting expectations for behavior or for the work to be completed over the course. Although certainly important in terms of class order, such expectations do little to motivate the actual process of learning. In cases where such directives dominate, they do more to create a culture of compliance and passivity than a culture of thinking. Learning needs a focus, and learners need directions for channeling their mental energies. If Dara had merely told students they would be going on a tour of the museum and then engage in some printmaking, students would have received the message that little was expected of them mentally. Likewise, in Lisa's classroom the continual push to make connections and synthesize one's thinking lead to rich reflections and not a mere reporting of what students had done or read.

Opportunities

Expectations provide the focus and direction for thinking, but opportunities are a mechanism by which those expectations will be realized. In all three of the cases, rich opportunities for the learners' thinking were created. Lisa provided challenging content that not only built on but also extended students' understanding of migration. Julie carefully chose readings that were provocative as much as they were useful. Dara took pains to choose works of art that would uncover different aspects of identity. The importance of selecting good content has been emphasized throughout this book, and certainly this is a cornerstone of creating rich opportunities for thinking. Rich content draws the learner in in some way. At the same time, it provokes or challenges the learner to move to a new place.

Opportunities are not solely about content, however. A rich thinking opportunity must also provide for meaningful interaction with that content. Ultimately, it is what learners are asked to do with the content that makes it a rich opportunity for learning. As interesting as the artworks Dara used were, merely showing them to students and telling them about them would not have been a rich thinking opportunity. It was the building up of the experience, one work after another, the connection to students' own ideas about identity, the identification of techniques and methods of representation, and ultimately the chance to employ those methods in their own printmaking that was the truly powerful opportunity. Similarly, Julie's chosen articles might have been well received by individuals, but it was the opportunity to discuss them and make connections to practice that lifted the words off the page for the Breakfast Group.

Time

Embedded within the creation of opportunities is the provision of time for thinking. Whether in the classroom, at a professional gathering, in a museum, or other group learning situation, good thinking requires time. Without time, teachers and leaders cannot expect insights, connections, and understandings to develop. The influence of providing time was evident in all three of the cases presented. From her own learning, Lisa knew the value of reflecting over time to develop depth of understanding, and she wanted to create this for her students. She saw the effects of this provision of time in students' growth in the metaphorical and reflective thinking over the year. Dara chose just four works of art, out of a collection of over 150,000, because she recognized that if students were to do more than just look at each work, they would need time to examine it, discuss it, and draw insights from it.

Of course, time is one of the scarcest commodities in teaching and a constraint that every teacher feels. The Breakfast Group case clearly highlights this pressure. How does one provide a rich professional experience for a diverse group of teachers in just 90 minutes? Certainly, Julie's plan for the group's time packed a lot in. This was largely possible through the use of routines as common structures for discussion, enabling a high degree of autonomy and efficiency for the groups. Ultimately this saved time. While Julie looked for and developed efficiencies, she didn't try to shortcut people's thinking. Her focus remained on providing opportunities for engagement and thinking. As a consequence, she avoided the common trap of merely disseminating an abundance of ideas without the time to process them. Too often, many people take this to be a mark of efficiency: Can't we move faster and cover more? But coverage is the ultimate delusion of those who place the act of teaching (or presenting) above the act of learning. It is a deceit perpetuated on a grand scale in education. A deceit in which both teachers and learners implicitly agree that in the name of achieving coverage of the curriculum, only superficial and short-term learning will be expected. However, to achieve insight and understanding, one must have the time to think about and with ideas.

Modeling

In teaching, the idea of instructional modeling is familiar. In this instructional move, the teacher shows students how to do something: a process, procedure, task, or assignment. Instructional modeling has its place in instruction, but it isn't really a shaper of culture. The kind of modeling that creates culture is more subtle, ubiquitous, and embedded. It is the modeling of who the teacher is as a thinker and learner. This kind of modeling can't be "put on" for students' benefit; it must be real. Students know if a teacher is passionate about a topic, interested in ideas, engaged as a learner, thoughtful and deliberative, and so on. When Lisa engaged in the painted reflections with her students, she was conveying the message that the process of reflecting was valuable to her and so it should be of value to them. Imagine how different her class would have been if she had sat in the back grading papers. Similarly, Julie put herself into the learning groups with the other teachers, signaling her own interest in exploring ideas with others. In Dara's case, her interest and passion for art was what students got from being in her presence. The quote from Vygotsky (1978) shared earlier about learners growing into the intellectual life around them perfectly captures the importance and power of modeling. Modeling is not just picking up "how it's done"; it is about who one is becoming.

Language

Through language, teachers name, notice, and highlight the thinking and ideas that are important within any learning context, drawing students' attention to these concepts and practices in the process. Vygotsky (1978), whose work concerned itself with how learning unfolds within social contexts, wrote, "The child begins to perceive the world not only through its eyes but also through its speech. And later it is not just seeing but acting that becomes informed by words" (p. 78). Words mediate, shape, inform, and solidify experience. Lisa's students learned to talk about their thinking and to reflect on their learning as they developed the words to do so. Lisa shepherded this process through her constant talk about connection making and the ongoing discussion of metaphors. By continually naming and noticing this type of thinking, she made it the object of attention in her classroom.

Language shapes our thinking in more subtle ways as well. Julie noted that over time the teachers in the Breakfast Group took on a conditional (versus absolute) use of language in their interactions with one another. Rather than using a language of single perspectives and fixed ideas, conditional language acknowledges possibilities, alternatives, and perspectives (Langer, 1989). How differently people hear, "What you should do is . . ." and "One thing you might consider is . . ." Absolute language often makes people doubt their own thinking and experience as they defer to authority, whereas conditional language allows one to connect one's experience to new ideas and keeps one open to alternatives (Langer, Hatem, Joss, & Howell, 1989; Lieberman & Langer, 1995; Ritchhart & Langer, 1997). It is difficult to get a sense of both the power and nuance of language to shape experience from written cases alone. Unfortunately, too much of the dialogic interaction is left out when one writes about learning. However, as you view the DVD accompanying this book you might attend specifically to the way teachers' language supports and advances students' learning.

Environment

Imagine a trip to a school after hours: no students or teachers around. How much could you discern about the learning and thinking that goes on there just by walking the hallways and stepping into classrooms? What does the room arrangement tell you about how students are expected to interact? Where is the teacher's desk, and what does its placement reveal? What's up on the walls, and who put it there? What does a collection of finished, graded projects from the last unit taught say as opposed to a messy chart paper brainstorm of developing ideas? Or, are there both? What does a room without anything on the walls communicate?

The physical space of one's learning is yet another factor that shapes the learning culture. As human beings we are continually constructing and reconstructing our environments to fit our needs. What are the needs of learners that the environment can facilitate? There is the need to communicate, discuss, share, debate, and engage with other learners. The Breakfast Group led by Julie Landvogt was all about group interaction and discussion. Consequently, their meeting room consisted of six large tables, arranged by Julie and a helper before 7:30 A.M., one for each of the different groups. Likewise, Lisa Verkerk's classroom used flexible, nonassigned groups of tables that could seat four to six students. In this configuration it was easy to share materials as well as thinking. Dara Cohen had to recreate her seating in each gallery visited, sometimes using stools, sometimes standing, or sitting on the floor. In all these configurations pairs and groups could talk easily.

Learners also benefit from the records and documentation of the group's learning journey. This practice allows both individuals and the group to see where they have been, recognize growth, make connections, and raise new questions. All three of the teachers and leaders used some form of documentation. Each group in the Breakfast Group had a documenter to record their ideas. These could be referred back to in the moment, and afterward the documentation was posted on a Web-based wiki that everyone in the group could view and comment upon. This was a solution that fit the group's needs given the constraint of not having a meeting location where they could post and save their documentation. Similarly, Dara's group at the museum had no permanent space to record their ideas. Dara's solution was a red marker and a sheet of white construction paper that she carried along with her throughout the tour. Lisa's students, in a traditional classroom space, had the benefit of being able to post their documentation within the room itself. This certainly occurred as students studied poetry, migration, human rights, and other topics. In addition, the painted reflection journals provided a place for individual documentation of learning that students held on to long after leaving Lisa's classroom.

Interactions

Although we can infer a lot about learning from the physical environment of the classroom, perhaps nothing speaks louder about the culture of a classroom or learning group than the interactions that take place inside it. In Chapter Two, the importance of listening and questioning were discussed. At the heart of these two practices lies a respect for and interest in the learner's thinking. This is the basis for positive interactions that shape meaningful collaboration, which in turn help to build a culture of thinking. Individualized practice, whether framed in the context of competition or not, can be effective at consolidating and developing skills. However, such individualization is less effective in developing understanding and advancing deep learning (J. Biggs & Moore, 1993). Understanding benefits from listening to and taking in others' ideas and viewpoints, evaluating them, making connections to one's own thoughts, and then presenting one's thinking to others, knowing that it too will be challenged and must be backed by evidence and reasons. Within such a social context, robust understanding and innovation often flourish (Johnson, 2010). Such development depends on the interactions of the group. Even skill development is not truly an individual endeavor, as it usually requires feedback from others to advance.

Developing such positive interactions can seem a mysterious enterprise. For instance, teachers often ask, "How do I get my students to listen to one another?" which is just one manifestation of this concern with interactions. Although the nuance of interactional development doesn't come across fully in these three cases, there are some useful tips to be gained nonetheless. First, all of the teachers and leaders were models of learning themselves and showed that interest in and respect for thinking. Students pick up on this. If teachers are not interested, it is that much harder for students to show interest. Second, positive interactions, whether in the classroom or out, usually have a center of gravity. There has to be something for the two individuals or the group to come together around. This means worthwhile content, big ideas, or generative topics. David Hawkins (1967/1974) captured this beautifully in his seminal essay, "I, Thou, and It," in which he writes about the triangular relationship among teacher, student, and content. In all three cases this triangular relationship was central. Why is this important? Because interactions within a culture of thinking are not just about being civil or treating people decently through politeness. No, within a culture of thinking the interactions need to facilitate individual and group learning not just order and civility. This can be seen in the elaborated conversation Dara nurtured over the 90 minutes of her tour. At the center of this conversation was the issue of identity. Third, to facilitate these content-based interactions, the teachers and leaders used routines to structure learning interactions along specific paths. This was very evident in the Breakfast Group. Although adults can often discuss an article without difficultly; the routines encouraged an equanimity to the interactions that ensured everyone participated.

Routines

In Part Two of this book, a variety of thinking routines were presented with accompanying Pictures of Practice. These pictures sought to give an example of the routine being used in a rich and productive way that advanced learning of specific content. What these short examples could not do, however, was to provide readers with a feel for how the routine really became a true routine—that is, a pattern of behavior—in the classroom. We hope that the three cases here help to fulfill that need. In Lisa's case, we see how she embedded the routine of painted reflection over the course of a school year. Over time, she carefully monitors students' growth and continually pushes them in their use of abstract metaphors. Much of this occurs through Lisa's own modeling but also through the modeling done by other students. As a result, students develop a regular rhythm to their work with journals and their reflections deepen.

This regular rhythm can be seen in the Breakfast Group as well. One of the benefits of routines is that once they become established, individuals and groups can use them with minimal directions or support. By the fourth meeting, the Breakfast Group had clearly learned the routines and fell into their use almost effortlessly to structure their discussion. This was crucial to the group being able to maximize its learning time while decreasing its administrative time. Teachers working with routines will want to look for this increasing level of autonomy in their students. Less clear regarding the development of routines would be with the students visiting MoMA. In this case, a single 90-minute episode of learning is presented. Is it fair to say, then, that any routines were truly developed? The Think-Pair-Share routine (Lyman, 1981) is one that is so widely used that most students would be familiar with it. Consequently, Dara could draw on this familiarity in her teaching. Another routine she used—What Makes You Say That?—is one that students take hold of very quickly. When a student first makes an assertion, Dara asks him or her, "What makes you say that?" After a few times of doing this, students often spontaneously begin to answer the question without even being prompted, giving reasons and evidence immediately after stating their interpretation. This is confirmation that this routine is already taking hold even in a short time frame. Since thinking routines are designed to scaffold and support thinking, it is this sense of independence in engaging in the thinking, rather than just the formal steps of the routine, that we want to look for over time.

CHAPTER 8

Notes from the Field

M aking students' thinking visible is not without challenges. In this book we have offered a number of strategies—the use of documentation, listening, and questioning—as well as specific tools—namely the use of thinking routines—that can help to address these challenges. At the same time, rich Pictures of Practice have been presented to exemplify each of the routines or highlight the development of a culture in which thinking is valued, visible, and actively promoted. These examples are meant to highlight the power and potential of these practices. However, we as authors would be remiss if we didn't also acknowledge the common struggles, potential pitfalls, and successful learning paths we have witnessed in our work with educators. That is what this final chapter is about: our notes from the field. These are by no means cautionary tales; rather they represent the common, and sometimes even necessary, bumps in the road that occur naturally as one engages in the complexity of teaching. Recognizing where and how one might go off track and what the learning path might look like can be extremely helpful in charting one's own journey. It is also helpful to see how others have dealt with common challenges, so that we might learn from their experience.

This chapter looks first at two cases of teachers learning to use routines drawn from our research (Ritchhart, Palmer, Church, & Tishman, 2006): Mark Church working with the challenge of making students' thinking visible in a sixth grade mathematics classroom, and Sharonne Blum creating a culture of thinking in a ninth grade history class. These two cases highlight how teachers dealt with students' responses to the routines that were, at least initially, superficial in nature and not reflective of very deep thinking. From these cases, the usefulness of starting with routines to build a culture of thinking and the power of working with colleagues is examined. Following these two cases, a common trajectory of growth in working with routines for both teachers and students is presented. This trajectory has emerged from following hundreds of teachers and their students in a variety of settings over several years. Finally, we conclude this chapter by noticing and naming some common pitfalls and struggles we have seen in classrooms as teachers use thinking routines as tools to make students' thinking visible.

Some of these common struggles have received previous brief mention in the "Tips" sections of the routine descriptions. We explicitly restate here those issues that seem to frequently recur for closer examination and discussion. As professional developers, we have evolved a shorthand for referring to these common rough spots of implementation, such as Sticky Note Mania, Special of the Day, the "To Kill a Mockingbird" Syndrome, Death by Worksheet, and From Episodes to Arcs. Just as early explorers marked their maps with potential dangers—"Dragons lie here!"—we use these names to help mark your route through the field of making thinking visible.

The Challenges of Making Thinking Visible in a Mathematics Class and Beyond: The Case of Mark Church

In 2003, the Visible Thinking project funded by Stiftelsen Carpe Vitam in Sweden expanded to include three international schools in Europe, including the International School of Amsterdam (ISA). ISA is a preK–12 school of around nine hundred students from forty-five countries. More than 60 percent of the student body speaks a home language other than English. The language and cultural diversity of the school provides an extremely interesting backdrop from which to study the use of thinking routines as well as the development of a culture of thinking. Because students at international schools move frequently, the culture of the school and classroom is always being established, and teachers are aware of the fact that their instructional practices, whatever they are, may be new to many of their students.

In October of the 2003–2004 school year, eight teachers agreed to pilot the set of understanding routines we as researchers were developing and to meet regularly as a group to discuss our work with the routines. Among the members of this pilot group was Mark Church, a twelve-year veteran teacher in his fifth year at the school. Mark's university training was as an elementary school teacher; however, his strong interest in mathematics led him into middle school mathematics teaching. At ISA, Mark had become recognized as a leader in professional development around Teaching for Understanding (Blythe & Associates, 1998) and the implementation of the National Council of Teachers of Mathematics (NCTM) standards (NCTM, 1989). During his first year of involvement with the project, Mark taught two sections of sixth grade mathematics and a section of both seventh and eighth grade mathematics. Mark's classes were mixed-ability, standard-level classes following the International Baccalaureate Middle Years Programme using the Connected Mathematics series (Lappan, Fey, et al. 1997) .

Early on, Mark was enthusiastic about the Connect-Extend-Challenge (CEC) routine and thought it might help deepen his students' understanding in the "Covering and Surrounding" unit on which they were currently working. Mark felt the three steps of the routine were manageable for his sixth grade students, since the Connected Mathematics series explicitly stressed Applications, Connections, and Extensions (ACE) as an integral part of each unit. Still, Mark wondered how this thinking routine might create another way for students to think about the mathematics they were learning and was curious to see what kind of thinking might be revealed that wasn't coming out through the ACE questions. Mark commented, "Although I always felt that making connections was important for my students' learning, I never gave the idea of connection making much attention—other than superficially pointing out to students how a particular mathematics problem relates to the real world."

For his first use of the routine, Mark constructed a three-column worksheet with the labels "Connect," "Extend," "Challenge." He gave this to his students following a three-day, hands-on geometry investigation. In this investigation, students were given the task of designing all the rectangular dog-pen enclosures possible using a given amount of fence material, a changing area, fixed perimeter problem. In discussion of his goals, Mark stated that he hoped the CEC recording sheet might help push the students' reflections to go beyond simply reporting their answers to the problem, or their like or dislike for the investigation for that matter, and to look more closely for connections between ideas brought up in this investigation and previous unit investigations.

Mark thought his students had little difficulty filling in the column marked "Connect." However, the responses they gave were not always what he had hoped. For example, many students responded, "The dog-pen problem was like the bumper car problems we did before because they both involved area and perimeter." This kind of connection didn't strike Mark as particularly powerful. "It just doesn't seem to push the students' thinking into anything new," Mark reflected. Although these simplistic connections were dominant, Mark nonetheless felt that his students had gained something from the routine. For instance, Mark had overheard some students initially say the problem was the same as one about designing storm shelters (a fixed area, changing perimeter problem), but by the end of the dog-pen designing, many of his students voiced the difference between these two investigations.

Mark brought his students' CEC responses to his weekly study group to share and discuss. In reviewing the student work, the group noticed that some students were in fact making the richer kinds of connections Mark sought. One student wrote, "Just like when we laid the storm shelter floor plans out, the more 'bunched together' we make a shape, the less perimeter we'll use!" Although these kinds of responses were few compared to the entire set of CEC sheets collected, Mark commented that these rich responses weren't just the province of high-achieving students. This caused Mark and the group to wonder, "How might this thinking routine allow for students of different abilities to show significant thinking that we can then bring up for the entire class to consider?"

In taking time to examine students' responses in depth, a fundamental puzzle began to emerge for Mark and the group around the kinds of connections that are meaningful in advancing students' understanding. Furthermore, the group wondered how they might support the development of those kinds of connections. Thus, though the routine was grounded in a particular sixth grade mathematics lesson, the pedagogical issues raised were important to all the teachers in the group. As researchers, we have seen this scenario repeat itself in countless other contexts. Although it may seem that a sixth grade math teacher has little in common with a grade 12 English teacher or a kindergarten teacher, the fact is that when students' thinking and its development becomes the centerpiece of the professional conversation, rather than issues of delivering or assessing specific content, connections emerge that bind teachers together in a sense of common purpose. Furthermore, when one teacher uses a routine in a way that reveals students' thinking, a ripple effect occurs and other teachers find themselves willing to try out a routine they might not have thought appropriate for their content or their students.

Mark's experience demonstrates that, although the thinking move embedded in a particular routine may be ostensibly clear, teachers must still take on the issue of quality and depth in students' responses in using the routines to ensure that students don't merely complete the activity. Generally, this takes the form of providing models of appropriate responses accompanied by the expectation that students will go beyond the superficial and obvious. In reflecting on his first use of CEC, Mark identified this issue for himself: "I'm wondering if my students recognize the difference between types of connections—from the kind that seem more simplistic in nature to the kind that seem more elaborated and, well, that lead the learner somewhere further in understanding?" Although the language of "connections" was familiar to Mark's students, appropriate examples and clear models were needed to flesh out the meaning of connections for students. *This is something a routine itself cannot provide; it is something the teacher must bring to the routine.* However, by working with the routine over time and discussing it with colleagues, both Mark and his students were able to explore what it means to make meaningful connections.

The issue of language and deeper meaning also emerged in students' responses to the "Extend" and "Challenge" sections of the routine. Under "Extend," Mark and his colleagues noted that many students responded that they'd "learned a lot" through the investigation without articulating what exactly had been extended in their thinking. Many students wrote nothing at all in this column. However, a few had written that their thinking was extended because they never knew that the area could change so much given a fixed perimeter. Mark found one student's comment particularly interesting. This student asked a question about what would happen if the fence sections didn't have to come in one-meter segments. That is, if fence sections could be split into fractions, would there be even more possible enclosures? Mark felt this question represented a leap in the student's understanding, and in the study group he wondered aloud about how he might bring this thought up with the whole class to further students' thinking and provide a model of what "Extend" could look like. The group decided that part of making students' thinking visible was affording students the opportunity to hear and learn from others and that Mark should share this extension as one for the class to explore further.

Under the "Challenge" column, a large number of students responded, "I did not find anything hard," or "There wasn't anything difficult in this investigation—I understood everything I was supposed to do," causing Mark to ask his colleagues, "Why are students automatically jumping to terms like *difficult* and *hard* when asked what the challenge in this investigation was? Do my students view a challenge as a bad thing, as in, 'If I have a challenge, then there must be something wrong with me as a learner because I should be finding it more easy?'"

Mark was initially attracted to the CEC routines because he felt the routine matched many of his instructional goals. However, he found that what he had initially perceived as being very explicit—asking students to make connections, extensions, and identify challenges—was not so clear. The language of the routine needed to be unpacked for students and models provided. Mark summed up the issue: "It seems to me that my students really weren't engaged in significant connection making like I thought they would be by distributing this sheet. Rather than doing Connect-Extend-Challenge, it seems they've done 'Look for What Matches Up, Report That You Learned a Lot, and Say How Easy the Task Was.' I thought that if I distributed a worksheet with 'Connect,' 'Extend,' and 'Challenge' clearly marked at the top of each column, I might get something different than what I got from most of them." This prompted the entire group to wonder about what things—in addition to issue of language and a lack of models—might stand in the way of students' thinking or keep it invisible.

As a member of an ongoing study group, Mark found support and encouragement to continue with the routine. The puzzles raised by students' responses to the routine didn't defeat Mark; they energized him. Perhaps another teacher trying out this routine without the support of a colleague group or researchers might have found fault with the routine and abandoned it. "It didn't work; so much for that." However, Mark figured there might be some untapped potential in this thinking routine, and he wanted to "allow myself to intellectually mess about with it to see where it might take me and my students."

One thing Mark decided to do was to abandon the three-column worksheet and instead focus on using the language of the CEC routine in his instructions and interactions. In reflecting with the research team during an interview, Mark stated, "The three-column sheet itself wasn't a bad thing, but I felt perhaps my students got the idea this was just one more thing to do in order to complete assigned tasks. I wanted to give connection making its own arena—its own value and importance as a result of all the work we've done up to this point in our investigations." Subsequently, Mark decided to weave Connect-Extend-Challenge–type language into his instruction. For example, when launching assignments, Mark announced to his students, "As you work on this investigation in small groups today, not only do I want you to do the work the problem is asking of you, but I also want you to think about how this investigation connects with some of the problems we've done recently *and* what's new here? In what way does this investigation extend your thinking further or deeper from the place we left off at the last round of problems?"

At first, Mark said he needed to remind himself to ask these Connect-Extend-Challenge questions to the whole class by writing "CEC" in the corner of the whiteboard. Occasionally, he would stop the class and ask, "What are you noticing? How is this familiar to things we've been doing? What's new here? Is this just the 'same stuff' or is there something different?" Mark also made an intentional effort to use these kinds of questions as part of his talk with individual students as they came to show him work or when he'd check in with small groups.

Over time, Mark noted that this way of questioning became a natural part of the interactions he had with students, "It didn't seem forced or awkward after we'd done this a few times.... I was fascinated by the kinds of things they'd respond, which often helped me formulate new questions for an individual or group, and often, for the entire class. I was especially intrigued when students would make mention of other problems or investigations we'd done previously and how what they were doing presently seemed to remind them of something they'd seen or thought about before. In moments like that, I'd often pause the groups and say something like 'It seems like a lot of groups are making such-and-such a connection with the problems from last week, which is a great thing—seems like our theory last week is holding true for these problems too. However, I'm wondering, Are groups finding some new layers here? Is there something about these problems that adds another dimension to the theory we had last week? Make sure you consider that as you work through this investigation.'"

By the end of the school year, Mark returned to the three-column recording sheet and even used it to structure homework assignments occasionally. However, by this time the language of Connect-Extend-Challenge had been thoroughly unpacked for his students, and models of good thinking in each of the three steps had been made visible through numerous class interactions. Once these examples and experiences were in place, the explicitness of the routine became apparent to students, and they were able to engage with the routine independently at a high level. This became evident to Mark when he had a substitute teacher give his students Connect-Extend-Challenge as a homework assignment. Without any more instruction than that, students came to class the next day with a wealth of observations to discuss, indication that the CEC had truly become a routine in Mark's class (see the example of Mark's students using the routine in a social studies context on the DVD that accompanies this book).

When we observed Mark's classes near the end of the school year, this high level of independent routine use was noticeable, as was student use of the language of the routine. As outside observers in Mark's classroom, we frequently heard students making comments about their thinking being "extended" or "challenged" or their pointing out a "connection" they'd made. Another noticeable shift was observed in students asking questions during the classes' "Extend" and "Challenge" discussions. Recall that in Mark's initial use of the routine, only one student asked a question under "Extend," and many students commented, "Nothing was hard about this investigation" when asked about "Challenges." Through repeated modeling and making students' collective thinking visible, it appears that the idea that extending and challenging one's thinking involves asking questions about what you are studying became ingrained in the minds of Mark's students. This shift in students' responses seems to indicate more than a familiarity with the routine and expected types of responses. It suggests that students are internalizing the deeper messages about learning, namely that questions not only drive learning but are often outcomes of learning as well and that learning is more than gathering information, it involves uncovering the complexity of ideas and concepts.

Our observation of students' spontaneous connection making indicates that not only are students learning the routine, they are also developing in their disposition to think. While Mark observed significant improvement in students' ability over time, he also noticed that students became more inclined to look for connections and to see connection making as worthwhile. In addition, his comments suggested that students were spotting opportunities for connection making on their own. Thus, over time students' ability, inclination, and awareness of the disposition to make connections was being enhanced through Mark's use of CEC.

Content + Routines + Students = A Culture of Thinking: The Case of Sharonne Blum

Within weeks of its introduction, See-Think-Wonder (STW) had spread rapidly through Bialik College, a 1,000-student, preK–12, independent school outside Melbourne, Australia, and a funder of the Cultures of Thinking Project. From middle school students' study of planets in science using satellite images to first graders' exploration of portraiture based on museum reproductions, from high school students' probing of the Hurricane Katrina response in the United States through examination of political cartoons to second graders' study of animal habitats through nature photographs, teachers at Bialik found this routine a good and easy fit with their course content. Furthermore, See-Think-Wonder is highly accessible for both teachers and students and often provides a good introduction to a topic of study. The routine is usually launched by presenting a visual stimulus and asking students to observe closely and make note of what it is they actually "see." Based on these observations, students begin to make interpretations with justifications as they explain what they "think." The routine concludes with students posing questions and "wondering" about their observations and interpretations.

The attractiveness of See-Think-Wonder and its quick spread throughout the schools with which we have worked might in part be due to its ability to engage students in an open-ended exploration. As one teacher commented, "It has been taken by the kids in a very nonthreatening way, so they are prepared to take risks with their responses." Teachers also identified the routine as being useful for encouraging self-direction and personal involvement in learning for both strong and weak participants: "I love the fact that it empowers the usually silent students to participate. It gives them a voice." Another teacher stated, "It exposes the thought process of all, but specifically those children willing to challenge themselves in their thinking." At the same time, we as researchers and staff developers often witness STW being used as just an activity precisely because it is so accessible and engaging. When this happens, students quickly tire of it, and rather than enhancing their ability to observe, notice, interpret, and question; the routine can dull their thinking.

To better understand the power, nuance, and instructional implications of STW (as well as other routines) the case of high school history teacher Sharonne Blum's use of the routine across two school years is instructive. Sharonne has been teaching history to seventh, eighth, and ninth graders at Bialik for six years. She feels settled into teaching but not necessarily set in her ways. Like other secondary teachers (Bialik didn't have a separate middle school during this period), she teaches her classes in a variety of rooms and doesn't have a space to personalize or make her own. Hence, the documentation of thinking and capturing of artifacts of class discussions is often challenging, leading Sharonne to think about ways for students to self-document whenever possible. Recently she decided to have students begin saving their work so that they can look back and reflect on their group and individual progress. Sharonne found See-Think-Wonder a good fit for history: "I really like that [STW], because it is easy and so suitable for history. Like with political cartoons. We look at lots of visuals."

In using the routine initially, Sharonne drew her students into the process of her own pedagogical learning. "I am completely honest with the class and tell them I am learning it and ask them to try it. I let them know this is a new way. I don't pretend at all. Kids can read pretending." On those occasions when things don't work out the way she expected, she is open about that as well. "I learn it [the routine] by doing it. I told them, 'We tried it and I didn't think it was right.'

So, I told the class that we would do it again. Students respond to that. They like it. It makes them feel more equal since I am being honest, and they see that I am making a mistake and being honest about it."

In her second use of STW with her ninth graders, Sharonne presents the class with a political cartoon from a 1959 Australian publication, *The Bulletin*. The cover of this issue features a slightly distorted map of the Eastern Hemisphere with the outline of Australia's Northern Territory and Queensland visible in the lower right-hand corner. Over the map a large spider with a C on its back is spinning a web centered near Moscow. The web covers most of Eastern Europe and continental Asia with just one string of the web anchoring in Australia. Trapped in the web are what appear to be human figures. Sharonne chose this image because "the class has been learning about the Cold War, and the 'weapons' of the Cold War: propaganda, fear, paranoia, etc. They [the class] are familiar with cartoon analysis and have also experienced the See-Think-Wonder routine once before."

Sharonne hands out copies of the cartoon to pairs of students along with a recording sheet with four columns:

1. See: What do you see in this picture?
2. Think: What do you think this means?
3. Justify: What makes you say that?
4. Wonder: What do you wonder about what you see?

This addition of the "Justify" column represents not so much a modification of the routine as it does making an inherent part of the routine explicit for students. When the routine was done orally, Sharonne would question her students' interpretations by asking them, "What makes you say that?" thus, combining two routines. Many teachers have found that this simple question of elaboration and justification increases their understanding of students' responses and enhances class discussion. In her recording sheet, Sharonne makes this following-up questioning explicit. The intent of the recording sheet is to provide the basis for the class discussion and documentation of students' ideas rather than something that will be graded.

After 10 minutes of looking at the cartoon in pairs and recording responses, Sharonne brings the class together for a group discussion that will uncover the cartoon's symbolism and emotional connotations. Sharonne asks one student what she sees. "Australia in the corner of the picture." She says she thinks this means

"Australia is being cornered." Sharonne asks the class for other interpretations and gets "Australia is being attacked by the communist web." For both of these responses, Sharonne follows up with "What makes you say that?" Both students concur that it is because "the web is touching the tip of Australia." This seems a fairly straightforward response shared by many other students. When Sharonne asks these two students and the rest of the class what they "wonder" about this feature they have seen and interpreted, the discussion opens up. Students ask, "Are there communists in Australia? How did Australia react? Did the 'cornering' make sense or was it just propaganda?" These questions provide a rich basis for future exploration.

The class discussion follows this rhythm for the rest of the period. Since this is a fairly straightforward image, it is not surprising that most students "see" the same types of things and even make similar interpretations. The richness emerges as students provide justifications for their interpretations and begin to wonder, Why was the spider chosen? How can you stop the web from expanding? How did they get people to think like that and change their ideology? Why is there only one spider? What is the spider trying to achieve? In this way, students come to see the power of questions to drive learning and help to uncover complexity.

In reflecting on the routine, Sharonne is aware of how the routine has changed the way she approaches her content, though not the content itself. "The main difference between the way we used to analyze cartoons and this routine is we used to begin by identifying the overall message, and now that is the last stage of the analysis." She also finds the routine changes the class discussions and sends the message that learning can be a group process: "We have more discussions . . . and it is changing the way I run a discussion. Rather than just hearing an idea and asking students to justify their positions, now, the way the discussion runs is more open and free but also more structured. The structure gives freedom." Elaborating on the structure of the conversation, Sharonne adds, "I feel students are able to be more objective by having the 'See' as the first step. It stops them from jumping to conclusions. They learn to read a text more closely. Also, the 'Wonder' section gives the student a voice, and it is just as important [of a step] as the observation and thoughts."

Perhaps most significant, use of STW and other routines has changed the way Sharonne views students. "In previous years I was sometimes too quick to earmark a student as weak purely based on work output, his or her traditional comprehension skills and analytical skills. . . . What I had seen as a clever or good student was someone who gets it all the time rather than someone who raises questions. . . . However, this year I have been pleasantly surprised to see students whom I had labeled as weak actually shine, as the thinking routines gave many of them a way to structure, understand, and reflect on their own thoughts.'' Sharonne provides a concrete example: ''I have a student whose handwriting and spelling are terrible and his comprehension is challenging. He doesn't have learning difficulties in terms of needing support, but he is average. But, after hearing his thoughts and ideas it made me realize that what he knows about the world and politics is amazing. Apart from knowing information, he is developing his own identity about the world around him. If you give him something pedestrian to do in class he is just average, but in terms of developing himself he is head and shoulders above others. . . . For the first time I was able to acknowledge that this student really is capable of 'deep level thinking,' and I was able to acknowledge this because I believe that the thinking routines enabled me to recognize it. I have started to use terms like *deep-level thinking* and *sophisticated thought processes* more often in my reporting to parents and with less self-consciousness because I have actually *seen them,* and I therefore feel I can make comments about them.''

One of the big lessons Sharonne learned in using routines such as See-Think-Wonder was that they are not foolproof lessons but rather structures to work within and adapt to meet the needs of the content and students. This was driven home when she began the new school year confident that her ninth graders, having come from classrooms that used STW, would automatically engage deeply with images she had presented them of the Cronulla race riots that took place in Australia in December 2005. ''After class I reviewed their recordings, and I felt disappointed because the students' thinking seemed rather shallow and abbreviated.'' One problem she identified was that rather than stating a small detail that they could ''see,'' students were providing an overall interpretation of the picture or just picking up on the focus of the picture: a fight, flags, and people at a march. This response is not uncommon when people know something about an image. If you know you are looking at an image of the Gulf of Mexico oil spill disaster, say, or a painting by an artist you know, it is often hard to go beyond one's known labels to see new things unless one takes extra efforts to do so. Furthermore, interpretation can also be stunted as one relies on known facts and is hesitant to go beyond them. For these reasons, ambiguous images and artifacts often prove more successful with STW. However, this is not to say one cannot use familiar images as Sharonne did. It just means that some extra set-up and discussion may be needed.

The following day Sharonne brought this problem of general observation and interpretation to her students' attention and asked them to do the routine again but this time to focus on the details of the picture using a simple viewfinder cut out of cardboard. She modeled this process for the class, demonstrating how the cutout allowed one to see only a portion of the image at any one time. By elaborating a set of details in the picture rather than the whole, Sharonne helped her students to uncover the complexity in the images that was initially difficult to find since students were familiar with this event and had preformed interpretations. This is in contrast to the Cold War image discussed previously, which was comparatively unfamiliar to students and therefore not in need of this extra step.

This ongoing learning about the intersection of content, routines, and students is significant. The goal of all the routines is to provide a structure that engages students deeply with content, fosters their understanding, and uncovers their thinking in the process. As Sharonne states, "What has been most rewarding for me in this project is seeing how a thinking routine works in the classroom. It's when you can hear students talking about the idea outside of the classroom, not the routine but the idea. . . . I get excited hearing students' thoughts. Getting close to their minds." One way of thinking about the routines is that they are containers that must be filled with interesting and meaningful content. Just as a vase holds and supports a bouquet of flowers, the routine supports the exploration of the content. However, a vase is not meant to eclipse the bouquet, only to support it. So too a routine supports the content and allows our focus to be drawn to it. Weak content can no more benefit from the use of a thinking routine than a flimsy bouquet can benefit from being placed in a beautiful vase.

WHAT THESE CASES REVEAL ABOUT THE USE OF ROUTINES

Both Mark's and Sharonne's cases demonstrate that routines act as culture shapers. Thinking routines are more than strategies that cultivate students' ability or that simply engage them in interesting activities. Through the regular use of routines to explore meaningful content with students, teachers convey messages about the nature of thinking and learning. Chief among these are the notion that:

1. Learning is a consequence of thinking.
2. Learning is as much a collective endeavor as it is an individual process.
3. Learning is provisional, incremental, and evolving in nature.

4. Learning involves continual questioning aimed at uncovering the complexity of ideas.

5. Learning is an active process that entails getting personally involved.

These messages about learning have the power to shift the landscape of schools and classrooms by helping students to become more self-directed learners and teachers to see students as more thoughtful and engaged learners.

This shift doesn't occur through the simple application of a set of steps, however, but over time and with considerable thought. As teachers begin to unpack the thinking moves designed into a routine, for instance, what is meant by making connections or how to help students see beyond the obvious, they are able to lead students beyond superficial responses. As they develop models of and language for thinking in their classrooms, thinking is demystified and made visible to students. As teachers use routines to focus on thinking, they themselves are drawn into students' thinking and ideas. In this process, teachers come to see that assessing students' understanding requires that their thinking be made visible. In this way, thinking routines are often self-perpetuating. The response of students from their use encourages their continued use. Over time, the routines of a classroom do become explicit, and through their use, patterns of thinking are established, thus providing students with a truly powerful education that instructs them not only in content but in learning how to learn.

STAGES OF DEVELOPMENT IN THE USE OF THINKING ROUTINES

Mark and Sharonne are just two among thousands of teachers with whom we have worked in our capacity as coaches and researchers. Their stories show that creating a culture of thinking and making students' thinking visible is not merely a matter of inserting a thinking routine into a unit of study; rather it is an ongoing process of development in which both the teachers' and the students' expectations and ideas about learning shift and deepen over time. The learning and growth that both Mark and Sharonne experienced was greatly enhanced and facilitated through their involvement with colleagues in a regular focus or study group. These groups were true professional learning communities (though we didn't label them as such) that met regularly to support and learn from each other. At each weekly meeting, a member of the group brought student work from one of the thinking routines, and the group discussed the work in a structured manner using the Looking At Students' Thinking (LAST) Protocol (Table 8.1). On the accompanying DVD, you can watch one of the focus groups at Bialik College use the LAST Protocol to discuss a compass points routine done by seventh

Table 8.1   Looking At Students' Thinking (LAST) Protocol

Roles	
Presenting Teacher	Brings work to share, listens to the discussion, responds at the end
Facilitator	Keeps track of time, asks the lead questions for each phase, redirects as needed
Documenter	Records the group's discussion

1. Presenting the Work (5 minutes)	Presenting teacher provides the context, goals, and requirements of the task. Ask questions of clarification that will help you to understand and read the work.
2. Reading the work (5–10 Minutes)	Read the work silently. Take notes for later comment. Categorize your notes to fit in with the stages of the protocol.
3. Describing the work (5 Minutes)	What do you see? Raise one another's awareness of all the features of the work. Avoid interpretation and just point out what things can be seen.
4. Speculating about students' thinking (10 minutes)	Where in the work do you see thinking? What aspects of the work provide insights into students' thinking? Interpret the features of the work. Make connections to different types and ways of thinking.
5. Asking questions about the work (10 minutes)	What questions does this work raise for you? Frame questions to get at broad issues as well as specifics. Ask the question behind the question. Rather than, "How long did this take?" ask, "This raises questions for me about the time needed to do this kind of work." *Note:* Presenting teacher does not respond to the questions at this point.
6. Discussing implications for teaching and learning (10 minutes)	Where might this work go next to further extend and build on students' thinking? Suggest practical possibilities and alternatives for the presenting teacher. Raise general implications the work suggests for promoting students' thinking.
7. Presenting teacher responds to the discussion (5 minutes)	What have you as presenting teacher gained from listening to the discussion? Highlight for the group what you found interesting in the discussion. Respond to those questions that you feel need addressing by you. Explain briefly where you think you might now go with the work.
8. Reflecting on the protocol (5 minutes)	How did the process go and feel? Reflect general observations. Notice improvements and changes since the last time the group used the protocol. Make suggestions for next time.
9. Thanking the presenting teacher, the documenter, and the facilitator	The group acknowledges everyone's contribution. Decide how the documentation will be shared, used, and archived for the group. Establish roles for the next meeting.

Source: © Cultures of Thinking Project 2005, Project Zero, Harvard.

graders in science. Although these groups learned to use the thinking routines, this was not their primary purpose. The routines were just tools used to explore the complexity of making students' thinking visible.

As researchers, we have studied teachers as they have worked with thinking routines as tools for making thinking visible in their classrooms. Through our case studies and classroom observations, we have been able to identify common stages through which both the teachers and their students pass as they work with thinking routines over a sustained period of time (Ritchhart, 2009). Of course, every teacher is different and every group of students unique. Consequently, these stages represent general trends and a portrait of teaching painted with the broadest of strokes rather than a sharp, highly fixed image. Nonetheless, these stages can be helpful in charting and recognizing your and your students' own growth in using routines. Knowing that certain behaviors can be expected, in yourself as well as among students, at the beginning provides a sense of freedom to take risks and not worry about perfection. The stages can also provide a way of pushing both yourself and your students to make sure everyone's thinking about thinking is deepening.

Getting Started: The Initial Stage

When teachers first try out a routine in their classrooms, it is not uncommon for the routine to feel like a stand-alone activity, planned and carried out in a deliberate step-by-step manner. This is to be expected when trying anything new. One needs to see how the routine feels and how it plays out initially. Many teachers stick closely to the script of the routine in order to learn the steps and get comfortable with the language of routine. In fact, in working with teachers, we generally encourage this approach initially. If one starts off changing the routine too much, it will be hard to diagnose and learn from the problems and difficulties that may appear. In Mark's case study, it might have occurred to Mark to just change the language of the routine initially, but in doing so he would have missed the opportunity to delve into the importance of developing language and models of thinking with his students.

As students experience routines for the first time, it is not uncommon for them to have a sense of confusion about expectations and to wonder aloud what they are meant to do. To the extent that the thinking routines are a departure from the kinds of work students typically engage in at school, this is to be expected. Worksheets are a known quantity on which students are used to providing answers that will be evaluated as correct or incorrect. Being asked to think and to offer one's ideas can feel quite different from this familiar script. Some students may be eager to please the teacher and concerned with being wrong or appearing "dumb." Such feelings may cause some to freeze up until they have examples of the kinds of responses being solicited. Other students may give narrow, superficial, or simplistic responses, as Mark's students did the first time they tried Connect-Extend-Challenge. Still others may wonder, "Why are we doing this?" not seeing the connection between the class's activity and the typical amassing of content knowledge with which they are used to engaging. This response can be particularly true of older students who have learned how to play the game of school and expect teachers just to present information and to answer questions that will help students prepare for the test.

Some of these common responses might be mitigated, at least partially, by teachers at the outset. For instance, rather than announcing that the class is going to do a routine, it is more effective for teachers to establish the purpose for using a thinking routine and to let students know how using the routine will advance both students' individual and collective understanding. Teachers should also try out the routine with the content themselves to see how it will play and what examples might be given. Many times when a particular thinking routine doesn't work, it might have been possible to identify in advance that the content being used simply doesn't offer enough of a provocation to stimulate thinking. However, not all of these initial challenges can be avoided simply through advance planning. As both Mark's and Sharonne's cases demonstrate, students sometimes give responses that lack depth and don't reveal much thinking. In such instances, teachers need to analyze students' responses, one hopes with the assistance of colleagues, to determine how they as teachers might promote better and deeper thinking from their students in the future. This step should be recognized as a natural part of what it means to make students' thinking visible and not as a failing of either the teacher, the students, or the routine.

Getting Comfortable: The Developing Stage

Once students and teachers have experienced a routine and become more comfortable with it, new possibilities for the use of the routine often emerge. This can be greatly facilitated by teachers sharing their experiences in working with routines with each other in ongoing professional groups. During this stage, teachers generally report that their thinking moves from a focus on the routine as an activity that they will try to a tool that they will use to explore content and to enhance specific understandings they have targeted. A common refrain from teachers at this stage is, "I used to begin my planning by thinking about what routines I could use in the unit. Now I think about what kinds of thinking I want my students to do and choose a routine to scaffold and support those kinds of thinking. It may not sound like much on the surface, but the shift is huge."

My mind is always on students' thinking now." To accomplish this goal, teachers may find that they slightly vary the routine to get at the thinking they are after. Such modifications are certainly appropriate once the routine has been learned.

For students, additional exposure to and use of the routines provides them with a growing confidence in the power and importance of their own ideas. With this confidence comes a greater independence in working with routines as well as an increased richness of responses that reveal a depth of thinking. When teachers consistently use the routines to uncover students' thinking and then build on and develop that thinking, students come to feel that the teacher really is interested in what they think and have to say, as opposed to simply giving an expected answer. As a consequence, students will generally mirror back the level of interest shown in them to the other members of the class. Thus, a sense of a community of learners develops in the classroom over time, and a culture of thinking starts to take hold.

Getting Confident: The Advanced Stage

With practice and reflection comes confidence. This is as true when learning to use a new thinking routine as it is a new sport, workout regime, or cooking technique. What initially feels awkward and rigid gradually becomes intuitive and flexible. At this more advanced stage there is a sense of personal ownership that allows teachers to fit thinking routines seamlessly into their orchestration of the learning process. Teachers at this stage, many of whom have been featured in the Pictures of Practice, sometimes find that they modify and adapt the routines slightly to better fit their needs and objectives. At this stage, teachers usually become more aware of the other cultural forces, discussed in Chapter Seven, that are always operating in the classroom. For instance, when one is continually reflecting on the way routines play out, one begins to notice the significance of language, time, and interactions in shaping the discourse of the classroom. As one thinks about documentation, the importance of models and the use of the environment come into play. The routines become embedded in the opportunities that are created, and the expectations for thinking become the drivers of action in the classroom. Thus, although routines tend to be a great starting point, teachers' attention broadens and shifts from "How do I use these thinking routines?" to "How do I create a culture of thinking in my classroom?"

The ownership of routines that teachers come to experience with time is also felt by students as they become more practiced. Indeed, one of the powerful things about thinking routines is that they are not just classroom structures. Routines can and should be used by individual learners. This means that over time one should expect and look for students to use routines more and more independently to guide their learning. For instance, grade 12 teachers at Bialik College noticed students using the Generate-Sort-Connect-Elaborate and the Claim-Support-Question routines as they prepared their responses on the Victorian Certificate of Education Exam they take at the end of the year. In Mary Kelly's sixth grade science class at the International School of Amsterdam, students regularly suggest routines that the class might use to further their collective understanding.

COMMON PITFALLS AND STRUGGLES

The stories of Mark and Sharonne and the stages of development presented provide a glimpse into what it feels like for teachers and students to work with thinking routines over time. In addition, there are several common pitfalls and struggles that we have been able to document in our work with teachers striving to make students' thinking visible through the use of documentation, thinking routines, and other strategies. We present them here, not as practices to studiously avoid, but more as phenomena to look out for and possibly recognize in your own development. Indeed, although it may be helpful to read through this set of identified pitfalls to alert yourself to them now, the list may be more useful and meaningful to you in the future. If you come back to this section of the book after six months or a year of working with these ideas and strategies for making thinking visible, you might recognize some of your struggles in a new way and be ready to act on the implications associated with them in a way that is reflective of your deeper experience.

Sticky Note Mania

Nearly all of the teachers we've collaborated with in this project recall former days in their classrooms where great discussions had taken place, where really interesting questions had been posed, and where wonderful ideas had been shared, but at the end of the lesson these exciting moments of learning evaporated—vanished at the sound of a bell. Teachers quickly realize that making students' thinking visible and prominently displaying it for all to see not only helps with the evaporation tendency of rich classroom discourse but communicates a sense of value for students' thinking physically in the very setting where their learning is taking place. Asking a student to write a connection she or he has noticed on a sticky note placed on chart paper in the front of the classroom, or to create a headline that captures a big idea on a strip of paper that can easily be tacked to a classroom display board are but a few ways teachers begin to make invisible thinking visible and present in the classroom environment.

Once interest in student thinking begins to grow within a teacher, it is hard not to want to capture every idea, reflection, or connection that students are coming up with. The walls begin to crawl with sticky notes, and many teachers in our research admit to going a little overboard with them at first. Overcome by sticky note mania, there seems to come a defining moment when teachers begin to find it critical to ask themselves, "Just how am I using my classroom space to be an archive of the history and power of ideas that have happened in this place?" Rather than plastering the walls with bits and pieces of paper strips, teachers begin finding it useful to ask themselves, "What ideas and thoughts do I want my students to come back to over and over again so that we can change them around, add on to them, and even revise some initial ideas or perhaps take some of them away as we develop and deepen understanding in a topic?" Mary Beth Schmitt's use of Claim-Support-Question prominently displaying "Claims on Trial" in her middle school mathematics classroom and Clair Taglauer's Tug-of-War posters in her middle school language arts classroom are just two examples of students' ideas captured and made visible in public ways that helped to archive, anchor, and frame the ongoing learning taking place within the classroom space.

Special of the Day

As teachers begin using thinking routines in their classrooms and experience some initial success, many describe a tendency to "try them all out." Who can blame them? Once students begin making insightful connections, surfacing complex puzzles, or generating interesting inquiry, it is rather exciting for a teacher. "What other routine could I try out?" becomes the driving question and a new and different thinking routine-of-the-day habit begins to form. However, when routines begin to take on a "one-off special" feel, a kind of fatigue begins to emerge among students. A good example of this initial over-use can be found in Mary Kay Archer's Picture of Practice of "What Makes You Say That?"

Many teachers find that what becomes helpful to them is to consider just what type of thinking a given situation calls for rather than just doing a thinking routine for the routine's sake. For example, connection-making routines are very natural and appropriate when a given situation begs learners to tie things together. Capturing the essence of a concept seems a good fit when the learning scenario seems opportune for putting one's thumb on the pulse of an idea. Rather than trotting out a thinking routine like a menu's "Special of the Day," with time and experience, teachers become aware of the ongoing pattern of cognitive behavior and types of thinking they desire to be a part of the "regular fare" of their classroom. While initially teachers do need opportunities to try out thinking routines with their students to get a sense of the routine's steps, flow, and purpose, in time it is important for teachers to become more selective in both the choice and positioning of the thinking routine when used with students. A defining moment we have observed among teachers is when they change their questions from "What thinking routine should I use?" to "What kind of thinking would make sense to invite here in this moment?" and begin making instructional choices and decisions accordingly. Likewise, these teachers make a shift from announcing the use of a thinking routine to highlighting the kinds of thinking that will be important in the situation and then the thinking routine that will be used as the vehicle for supporting that thinking.

The "To Kill a Mockingbird" Syndrome

Another struggle teachers in our project often experience relates to choosing content that lends itself well to particular thinking routines. A few years ago, we worked with a high school teacher in New York City who was enthusiastic about creating a culture of thinking in his classroom. His students were reading Harper Lee's To Kill a Mockingbird and he had found some images on the Internet of the late Gregory Peck playing the role of Alabama lawyer Atticus Finch in the film version of this classic literary work. This teacher had chosen the thinking routine See-Think-Wonder to make use of with his students while looking at this film image he projected on the classroom wall.

He asked students "What do you see and notice?" to which they responded: A man. A white man. A hat. The inside of a courtroom. An upstairs and a downstairs. All the people sitting downstairs are white, all the people sitting in the balcony are black, etc. Though not much of what the students offered in response reached beyond the surface of the image, the teacher diligently documented their responses, hoping that in the next step of the routine, he would press them to think a little more deeply.

He then asked, "So, what do you think is going on here?" The students looked at one another and stayed silent. Eventually, one student responded, "Uhm, it's To Kill a Mockingbird." Our colleague paused and asked, "So what makes you say that?" Again, silence, until the student replied, "Because it's To Kill a Mockingbird," with a tone of speaking the obvious clearly heard in her voice.

A bit frustrated, but not willing to retreat, the teacher pressed on. "So, what does this make you wonder?" Not quite sure they understood what he was getting at, the students said with a frustrated, yet questioning tone, "We wonder if this is To Kill a Mockingbird?"

Clearly there was a dilemma unfolding here. The students were not coming up with any unique insight, discovery, or thought that would help them understand any key literary or thematic idea more deeply, and certainly Harper Lee's novel is one full of complex and passionate ideas to be examined. But rather than blaming the students for not coming up with some great insight, one might begin to recognize that, though the teacher's intentions were certainly noble, there simply was not much for the students to see, think, or wonder about as inspired by this image. The image chosen was too obvious—indeed it was a direct scene from *To Kill a Mockingbird*. Used in this way, See-Think-Wonder played out more as a game of "Name This Photo," offering students not much more than a "Guess and See If You're Right" opportunity rather than an opportunity to consider a bigger content-related idea such as prejudice, segregation, injustice, or any other theme that a study of *To Kill a Mockingbird* might provide readers.

To Kill a Mockingbird Syndrome is a fitting name for this pitfall teachers experience when understanding goals within the content aren't quite clear and thinking routines unfold as a guess-the-obvious scenario rather than as a tool to push students toward novel thinking. Teachers who wish to create a culture of thinking in their classrooms not only need to make intentional choices about what thinking routines to use with students but also with what content to use the thinking routines. One lesson many teachers have learned along the way is that it's hard to provoke or elicit good thinking from students when there is not much to think about to begin with.

As Tammy Lantz became familiar with the thinking routine Red Light, Yellow Light, she quickly realized that this routine works well and generates rich classroom discourse when the passage students are reading or the materials they are examining have a stance or viewpoint worth questioning or challenging. In the absence of a variety of perspectives, there isn't much to have "red lights and yellow lights" about. Likewise, as Mary Beth Schmitt realized, mathematical situations that could be reasoned from a variety of perspectives were more well suited for asking her students to surface their initial ideas in the form of claims than those mathematical contexts that are straightforward, without much complexity.

Death by Worksheet

There seems to be some kind of force at work in some classrooms that tends to pull instruction toward worksheets. Many teachers feel they have to have them. Perhaps it is due to the fact that schools have for such a long time focused on learning as work and not trusted students to do that work. Perhaps it is because the pressure to grade, evaluate, and report out every instance of learning has caused teachers to want something tangible that they can look at to see whether learning has happened or at least work been done. Whatever the forces at work here, we have seen time and time again teachers taking routines and creating worksheets to go with them. This happens despite the fact that you won't find a single blackline master in this book or on the Visible Thinking website and that the teachers with whom we have worked in professional development settings weren't introduced to the routines using a worksheet.

The reason we haven't provided worksheets is that the routines are designed to foster engagement and discussion around the content. As was discussed in Chapter Seven, "interactions" are a key cultural force and central to learning. When a worksheet is being filled out, invariably the amount of interaction is reduced and the focus becomes doing the work rather than the learning. For instance, having students record their individual responses to See-Think-Wonder doesn't allow individuals to hear and thus build on the ideas of others. Furthermore, there is just too much to see in almost any image to capture it all. Thus, students edit and ask, "How many things do we have to write down?" We once saw a collection of student work from this routine using a worksheet in which every student had exactly five "Sees," three "Thinks," and one "Wonder." Not surprisingly there wasn't much thinking evident in this collection. The worksheet killed the thinking.

This is not to say that documentation of one's thinking isn't valuable. However, there is a big difference between a recording sheet and a worksheet. Recording sheets are for learners to track their ideas so they can refer back to them. In the DVD, you'll notice Lisa Verkerk used a recording sheet to help students capture their thinking in Sentence-Phrase-Word. Likewise Ravi Grewal had students record their thinking in the Generate-Sort-Connect-Elaborate routine. Indeed, these routines demand some kind of recording, as does CSI: Color-Symbol-Image. In all of these cases, you will see students listening to and building on other's ideas. In contrast, a worksheet is something to be filled in for the teacher. It then becomes the goal rather than the thinking. This may seem a very fine distinction to make, since both worksheets and recording sheets can look the same, but it is a distinction that produces a major difference in the learning and thinking that results.

From Episodes to Arcs

A last struggle teachers seem to bump up against is how they use thinking routines to weave together a storyline of learning rather than present them to their students as isolated activities. Much like television programs of the past when each episode within a series sat in isolation from the next, many of the teachers we've worked with report that their classroom activities used to be nothing more than a string of single episodes: a particular task was assigned, the students worked through it, and it came to a end, tied up neatly, today's episode complete. The following day another isolated episode of activity would be assigned to students with little connection to the episode that came the day before or leveraging toward the episode to come after. In other words, learning was conveyed as activity to activity, episode by episode, and teachers reported that their time and energy was spent in making sure each episode seemed interesting enough to keep the students' attention and help them learn something along the way.

Once thinking routines became an established part of their classroom cultures, many of our teachers spoke of transitioning toward using each day's time for learning to pursue a variety of interrelated story arcs within a topic. Some teachers liken this reframing of their teaching to how television programs have become in recent years. While a series still has an appointed time within a network's lineup, the threads of various stories within a series keep weaving in and out from episode to episode. Different characters play different roles to advance a story arc or trajectory of an idea that seems significant to the overall series' narrative. By considering deeply what big ideas seem to be powerful in the topics they are exploring together with students, teachers begin crafting their use of routines and other classroom endeavors to be a pursuit of those ideas—following the trajectory of important story arcs rather than presenting instruction as isolated episodes with relatively little connection to one another.

As written about in Connect-Extend-Challenge, Josh Heisler's attempt to help his high school students put together ideas within a study of "Race and Membership in Society" or the complexity and controversy of Social Darwinism are good examples of pursuing intricate and interrelated story arcs within curricular topics. As his students read novels, watched video, researched on the Internet, and developed journal responses and essays, Josh found that he could keep weaving students' thinking along the arc of some significant ideas through his use of Connect-Extend-Challenge, which then led to Headlines, which then led to I Used to Think . . . , Now I Think . . . Like many teachers we've worked with, Josh felt that his teaching seemed more purposeful as he helped his students explore the complexity of ideas over time rather than trying to force big ideas into singular, isolated episodes of learning that would be wrapped up lesson by lesson, day by day.

IN CONCLUSION

Learning is at once the most natural and complex of processes. We who bear the task of shepherding this process often find ourselves amazed and energized as we watch the process unfold before us even as we respect, and are sometimes overwhelmed by, its complexity and nuance. Herein lies the promise and power of making students' thinking visible: it offers us a window into the learning process itself. By using the various tools presented in the book—questioning, listening, documenting, and using of routines and protocols—we as educators can support the thinking of our students and thus their learning. However, we must keep in mind that the strategies provided in this book are just tools and, like any tool, must be applied in the right context and in skilled hands to see their full potential.

As you begin your own journey to make thinking visible, take inspiration from the stories of the teachers presented. At the same time, recognize that they too once encountered these tools as new and foreign practices that needed to be tried out, reflected upon, and then retried. Allow yourself to make mistakes and to learn from your students. Find colleagues with whom you can share and discuss your efforts and ongoing learning. Each time you make students' thinking visible, use it as a natural springboard for your next teaching move that will ensure you are building arcs of learning and not just individual episodes of activity. In this way, working step-by-step, with your focus on the broader goal of promoting deeper learning and understanding for your students, you will find yourself well on the way to making thinking a valued, visible, and actively promoted part of your classroom.

REFERENCES

Abeles, V., & Congdon, J. (Directors/Writers). (2010). *Race to nowhere*. In V. Abeles (Producer). United States: Reel Link Films.

Anderson, D., Kisiel, J., & Storksdieck, M. (2006). Understanding teachers' perspectives on field trips: Discovering common ground in three countries. *Curator, 49*(3), 365–386.

Anderson, L. W., & Krathwohl, D. R. (Eds.). (2001). *A taxonomy for learning, teaching and assessing: A revision of Bloom's Taxonomy of educational objectives* (complete ed.). New York: Longman.

Barnes, D. R. (1976). *From communication to curriculum*. New York: Penguin.

Barron, B. (2003). When smart groups fail. *Journal of the Learning Sciences, 12*(3), 307–359.

Biggs, J., & Moore, P. (1993). *The process of learning*. New York: Prentice Hall.

Biggs, J. B. (1987). *Student approaches to learning and studying*. Research monograph. Hawthorn, Victoria: Australian Council for Educational Research.

Bliss, A. (2010). Enabling more effective discussion in the classroom. *Stories of Learning*. Retrieved from http://www.storiesoflearning.com

Blythe, T., & Associates (1998). *The teaching for understanding guide*. San Francisco: Jossey-Bass.

Boaler, J., & Brodie, K. (2004). *The importance, nature and impact of teacher questions.* Paper presented at the proceedings of the twenty-sixth annual meeting of the North American Chapter of the International Group for Psychology of Mathematics Education.

Boaler, J., & Humphreys, C. (2005). *Connecting mathematical ideas: Standards-based cases for teaching and learning, grades 6–8*. Portsmouth, NH: Heinemann.

Bruner, J. S. (1973). *Beyond the information given: Studies in the psychology of knowing*. New York: Norton.

Cazden, C. B. (1988). *Classroom discourse*. Portsmouth, NH: Heinemann.

Colby, A., Beaumont, E., Ehrlich, T., & Corngold, S. (2009). *Educating for democracy: Preparing undergraduates for responsible political engagement*. San Francisco: Jossey-Bass.

Cone, C. A., & Kendall, K. (1978). Space, time and family interactions: Visitors behavior at the science museum of Minnesota. *Curator, 21*(3), 245–258.

Costa, A., & Kallick, B. (2009). *Learning and leading with habits of mind: 16 characteristics for success*. Alexandria, VA: Association for Supervision and Curriculum Development.

Craik, F.I.M., & Lockhart, R. S. (1972). Levels of processing: A framework for memory research. *Journal of Verbal Learning and Verbal Behavior, 11*, 671–684.

Dobbs, S. M., & Eisner, E. (1990). Silent pedagogy in art museums. *Curator, 33*, 217–235.

Duer Miller, A. (1915). *Are women people?* New York: George H. Doran Company.

Eyleer, J., & Giles, D. E. (1999). *Where's the learning in service-learning?* San Francisco: Jossey-Bass.

Facts about language. (2009). Retrieved July 25, 2009, from http://www.askoxford.com/oec/mainpage/oec02/?view=uk

Fried, R. L. (2005). *The game of school: Why we all play it, how it hurts kids, and what it will take to change it*. San Francisco: Jossey-Bass.

Fry, E. B., Kress, J. E., & Fountoukidis, D. L. (2000). *The reading teacher's book of lists* (4th ed.). San Francisco: Jossey-Bass.

Gallagher, K. (2010, November 12). Why I will not teach to the test. *Education Week*.

Gardner, H. (1983). *Frames of mind*. New York: Basic Books.

Gardner, H. (1991). *The unschooled mind*. New York: Basic Books.

Giudici, C., Rinaldi, C., & Krechevsky, M. (Eds.). (2001). *Making learning visible: Children as individual and group learners*. Reggio Emilia, Italy: Reggio Children.

Given, H., Kuh, L., LeeKeenan, D., Mardell, B., Redditt, S., & Twombly, S. (2010). Changing school culture: Using documentation to support collaborative inquiry. *Theory into Practice, 49*, 36–46.

Harre, R., & Gillet, G. (1994). *The discursive mind*. Thousand Oaks, CA: Sage.

Hatch, T. (2006). *Into the classroom: Developing the scholarship of teaching and learning.* San Francisco: Jossey-Bass.

Hawkins, D. (1974). I, thou, and it. In *The informed vision: Essays on learning and human nature* (pp. 48–62). New York: Agathon. (Original work published 1967)

Hiebert, J., Carpenter, T. P., Fennema, E., Fuson, K. C., Wearne, D., Murray, H., et al. (1997). *Making sense: Teaching and learning mathematics with understanding.* Portsmouth, NH: Heinemann.

Housen, A., & Yenawine, P. (2001). *Understanding the basics.* New York: Visual Understanding in Education.

Housen, A., Yenawine, P., & Arenas, A. (1991). *Visual thinking curriculum.* New York: Museum of Modern Art.

Intrator, S. (2002). *Stories of the courage to teach: Honoring the teacher's heart.* San Francisco: Jossey-Bass.

Intrator, S. (2006). Beginning teachers and the emotional drama of the classroom. *Journal of Teacher Education, 57*(3), 232–239.

Johnson, S. (2010). *Where do good ideas come from: The natural history of innovation.* New York: Riverhead.

Johnston, P. (2004). *Choice words: How our language affects children's learning.* Portland, ME: Stenhouse.

Keene, E., & Zimmermann, S. (1997). *Mosaic of thought.* Portsmouth, NH: Heinemann.

Keene, E. O. (2008). *To understand.* Portsmouth, NH: Heinemann.

Langer, E. (1989). *Mindfulness.* Reading, MA: Addison-Wesley.

Langer, E., Hatem, M., Joss, J., & Howell, M. (1989). The mindful consequences of teaching uncertainty for elementary school and college students. *Creativity Research Journal, 2*(3), 139–150.

Lappan, G., Fey, J. T., Fitzgerald, W. M., Friel, S. N., & Philips, E. (1997). *Connected Mathematics Series*: Dale Seymour Publications.

Leinhardt, G., & Crowley, K. (1998). *Museum learning as conversational elaboration: A proposal to capture, code, and analyze talk in museums* (Technical Report #MLC-01). Pittsburgh: Museum Learning Collaborative.

Leinhardt, G., & Steele, M. D. (2005). Seeing the complexity of standing to the side: Instructional dialogues. *Cognition and Instruction, 23*(1), 87–163.

Leinhardt, G., Weidman, C., & Hammond, K. M. (1987). Introduction and integration of classroom routines by expert teachers. *Curriculum Inquiry, 17*(2), 135–175.

Lieberman, M., & Langer, E. (1995). Mindfulness and the process of learning. In P. Antonacci (Ed.), *Learning and context*. Cresskill, NJ: Hampton.

Lyman, F. T. (1981). The responsive classroom discussion: The inclusion of all students. In A. Anderson (Ed.), *Mainstreaming digest* (pp. 109–113). College Park: University of Maryland Press.

Marton, F., & Saljo, R. (1976). On qualitative differences in learning: I. Outcome and process. *British Journal of Educational Psychology, 46*, 4–11.

McDonald, J. P. (1992). *Teaching: Making sense of an uncertain craft*. New York: Teachers College Press.

National Council of Teachers of Mathematics. (1989). *Curriculum and evaluation standards for school mathematics*. Reston, VA: National Council of Teachers of Mathematics.

Nystrand, M., Gamoran, A., Kachur, R., & Prenergast, C. (1997). *Opening dialogue*. New York: Teachers College Press.

Palmer, P. (1998). *The courage to teach: Exploring the inner landscape of a teacher's life*. San Francisco: Jossey-Bass.

Perkins, D. N. (1992). *Smart schools: From training memories to educating minds*. New York. Free Press.

Perkins, D. N., Tishman, S., Ritchhart, R., Donis, K., & Andrade, A. (2000). Intelligence in the wild: A dispositional view of intellectual traits. *Educational Psychology Review, 12*(3), 269–293.

Ravitch, D. (2010). *The death and life of the great American school system: How testing and choice are undermining education*. New York: Basic Books.

Ritchhart, R. (2001). From IQ to IC: A dispositional view of intelligence. *Roeper Review, 23*(3), 143–150.

Ritchhart, R. (2002). *Intellectual character: What it is, why it matters, and how to get it*. San Francisco: Jossey-Bass.

Ritchhart, R. (2009, August). *Becoming a culture of thinking: Reflections on our learning*. Bialik College Biennial Cultures of Thinking Conference. Melbourne, Australia.

Ritchhart, R., & Langer, E. (1997). Teaching mathematical procedures mindfully: Exploring the conditional presentation of information in mathematics. In

J. A. Dossey, J. O. Swafford, M. Parmantie, & A. E. Dossey (Eds.), *Proceedings of the nineteenth annual meeting of the North American chapter of the International Group for the Psychology of Mathematics Education*. Columbus, OH: ERIC Clearinghouse for Science, Mathematics, and Environmental Education. (ED420494)

Ritchhart, R., Palmer, P., Church, M., & Tishman, S. (2006, April). *Thinking routines: Establishing patterns of thinking in the classroom*. Paper presented at the annual meeting of the American Educational Research Association, San Francisco.

Ritchhart, R., & Perkins, D. N. (2005). Learning to think: The challenges of teaching thinking. In K. Holyoak & R. G. Morrison (Eds.), *Cambridge handbook of thinking and reasoning* (pp. 775–802). Cambridge, UK: Cambridge University Press.

Ritchhart, R., Turner, T., & Hadar, L. (2009a). Uncovering students' thinking about thinking using concept maps. *Metacognition and Learning, 4*(2), 145–159.

Ritchhart, R., Turner, T., & Hadar, L. (2009b). Uncovering students' thinking about thinking using concept maps. *Metacognition and Learning, 4*(2), 145–159.

Robinson, K. (2010, October 14). Changing Education Paradigms. [Video file]. Retrieved from http://www.thersa.org

Ryder, L. (2010). Wondering about seeing and thinking: Moving beyond metacognition. *Stories of Learning*. Retrieved from http://www.storiesoflearning.com

Schwartz, M., Sadler, P. M., Sonnert, G., & Tai, R. H. (2009). Depth versus breadth: How content coverage in high school science courses relates to later success in college science coursework. *Science Education. 93*(5), 798–826.

Seidel, S. (1998). Wondering to be done: The collaborative assessment conference. In David Allen (Ed.), *Assessing student learning: From grading to understanding*. New York: Teachers College Press.

Skemp, R. (1976). Relational understanding and instrumental understanding. *Mathematics Teaching, 77*, 20–26.

Tishman, S., Perkins, D. N., & Jay, E. (1993). Teaching thinking dispositions: From transmission to enculturation. *Theory into Practice, 3*, 147–153.

Vygotsky, L. S. (1978). *Mind in society*. Cambridge, MA: Harvard University Press.

Whitehead, A. N. (1929). *The aims of education and other essays*. New York: Simon & Schuster.

Wiggins, G., & McTighe, J. (1998). *Understanding by design*. Alexandria, VA: Association of Supervision and Curriculum Development.

Wiske, M. S. (Ed.). (1997). *Teaching for understanding*. San Francisco: Jossey-Bass.

Yinger, R. J. (1979). Routines in teacher planning. *Theory into Practice, 18,* 163–169.

Zee, E. V., & Minstrell, J. (1997). Using questioning to guide student thinking. *Journal of the Learning Sciences, 6*(2), 227–269.

Zohar, A., & David, A. B. (2008). Explicit teaching of meta-strategic knowledge in authentic classroom situations. *Metacognition and Learning, 3*(1), 59–82.

INDEX

Long Lake Elementary School (Traverse City, Michigan), 188

Looking At Students' Thinking (LAST) Protocol, 95, 262–263

Lowry, Lois, 203–206

Lyman, F. T., 246

M

Making Learning Visible project (Harvard University), 38

Mao's Last Dancer (Cunxin), 66

Mardell, B., 38

Marks, Roz (Bialik College), 142–143

Martin, Stephanie (International School of Amsterdam), 33, 38

Marton, F., 7

Marylyn Monroe, 1 (Rosenquist), 236–237

McDonald, J. P., 26

McTighe, J., 7

Melbourne, Australia, xvi, 58, 90, 91, 201–202, 229, 256

Melbourne Grammar School, 151, 232

Memorization: beyond, 8–11

Memory-based strategies, 21. *See also* Strategic responses

Mentone Grammar (Melbourne, Australia), 149

Mercer Island High School (Washington State), 35

Meta responses, 17, 21

Metacognition, 12, 15, 21

Metacognition and Learning (Ritchhart, Turner, and Hadar), 17

Metacognitive awareness, 15

Meta-learning, 15

Metaphor, 119, 124

Meta-strategic knowledge, 15

Methodist Ladies College (Melbourne, Australia), 59, 149, 232, 233

Methods courses, 25

Micro Lab Protocol routine, 52; assessment in, 150; picture of practice for, 151–154; purpose of, 147–148; selecting appropriate content for, 148; steps in, 148–149; tips for, 150–151; uses and variations of, 149–150; and year 8 student's Wiki conversation on Atlantis, 153

Mikaelsen, Ben, 113

Miller, Alice Duer, 37

Miller, Andrea (Bialik College), 90–92

Miller, Lindsay, 209

Minds of Their Own (video; Harvard Smithsonian Center for Astrophysics), 27

Minstrell, J., 35

Minter, Emily (Bialik College), 96, 97

Mistakes, 29

Mitchell, Julie (Brighton Elementary), 112–113

MLC. *See* Methodist Ladies' College (Melbourne, Australia)

Modeling, 242; intellectual engagement, 31; interest in ideas, 31–32; thinking and learning, 29

MoMA. *See* Museum of Modern Art (MoMA; New York City)

Moore, P., 245

Morrison, K., xvi, xvii, 16

Motivation strategies, 21. *See also* Strategic responses

Murray, H., 8

Museum of Modern Art (MoMA; New York City), 234, 235, 236, 240, 246

N

"Name This Photo" game, 270

Naming, 29

National Coalition for Equality in Education, 147

National Council of Teachers of Mathematics (NCTM), 250

National Gallery of Victoria, 73

National School Reform Faculty, 207

NCTM. *See* National Council of Teachers of Mathematics (NCTM)
New York City, 269
Noticing, 29
Nystrand, M., 31

O

Oberman, Helene (Bialik College), 73
O'Brien, Tim, 128–131
Of Mice and Men (Steinbeck), 95
O'Hara, Debbie (International School of Amsterdam), 103, 104, 167
Open-ended questions, 30
Opportunities, 241
Oxford English Dictionary, 5

P

Palmer, P., xv, 11, 26, 48, 49, 249
Patterson, Fredrik, 12
Peck, Gregory, 269
Pencil Talk. *See* Chalk-Talk routine
Perella, Marc (Fairfax, Virginia), 64
Perkins, D. N., xvi, 11, 16, 26, 29, 49, 185
Perspective taking, 14
Philips, E., 251
Picasso, P., 237, 238
Picture of Practice: for 3-2-1 Bridge routine, 90–92; for 4 C's routine, 144–146; for Chalk Talk routine, 82–85; for Circle of Viewpoints routine, 175–177; for Claim-Support-Question routine, 195–198; for Compass Points routine, 96–100; for Connect-Extend-Challenge routine, 136–139; for CSI: Color, Symbol, Image routine, 122–124; for Explanation Game routine, 104–108; for Generate-Sort-Connect-Elaborate routine, 128–131; for Headlines routine, 115–119; for I Used To Think . . . , Now I Think . . . routine, 157–161; for Micro Lab Protocol routine, 151–154; for Red Light, Yellow Light

routine, 188–190; for See-Think-Wonder routine, 59–63; for Sentence-Phrase-Word routine, 211–213, 225; for Step Inside routine, 182–184; for Think-Puzzle-Explore routine, 75–77; for Tug-of-War routine, 203–206; for What Makes You Say That? routine, 168–170, 268; for Zoom In routine, 67–70
Pictures of Practice, 22, 48–49, 245–246
Plans, formulating, 14
+ *And* − (Hatoum), 239
Prenergast, C., 31
Primary Source Learning (Virginia), 64
Problem solving, 21
Project Zero (Harvard University), xv, 7, 38, 48, 263; Complex Causality Project, 28
"Promise and Perils of Praise" (Dweck), 232
Protocol, 78
Psychomotor domain (Bloom's taxonomy), 6
Purpose, 7

Q

Questioning, 13; and making thinking visible, 30–31; sequence of, 35
Questions: authentic, 31; constructive, 33, 34; essential, 32; generative, 31; review-type, 31

R

Rabbit-Proof Fence (film; Noyce), 173
Race to Nowhere (documentary; Abeles and Congdon), 221
Ravitch, D., 8–9
Recall, simple, 31
Reconstruction era, 136
Red Light, Yellow Light routine (RLYL), 52, 270; assessment in, 187–188; picture of practice for, 188–190; purpose of, 185; selecting appropriate content for, 185–186; steps in, 186; tips for, 188; uses and variations of, 187

3–2–1 Bridge routine, 51; assessment in, 89–90; picture of practice for, 90–92; purpose of, 86–87; selecting appropriate content for, 87; steps in, 87–88; tips for, 90; uses and variations of, 87–88

Threlkeld, John, 31

Time, 241–242

Tishman, S., xv, 11, 29, 48, 49, 249

To Kill a Mockingbird (Lee), 269, 270

"To Kill a Mockingbird" Syndrome, 250, 269–270

Tomlinson, Carol Ann, 232

Tooke, Alma (Methodist Ladies College), 233

Touching Spirit Bear (Mikaelsen), 113

TPE. *See* Think-Puzzle-Explore routing (TPE)

Traverse Area Public Schools (Michigan), 115, 168, 187

Traverse City, Michigan, 134, 188, 195, 203

Trinity Grammar (Melbourne, Australia), 201–202

Truth claims, 191

Tufts, Karrie (Traverse Area Public Schools), 115–118

Tug-of-War routine, 52, 268; assessment in, 202; and eighth grade Tug-of-War about makings of ideal society, 205; picture of practice for, 203–206; purpose of, 199–200; selecting appropriate content for, 200; steps in, 200–201; tips for, 202–203; uses and variations of, 201–202

Turner, T., 12, 16, 17, 38

Twombly, S., 38

U

"Uncovering Students' Thinking About Thinking Using Concept Maps" (Ritchhart, Turner, and Hadar), 17

Understanding, 6, 9, 21; in Bloom's taxonomy, 7; constructing, 31, 32–34; as goal of thinking, 8, 14; map, 13, 15; map of thinking involved in, 11–14; as type of thinking, 8

Understanding by Design (UBD; Wiggins and McTighe), 8

V

Vanguard High School (New York City), 136, 156, 157

Vellman, Paul (Bialik College), 66, 67

Verkerk, Lisa (International School of Amsterdam), 30, 58, 167, 211–213, 222–229, 240–241, 244, 245, 271

Victorian Certificate of Education (VCE) exam, 232, 267

Vietnam War, 129

Virginia, 64

Visibility, 27–30

Visible thinking: and challenge of making things visible in mathematics class and beyond (case study), 250–256; and constructing understanding, 32–34; and content plus routines plus students equals culture of thinking, 256–261; and documenting, 37–39; and facilitating and clarifying thinking, 34–36; and how to make invisible visible, 30–39; and how visibility serves both learning and teaching, 27–30; as important assessment tool, 28; and listening, 36–37; making students' thinking, 26; and modeling interest in ideas, 31–32; role of questioning in, 30–31

Visible Thinking Project, xv, xvi, 47, 49, 166, 221, 250; web site, xvi, xvii, 270–271

Vygotsky, L. S., 28, 220, 221, 242

W

Waliczek, Jill (List Elementary school), 80

Warhol, A., 236–237

Way Elementary (Bloomfield Hills, Michigan), 127

HOW TO USE THE DVD

SYSTEM REQUIREMENTS

PC with Microsoft Windows 2003 or later
Mac with Apple OS version 10.1 or later

USING THE DVD WITH WINDOWS

To view the items located on the DVD, follow these steps:

1. Insert the DVD into your computer's DVD drive.

2. A window will open asking you to select "Run start.exe" or "Open folder to view files."

3. Double-click "Run start.exe" to launch the DVD

If you do not have autorun enabled, or if the autorun window does not appear, follow these steps to access the DVD:

1. Click Start → Run.

2. In the dialog box that appears, type d:\start.exe, where d is the letter of your DVD drive. This brings up the autorun window described in the preceding set of steps.

3. Choose the desired option from the menu. (See Step 2 in the preceding list for a description of these options.)

Using the DVD With Apple OS

1. Insert the DVD into the DVD drive. When the DVD is mounted, a window showing the DVD contents will automatically launch.

2. Double-click the file named "Start". The DVD interface will open.

IN CASE OF TROUBLE

If you experience difficulty using the DVD, please follow these steps:

1. Make sure your hardware and systems configurations conform to the systems requirements noted under "System Requirements" above.

2. Review the installation procedure for your type of hardware and operating system. It is possible to reinstall the software if necessary.

To speak with someone in Product Technical Support, call 800-762-2974 or 317-572-3994 Monday through Friday from 8:30 a.m. to 5:00 p.m. EST. You can also contact Product Technical Support and get support information through our website at www.wiley.com/techsupport.

Before calling or writing, please have the following information available:

- Type of computer and operating system.
- Any error messages displayed.
- Complete description of the problem.

It is best if you are sitting at your computer when making the call.